Bibliographical guide to the study of the literature of the U.S.A.

Clarence Gohdes. **Bibliographical guide to the study of the literature of the U.S.A.** Fourth edition, revised and enlarged. Durham, N.C. 1976; Duke University Press

To

Jay Broadus Hubbell

Tu memineris sui cuiusque generis auctores diligenter eligere.
Aiunt enim multum legendum esse, non multa.   Pliny I.

Preface

The present volume undertakes to provide lists of books which will aid the professional student of the literature of the United States in the acquiring of information and in the techniques of research. It is believed that it will prove useful to college teachers of American literature and to reference librarians, as well as to graduate students writing master's or doctor's theses. In its way, it is comparable to the bibliographical guides to English literature compiled by Arthur G. Kennedy, Tom P. Cross, John W. Spargo, and others. Their manuals, with varying emphasis and method, contain material on American as well as British literature, but their treatment of the former is relatively incidental and for sound reasons has proved unsatisfactory to Americanists. This book was the first of its kind to see print.

In addition to materials having to do with methods of research and with American literature in its several phases, essential tools are herein listed for the study of American history, biography, art, religion, philosophy, etc., not only because of the patent need for backgrounds but also because of the special interests of a large number of students or scholars who investigate the literature of the United States in interdepartmental programs usually spoken of as *American Studies* or *American Civilization*. Historians of ideas will find that their favored approach has also been recognized in the selection of titles for this guide. Calculated consideration has, furthermore, been given to American literature as a part of comparative studies, and a special section is devoted to the relationship of the national letters with foreign countries and foreign literatures. The compiler has borne in mind not only the manifest importance of foreign influences upon the belles lettres of the United States but the repercussions, so to speak, of the national literature in foreign countries.

The various headings for the individual sections of the guide will usually provide sufficient direction to the reader, but indexes of subjects and of authors, compilers, or editors are appended as additional aids to the locating of information. In many cases the individual items that make up the contents of this book are recorded in "short title" style, but whenever a subtitle seemed advantageous in calling attention to the contents or purpose of a given work it has been printed.

By abandoning an alphabetical order for the works listed in this guide I have at times been able to begin the various sections with the most generally used bibliographies or to group titles which have a special affiliation. For example, in Section 32, "American Literature in Relations with Other

Countries and Literatures," all the works dealing with the relationship with France appear in consecutive order rather than scattered as they would be if an alphabetical arrangement were followed. Cross-references are supplied at the ends of various sections calling attention to important items classified elsewhere, but the index of subjects will usually provide further aid in locating items dealing in part with a given topic. Very few anthologies have been included, and most of those that do appear are listed because of their special editorial or bibliographical contents.

The long dashes indicate that publication is still in process. The dates following semicolons indicate the year of a reprinting. The reader should be warned, however, that the indication of reprints is bound to prove incomplete, for so many books of a scholarly or semischolarly sort are now being reproduced by offset that the record can never be kept up to date.

In preparing this edition I have been astounded at the vast number of reprints waiting to be recorded and bewildered by the array of new titles demanding inclusion. Every page of the preceding edition has been changed. More than four hundred new items have been added. In selecting titles I, of course, have assumed the responsibility of making the final decisions, but I have had the advice of a very considerable number of the ablest scholars.

For information and suggestions of one sort or the other I am grateful to many people who have aided me. Of my own colleagues at Duke University I wish to thank especially John Alden, Robert Durden, Irving B. Holley, Jr., Richard Watson, and Robert Woody, of the History Department; Stuart Henry and H. Shelton Smith, of the Divinity School; Louise Hall, of the Art Department; Bernard Duffey, Holger Nygard, and George Williams, of the English Department; and Ashbel Brice, John Menapace, and the late William Owens, of the Duke University Press.

I am grateful also to the following scholars and experts from other institutions: Alfred O. Aldridge (Illinois), George Arms (New Mexico), Roger Asselineau (Paris), Roy P. Basler (Library of Congress), Charles Boewe (Pennsylvania), Robert A. Bone (UCLA), Fredson Bowers (Virginia), Clarence A. Brown (Marquette), Milton Byrd (Northern Michigan), Hennig Cohen (Pennsylvania), F. W. Conner (Alabama), Alexander Cowie (Wesleyan), Richard Dorson (Indiana), David Erdman (N.Y. Public Library), Marvin Felheim (Michigan), Max Fisch (Illinois), Horst Frenz (Indiana), Werner P. Friederich (North Carolina), Hans Galinsky (Mainz), Frederick L. Gwynn (Trinity), James D. Hart (California, Berkeley), Ima H. Herron (Southern Methodist), C. Hugh Holman (North Carolina), William Hutchison (Harvard), James P. Johnson (Howard), Helen D. Jones (Library of Congress), Joseph Jones (Texas), Albert R. Kitzhaber (Oregon), Robert H. Land (Library of Congress), Lewis Leary (North Carolina), Raven I. McDavid, Jr. (Chicago), James B. Meriwether (South Carolina), Lawrence C. Powell (UCLA), S. J. Riccardi (N.Y. Public Library), Edgar P. Richardson (Winterthur Museum), Lyon C. Richardson (Western Reserve), Walter Rideout (Wisconsin), Albert J. Robbins (Indiana), Louis Rubin (North Carolina), Ernest Samuels (Northwestern), Rollo Silver (Boston, Mass.),

Louis P. Simpson (Louisiana), Sigmund Skard (Oslo), Nelle Smither (Douglass), Theodore Spencer (Ohio Wesleyan), David H. Stam (N.Y. Public Library), Madeleine B. Stern (N.Y. City), Floyd Stovall (Virginia), Heinrich Straumann (Zurich), Robert Walker (George Washington), Edward N. Waters (Library of Congress), and Harvey Wish (Western Reserve).

No words can ever express how grateful I am for the help received from members of the staff of the Duke University Library. Their patience was given the acid test by my multitude of inquiries. Especially kind to me have been Samuel Hammond, Gertrude Merritt, and the wizards of the Reference Department: Florence E. Blakely, Mary W. Canada, and Edith Hassold.

Clarence Gohdes

Duke University
February, 1976

Table of contents

Contents

Bibliographical guide to the study of the literature of the U.S.A.

1. Aids to information on all subjects

1.1   Besterman, Theodore. A world bibliography of bibliographies: and of bibliographical catalogues, calendars, abstracts, digests, indexes, and the like. 4th ed. 5 v. Lausanne, [1965–1966].

International in scope, this work lists by subjects separately published bibliographies in all fields—from "academic writings" to "zoology." This is the most comprehensive bibliographical guide available, 117,000 items under 16,000 headings.

1.2   Bibliographic index: a cumulative bibliography of bibliographies 1937——. N.Y., 1945——.

Issued quarterly; cumulated annually. Separate bibliographies and bibliographies in books as well as in many periodicals are listed under several thousand different headings.

1.3   Winchell, Constance M. Guide to reference books. 8th ed. Chicago 1967. Supplements. Comp. Eugene P. Sheehy, Chicago, 1968——.

Standard guide to reference works on all subjects; periodically revised and brought up to date. The 8th edition can often be supplemented by the following item.

1.4   Wynar, Bohden S., ed. American reference books annual 1970——. Littleton, Colo., 1970——.

Coverage begins with 1969 imprints. Descriptive and evaluative annotations, increasingly generous, are often derived from reviews published in librarians' journals and from consultants. Contents of the first five annuals are indexed in Joseph W. Sprug, *Index to American Reference Books Annual 1970–1974: A Cumulative Index to Subjects, Authors, and Titles*, Littleton, Colo., 1974.

1.5   Downs, Robert B., and Jenkins, Frances B., eds. Bibliography: current state and future trends. Urbana, Ill., 1967.

A collection of essays by various hands, including one on "American Literature Bibliography in the Twentieth Century" (pp. 214–236), by John T. Flanagan. The book was previously published in the January and April, 1967, numbers of *Library Trends*.

1.6   Malclès, Louis N. Les sources du travail bibliographique. 4 v. Geneva and Lille, 1950–1958.

A well-indexed general bibliographical guide. V. 2 and 3 are principally concerned with the humanities, and v. 4 with the exact sciences and technology. An updated abridgment appeared in Paris, 1963.

1. Aids to information

1.7 Totok, Wilhelm, and Weitzel, Rolf. Handbuch der bibliographischen Nachschlagewerke. 4th ed. rev. Frankfurt a.M., [1972].

Not so full as Malclès but more systematically arranged.

1.8 Murphey, Robert W. How and where to look it up: a guide to standard sources of information. N.Y., [1958].

Contains numerous subject headings for more than 10,000 annotated reference sources. Explanations of the ways to use them are prepared for the layman's needs. Often uneven and inaccurate in details.

1.9 Walford, A. J., ed. Guide to reference material. 3d ed. 3 v. London, 1973——.

"The aim is to provide a guide to reference books and bibliographies, with emphasis on current material and material published in Britain." The annotations are especially helpful.

1.10 American Library Association index . . . to general literature. 2d ed. Boston and N.Y., 1901. Supplement, Chicago, 1914.

Subject classification of books in English devoted to essays and other factual works, including biography, literary and art criticism, history, and other social studies. The first volume covers books published before 1900; the supplement, books published 1900–1910. Predecessor to the following item.

1.11 Essay and general literature index, 1900——. N.Y., 1934——.

Now kept up to date by regularly appearing supplements; all materials indexed have appeared in book form.

1.12 Library of Congress catalog: a cumulative list of works represented by Library of Congress cards: books: subjects 1950–1954. 20 v. Ann Arbor, Mich., 1955.

Since 1955 continued with the Library of Congress as publisher. Books from the U.S. or abroad received by the Library of Congress or co-operating libraries are classified alphabetically under headings such as "American Wit and Humor," "English Drama," "French Literature," "Zoological Parks." (Very useful also is *The British National Bibliography 1950——: A Subject List of the New British Books Published in 1950——*, ed. A. J. Wells, London, [1951]——.)

1.13 The cumulative book index: a world list of books in the English language. N.Y., 1933——.

An author-title-subject catalog in one alphabet of books in English published in all parts of the world since January 1, 1929.

1.14 Subject guide to books in print: an index to the Publishers' Trade List Annual 1957——. N.Y., [1957]——.

Under more than 20,000 topics or headings, the works currently listed in the catalogs of all the principal U.S. publishers are recorded; volumes of poetry and plays by a single author are omitted.

1.15 The national union catalog of manuscript collections 1959–1961――.
Ann Arbor, Mich., [1962]――.
   Reproduces cards for several thousand manuscript collections issued
by the Library of Congress. The names and subjects covered by the collections are indexed. Compiled by the L. of C. but based on reports from
about 400 repositories.

1.16 Hamer, Philip M., ed. A guide to archives and manuscripts in the U.S.
Compiled for the National Historical Publications Commission. New
Haven, Conn., 1961.
   Indicates the chief holdings of more than 1,300 repositories arranged
by state, and is not confined to material dealing with the U.S.

1.17 American library directory, 1968/69――. N.Y., 1968――.
   A classified list of libraries with names of librarians and statistical data;
compiled biennially.

1.18 Ash, Lee, *et al.* Subject collections: a guide to special book collections
and subject emphases as reported by university, college, public and special libraries and museums in the U.S. and Canada. 4th ed. rev. N.Y.,
1974.
   The intention is to revise this work triennially.

1.19 Kruzas, Anthony T., and Young, Margaret L. Directory of special libraries and information centers. 3d. ed. 2 v. Detroit, [1974].
   Lists specialized collections in many corporate and private institutions
as well as in college and research libraries.

1.20 Freitag, Ruth S. Union lists of serials: a bibliography. Washington,
1964; Boston, 1972.
   Records union lists of serials broadly defined: newspapers, periodicals,
annuals, services, etc., for fifty-six nations.

1.21 Brummel, L., and Egger, E. Guide to union catalogues and international
loan centers. Amsterdam, 1962.

1.22 Bulletin of bibliography. April, 1897――.
   A periodical which specializes in publishing checklists and records of
magazines newly started or ended. From October, 1909, to May–August,
1953, it carried a quarterly Dramatic Index of periodical articles (chiefly
from popular magazines) concerned with all aspects of the theater; inter-
filed in a single alphabet as *Cumulated Dramatic Index*, 1909–1949, 2 v.
Boston, 1965.

1.23 Union list of microfilms. Rev. ed. Ann Arbor, Mich., 1951. 1949–
1959 cumulation. 2 v. Ann Arbor, Mich., 1961――.
   Co-operating libraries reported their microfilm accessions for this
work. Theses from American universities are not included. Newspapers
are listed in *Newspapers in Microform*, Washington, 1948――.

1.24   Tilton, Eva M.   A union list of publications in opaque microforms.   2d ed.   N.Y., [1964].

Includes listings of both American and European publishers.

1.25   Guide to microforms in print 1961——.   Washington, 1961——.

"Lists or refers to all that is available in microform from domestic (U.S.A.) commercial publishers. Titles or projects of some non-commercial publishers are also included." Beginning in 1962, an annual *Subject Guide to Microforms in Print* has appeared as a biennial companion to the above.

1.26   Hale, Richard W., Jr.   Guide to photocopied historical materials in the United States and Canada.   Ithaca, N.Y., [1961].

Follows the fields of history in the sequence employed in *American Historical Association's Guide to Historical Literature* (2.2), but most of the entries relate to American history; private holdings are not indexed.

1.27   Doctoral dissertations accepted by American universities 1933–34—1954–55.   17 v.   N.Y., 1934–1955.

Covers doctoral theses in all fields. The preliminary matter in each volume contains a list of current university serials which publish abstracts of theses. Superseded by "Index to American Doctoral Dissertations," in the following item, v. 16, no. 13—v. 24, no. 13. (For a special list in American literature, see 20.14, Woodress. See also *Dissertations in English and American Literature: Theses Accepted by American, British and German Universities, 1865–1964*, comp. Lawrence F. McNamee, N.Y., 1968. Supplement, 1969——).

1.28   Comprehensive dissertation index, 1861–1972.   37 v.   Ann Arbor, Mich., 1973——.   Microfiche.

Over 400,000 doctoral dissertations, chiefly from the U.S. The first 32 volumes covered 22 general subjects; the remainder list the authors. Volumes 29 and 30 are devoted to language and literature. Annual supplements.

1.29   Dissertation abstracts: a guide to dissertations and monographs available on microfilm.   (Originally entitled Microfilm abstracts.)   Ann Arbor, Mich., 1938——.

The number of co-operating universities has greatly increased, and this compilation of abstracts of dissertations which have been microfilmed now appears monthly. The "Index" is the standard current list of dissertations in all fields accepted by American universities. With v. 25 (1964–1965), no. 13, the "Index" became "American Doctoral Dissertations," and from 1965–1966 it has been issued without *Dissertation Abstracts* volume numbering.

1.30   Collison, Robert L.   Encyclopaedias: their history throughout the ages.   2d ed.   N.Y., [1966].

A guide with historical notes on general encyclopedias issued in various countries.

1.31   Keller, Helen R.   The dictionary of dates.   2 v.   N.Y., 1934; 1971.
Among other good dictionaries of dates which include more recent dates are: Neville Williams, *Chronology of the Modern World, 1763 to the Present Time*, N.Y., 1966; and Robert Collison, *Newnes Dictionary of Dates*, 2d ed. rev., London, [1966]; N.Y., 1969.

1.32   Zaunmüller, Wolfram.   Bibliographisches Handbuch der Sprachwörterbücher.   Stuttgart, 1958.
More than 5,600 dictionaries covering about 600 languages are listed.

1.33   Vertical file index.   N.Y., 1935——.
A selective list of pamphlet material of interest to general libraries; issued monthly, accumulated annually. There are both a subject index and a title index. Begins with publications of April, 1932. V. 33 (1964) was the last annual accumulation. Thereafter monthly issues only.

1.34   Buchanan, William W., and Kanely, Edna M.   Cumulative subject index to the monthly catalogs of U. S. government publications 1900–1971.   15 v.   Washington, 1973–1975.
The years 1895–1899 were not covered because of the lack of earlier indexing. See also the *Document Catalog* for 1895–1940.

1.35   Wynkoop, Sally.   Government reference books: a biennial guide to U.S. government publications.   3d ed.   Littleton, Colo., 1974——.
Centers on bibliographies, directories, indexes, statistical reports, etc.

1.36   White, Carl M., *et al.*   Sources of information in the social sciences: a guide to the literature.   2d ed.   Chicago, 1973.
International in scope, but the section on history is largely concerned with works in English. A public librarians' tool.

1.37   International maps and atlases in print.   London and N.Y., [1974].
An enlargement of the British *Stanford Reference Catalogue*.

1.38   Koehmstedt, Carol L.   Plot summary index.   Metuchen, N.J., 1973.
Covers 24 collections, chiefly those compiled by Frank N. Magill, such as *Masterplots*, 6 v., N.Y., [1964].

2. Philosophy and general methodology of literary and historical study

2.1   Wellek, René, and Warren, Austin.   Theory of literature.   3d rev. ed.   London, [1966].
Describes and criticizes the various methods of, and approaches to, the study of literature, with generalizations on literary theory, evaluation, re-

search, and history. An excellent international bibliography is appended, with the following subtopics: "Literature and Literary Study," "The Nature of Literature," "The Function of Literature," "Literary Theory, History, and Criticism," "National, Comparative and General Literature," "The Ordering and Establishing of Evidence," "Literature and Biography," "Literature and Psychology," "Literature and Society," "Literature and Ideas," "Literature and the Other Arts," "The Analysis of the Literary Work of Art," "Euphony, Rhythm, and Meter," "Style and Stylistics," "Image, Metaphor, Symbol, and Myth," "The Nature and Modes of Fiction," "Literary Genres," "Evaluation," "Literary History," and "The Study of Literature in the Graduate School." Contains a bibliography.

2.2 Howe, George F., *et al.*, eds. The American Historical Association's guide to historical literature. N.Y., 1961.
A somewhat uneven bibliography of selected historical works treating various nations, peoples, and religions which lists in Part I, Section A, books dealing with the methodology of history and related studies.

2.3 History and theory: studies in the philosophy of history. 1960———.
An international periodical which issues also *Beihefte*, several of which are bibliographies covering works on the philosophy of history, 1945———.

2.4 Historical abstracts. (Published by the American Bibliographical Center, Santa Barbara, Calif.): March, 1955———.
Carries regularly sections on methodology, research methods, and historiography. International coverage.

2.5 Greenlaw, Edwin. The province of literary history. Baltimore, [1931]; Ann Arbor, Mich., 1968.
Literary history is viewed as a province distinct from that of criticism or literary biography, and certain of its problems and methods are set forth.

2.6 Boas, George. "Some problems of intellectual history." Studies in intellectual history, pp. 3–21. [Baltimore], 1953.
Points out "some of the peculiarities of historiography" and some of its problems as they pertain to the history of ideas.

2.7 Langlois, Charles V., and Seignobos, Charles. Introduction to the study of history. Tr. G. G. Berry. N.Y., [1926].

2.8 The social sciences in historical study: a report of the committee on historiography. Social Science Research Council bulletin, no. 64. N.Y., 1954.
Discusses, among other matters, the methods dominant in various social sciences that have relevance for historians.

2.9 Berkhofer, Robert F. A behavioral approach to historical analysis. N.Y., 1969.

Attacks traditional historiography and views a panoply of writings on the other social studies with an eye to emulation.

2.10 Collingwood, R. G. The idea of history. Oxford, 1946; N.Y., 1956.
A philosophical attempt to define the special character of historical knowledge.

2.11 Marrou, H.-I. De la connaissance historique. 2d ed. Paris, 1956.
An introduction to historical method presently in favor in certain quarters.

2.12 Iggers, Georg G. New directions in European historiography. Middletown, Conn., 1975.
Attempts to find a common demoninator among the very recent West German scholars, the Marxists, and the French historians associated with the review *Annales* in the pursuit of "total history." (The Johns Hopkins Press has published examples of the *Annales* writers.)

2.13 Jones, Howard M. The theory of American literature. 2d ed. Ithaca, N.Y., [1965].
Attitudes pervading scholarship on American literature from colonial times to the present are briefly surveyed.

2.14 Altick, Richard D. The art of literary research. 2d ed. N.Y., [1976].
Discusses purposes and methods of literary research on the level of a beginning graduate student. A selected bibliography of a set of exercises points up the fact that it is designed as a textbook.

2.15 Thorpe, James. Literary scholarship: a handbook for advanced students of English and American literature. Boston, [1964].
A practical manual which outlines principles and methods and calls attention to a limited number of essential bibliographical aids to research.

2.16 Hockett, Homer C. The critical method in historical research and writing. N.Y., [1955]; [1967].
Both a bibliography of essential tools and a lucid guide to research in American history. Part II, "The Master's Essay," describes the processes of finding and developing a topic, note taking, outlining, making a bibliography, etc. Included also are brief surveys of American historiography, of the historical projects of the WPA and of the armed services, and of the various types of U.S. government publications. Much of the discussion of method is as pertinent for the student of literature as for the student of history. The list of chief bibliographies dealing with the history of the various regions and the several states (pp. 281–295) is especially helpful. (For methodology in the study of American history, see also the first chapters of 9.1, *Harvard Guide*.)

2.17 Shafer, Robert J., *et al.*, eds. A guide to historical method. Homewood, Ill., 1969; 1973.
Primarily for beginning researchers in American history. The chapters are the products of Syracuse University faculty members.

2. Philosophy and general methodology

2.18 O'Neill, William L., ed. Insights and parallels: problems and issues of American social history. Minneapolis, 1973.
An anthology which illustrates varieties of methods.

2.19 McDermott, John F., ed. Research opportunities in American cultural history. Lexington, Ky., [1961].
Papers by various authorities on such topics as "Travel Literature" (Thomas D. Clark), "Folklore and Cultural History" (Richard Dorson), "Middlewestern Regional Literature" (John T. Flanagan), and "The Book Trade and Publishing History" (David Kaser).

2.20 Sanders, Chauncey. An introduction to research in English literary history. N.Y., [1952]; [1960].
Many of the illustrations of problems in editing, source study, etc., are taken from the American field. Part 4, "Suggestions on Thesis-writing" is elementary but clear-cut.

2.21 Wetherill, Peter M. The literary text: an examination of critical methods. Berkeley, 1974.
"My aim is basically to point to the problems which I think arise when a text is examined closely."

2.22 Morize, André. Problems and methods of literary history, with special reference to modern French literature: a guide for graduate students. Boston and N.Y., [1922]; 1966.
Valuable for students of literature in any language, since it surveys the techniques employed in scholarly research: preparing an edition, use of sources, questions of verification and influence, preparation and redaction of a dissertation, etc.

2.23 Vigneron, Robert. Explication de textes, and its adaptation to the teaching of modern languages. Chicago, [1928].
Reprinted from *Modern Language Journal* for October, 1927. Outlines the system of *explication* as developed in France.

2.24 Richards, Ivor A. Practical criticism: a study of literary judgment. London and N.Y., 1929; 1968.
This work is the grandfather, if not the father, of a considerable element in the recent analytical study of poetry.

2.25 Stallknecht, Newton P., and Frenz, Horst, eds. Comparative literature: method and perspective. Rev. ed. Carbondale, Ill., [1971].
Thirteen essays on topics like definition, translation, indebtedness, relations of literature and psychology, literature and the arts, modes of criticism, and Romanticism. See also 35.28–29.

2.26 Aldridge, A. Owen, ed. Comparative literature: matter and method. Urbana, Ill., 1969.
A collection of articles illustrating the principal methods of comparative literature, accompanied by the editor's explanatory introductions.

2.27 Weisstein, Ulrich. Comparative literature and literary theory. Rev. ed. Tr. William Riggan. Bloomington, Ind., 1974.

A substantial and respected manual.

2.28 Prawer, Siegbert S. Comparative literary studies: an introduction. N.Y., [1973].

Covers in a compact way the main concerns of comparative studies. Intended for beginners.

2.29 Brack, O. M., and Barnes, Warner, eds. Bibliography and textual criticism: English and American literature, 1700 to the present. Chicago, 1969.

Varied essays on aspects of textual methodology followed by a selective bibliography. Many of the illustrations are taken from the American field.

2.30 Poletta, Gregory T., ed. Issues in contemporary literary criticism. Boston, [1973].

An anthology which reflects many of the more recent "issues" from abroad. See also, for phenomenology and structuralism, another anthology, more philosophical: *European Literary Theory and Practice*, ed. Vernon W. Gras, N.Y., [1973].

2.31 Bowers, Fredson. "Textual criticism and the literary critic." Textual and literary criticism. Cambridge, 1959; N.Y., [1964].

Points out the usefulness of textual criticism to aesthetic literary discussion.

2.32 Van Hoof, Henry. International bibliography of translation. Totowa, N.J., 1973.

Coverage to July, 1971. This is an American edition of a European work. The history and theory of written translation form part of the contents. See also 35.3.

2.33 Arrowsmith, William, and Shattuck, Roger, eds. The craft and context of translation: a critical symposium. Garden City, N.Y., [1964].

Most of the papers collected here are the products of experienced translators. (The University of Texas has sponsored a kind of institute of translation.)

2.34 Thorpe, James, ed. Relations of literary study: essays on interdisciplinary contributions. N.Y., [1967].

Seven scholars discuss the relations of literary studies with history, myth, biography, psychology, sociology, religion, and music.

2.35 Rehder, Helmut, ed. Literary symbolism: a symposium. Austin, Tex., [1965].

Five essays discussing aspects of symbolism in modern literature.

2.36 Yule, G. Udny. The statistical study of literary vocabulary. Cambridge, 1944; Hamden, Conn., 1968.

The pioneer study in its field.

2. Philosophy and general methodology

2.37 New literary history: a journal of theory and interpretation. October, 1969——.

Each issue "examines a theoretical problem which, while specifically literary, has ramifications or analogues in other disciplines."

3. Technical procedures in literary and historical research

3.1 Studies in bibliography: papers of the Bibliographical Society of the University of Virginia, 1947——. Charlottesville, Va., 1948——.

An annual devoted to bibliographical studies pertaining especially to English and American literature. Regularly includes a selective checklist of bibliographical scholarship published during the preceding year, with emphasis on printing, publishing, and textual studies. The checklists for 1949–1955 have been assembled in a decennial extra volume, v. 10, 1957.

3.2 Bowers, Fredson. Principles of bibliographical description. Princeton, N.J., 1949; N.Y., 1962.

A standard work on the methods of analyzing a book with a view to making a scientific description of it as a physical entity. Offers expert technical explanations of such matters as edition, impression, issue, state, format. Of special interest is the section on books of the 19th and 20th centuries.

3.3 Gaskell, Philip. A new introduction to bibliography. N.Y., 1972.

Based often on Bowers (3.2), this opus incorporates discussions of recent research and updates the selective lists of references.

3.4 Thorpe, James. Principles of textual criticism. San Marino, Calif., 1972.

A major corrective to some of the views identified with Greg, Bowers, and the MLA Center for Editions of American Authors, as well as an exposition of sound practices in collecting and editing literary texts.

3.5 Esdaile, Arundell. A student's manual of bibliography. Rev. by Roy Stokes. 4th rev. ed. London and N.Y., 1967.

History of printing, methods of collating and describing books, types, and arrangement of bibliographies. Often outmoded by Bowers. (For a model arrangement of an extensive single-author bibliography, see Thomas F. Currier, *A Bibliography of J. G. Whittier*, Cambridge, Mass., 1937; N.Y., 1971).

3.6 Collison, Robert. Published library catalogues: an introduction to their contents and use. London, 1973.

About 600 catalogs or union lists of the English-speaking countries are considered with a particular slant toward resources and collections.

3.7 Parker, Donald. Local history: how to gather it, write it, and publish it. Rev. and ed. by Bertha E. Josephson. N.Y., 1944.
Useful for the study of minor authors of regional interest. Cf. also Philip D. Jordan, *The Nature and Practice of State and Local History*, Washington, [1958], a pamphlet issued by the Service Center for Teachers conducted by the American Historical Association.

3.8 Cumming, John. A guide to the writing of local history. Lansing, Mich., 1974.
A pamphlet outline.

3.9 Burnette, O. Lawrence, Jr. Beneath the footnote: a guide to the use and preservation of American historical sources. Madison, Wis., 1969.
Fundamentals of the uses of primary sources. Chapters deal also with national and state and local archives, private collections, and newspapers. Bibliography, pp. 379–437.

3.10 Gibson, Jeremy. Wills and where to find them. Baltimore, [1974].
A British work which may offer suggestions to those seeking to locate authors' papers.

3.11 Moss, William W. Oral history program manual. N.Y., [1974].
Profiting by the Kennedy Library experiences, this provides a guide to starting and conducting a project based on the tapes.

3.12 Haselden, Reginald B. Scientific aids for the study of manuscripts. [Oxford], 1935.
Contains much material on general procedures involved in studying manuscripts. (Practical advice on handling manuscripts appears also in 9.1, *Harvard Guide.*)

3.13 Greg, Walter W. The calculus of variants: an essay on textual criticism. Oxford, 1927.
A scientific treatise on the establishment of relationships among manuscripts of a given work and on the problems of handling variants.

3.14 Thorpe, James. The use of manuscripts in literary research: problems of access and literary property rights. N.Y., 1974.
A pamphlet that sets forth the elementary facts.

3.15 Halsband, Robert. "Editing the letters of letter-writers." Studies in bibliography, v. 11, pp. 25–37 (1958).
Practical suggestions for handling problems presented by the editing of collections of letters. (For a splendid example of techniques applied, see *The Letters of Ralph Waldo Emerson*, ed. Ralph L. Rusk, 6 v., N.Y., 1939.)

3. Technical procedures

3.16 Center for Editions of American Authors. Statement of editorial principles and procedures: a working manual for editing nineteenth-century American texts. Rev. ed. N.Y., 1972.

A pamphlet put out by the Center, an agency of the Modern Language Association, located first at New York University, then at the University of South Carolina, which ran out of funds in 1976.

3.17 Lewis, Chester M., and Offenhauser, William H., Jr. Microrecording. N.Y., [1956].

Description of various kinds of microrecording and copying devices and methods, including xerography. See also *Library Trends*, January, 1960.

3.18 American Library Association. Directory of library photoduplication services in the U.S., Canada, and Mexico. 2d ed. Chicago, 1962.

See also the annual *Guide to Microforms in Print*, Washington, 1961———.

3.19 National register of microform masters. Washington, September, 1965———.

Issued by the Library of Congress.

3.20 Microform review. January, 1972———.

Especially useful to librarians.

3.21 Ballou, Hubbard, ed. Guide to microreproduction equipment. 5th ed. Silver Spring, Md., 1971———.

Describes, with many illustrations, cameras, hand viewers, processors, contact printers, enlargers, etc. Issued under the auspices of the National Microfilm Association, which publishes also an annual volume of proceedings and a bimonthly *National Micro News*.

3.22 Garraty, John A. The nature of biography. N.Y., 1957; 1964.

Discusses the historical development of biography as a genre and contains a section on the methods of preparing a biography. A helpful list of sources is also provided. See also Catherine D. Bowen, *Biography: The Craft and the Calling*, Boston, [1969].

3.23 Clifford, James L., ed. Biography as an art: selected criticism 1560–1960. N.Y., 1962.

The list of works dealing with the problems and materials of biographies adds to the usefulness of this anthology.

3.24 Collison, Robert. Abstracts and abstracting services. Santa Barbara, Calif., 1971.

General practices in making abstracts are set forth as well as advice on editing and publishing them. There is also a hasty sketch of the history of abstract services in the U.S. "Selected Readings" take the place of a full bibliography.

3.25 Brower, Reuben, ed. On translating. Cambridge, Mass., 1959; N.Y., 1966.

Contains a critical bibliography. Cf. also 2.25.

3.26 Halkett, Samuel, and Laing, John. Dictionary of anonymous and pseudonymous English literature. New ed. Ed. James Kennedy *et al.* 9 v. Edinburgh and London, 1926–1962.

Many American works are included, especially in v. 8, which covers 1900–1949. This work is a standard one for English literature, from earliest times.

3.27 Cushing, William. Anonyms: a dictionary of revealed authorship. Cambridge, Mass., 1889; Hildesheim, Germany, 1969.

A standard work for English and American anonymous titles of the 18th and 19th centuries. (For a list of handbooks dealing with anonymously or pseudonymously published works, in various languages, see Adah V. Morris, "Anonyms and Pseudonyms, an Annotated List," *Library Quarterly*, v. 3, pp. 354–372, October, 1933; and the bibliography [pp. 207–279] of Archer Taylor and Fredric J. Mosher, *The Bibliographical History of Anonyma and Pseudonyma*, Chicago, 1951.)

3.28 Bauer, Andrew. The Hawthorn dictionary of pseudonyms. N.Y., [1971].

International in scope, this goes beyond literary works but may add an item to the literary record ever and anon.

3.29 Perman, Dagmar H., ed. Bibliography and the historian. Santa Barbara, Calif., and Washington, [1968].

Anthology of essays dealing with changes in progress in historical bibliography: new technology, new services of the Library of Congress, etc.

3.30 Youden, W. W., ed. Computer literature bibliography, N.Y., 1970————.

The first volume covers the years 1946–1963. A "special" publication by the National Bureau of Standards.

3.31 Shorter, Edward. The historian and the computer: a practical guide. N.Y., [1971]; [1975].

Contains bibliographical footnotes. Cf. also the articles in Robert P. Swierenga, ed., *Quantification in American History: Theory and Research*, N.Y., 1970.

3.32 Wisbey, R. A., ed. The computer in literary and linguistic research. London, 1971.

Selected revised papers from a Cambridge University conference which indicate the ways computers are used in dictionary making, editing texts, analyzing style, etc.

3.33 Bowles, Edmund A. Computers in humanistic research: readings and perspectives. Englewood Cliffs, N.J., [1967].

Of the twenty-four papers collected here six deal with language and literature. One of the better anthologies of its sort. (New York University supported an Institute for Computer Research in the Humanities which issued news of projects in a newsletter published monthly 1966——September, 1969. Nineteen sixty-six also marked the first appearance of

3. Technical procedures

Computers and the Humanities, published by Queens College of the City University of New York—a more formal periodical which offers surveys and an annual bibliography. Charles J. Sippl, *Computer Dictionary*, 2d ed., Indianapolis, [1974], is designed to help interpret the terminology of data processing, etc.; and *Computer Yearbook and Directory*, Detroit, 1966———, provides bibliography, articles on the "state of the art," and a section describing computer systems introduced since 1963. The MLA has computerized its annual bibliography, and Lewis Sawin and his colleagues at the University of Colorado (Boulder) have experimented with the storage of American literature bibliography. Cornell University has a center for the preparation of concordances with the use of computers.)

4. Definitions of literary and related terms

4.1 Wolf, Martin L. Dictionary of the arts. N.Y., [1951].
Briefly defines many terms used in literature, ballet, architecture, music, painting, etc.

4.2 Shipley, Joseph T., ed. Dictionary of world literary terms: forms, technique, criticism. Rev. ed. Boston, [1970].
An overhauled and sometimes updated edition of a work already revamped in 1953 and again in 1960. Lacks certain definitions of critical terms contained in earlier editions, which were entitled *Dictionary of World Literature*.

4.3 Abrams, Meyer H. A glossary of literary terms. 3d ed. N.Y., [1971].
The definitions are accompanied by examples intended for undergraduate use. Lee T. Lemon, *A Glossary for the Study of English*, N.Y., 1971, is aimed at the same market as Abrams but is arranged topically, e.g., types, plot, versification, bookmaking, periods, movements, etc.

4.4 Holman, C. Hugh. A handbook to literature. 3d ed. Indianapolis, [1972].
A generally useful work based on worthy predecessors.

4.5 Scott, Arthur F. Current literary terms. London and N.Y., 1965.
Includes also various foreign words and phrases.

4.6 Thompson, Elizabeth H. American Library Association glossary of library terms: with a selection of terms in related fields. Chicago, 1943.

4.7 Barnhart, Clarence L., and Halsey, William D., eds. The new Century handbook of English literature. Rev. ed. N.Y., [1967].

Contains entries on authors, titles, and characters from works of literature, etc.; includes a fair number of clear definitions.

4.8   Harvey, Paul, and Eagle, Dorothy, eds. The Oxford companion to English literature. 4th ed. Oxford and N.Y., 1967.
A standard handbook for the study of English literature.

4.9   Glaister, Geoffrey A. An encyclopedia of the book. Cleveland and N.Y., [1960].
Chiefly an alphabetical glossary of terms, explanations of practices, materials, etc., relating to paper-making, printing, bookbinding, and publishing. Leans heavily on the Swedish *Grafisk Uppslagbok* (1951).

4.10   Bookman's glossary. 4th ed. rev. N.Y., [1961].
Guide to terminology "used in the production and distribution of books new and old." A brief list of works on subjects reflected in the glossary appears as an appendix.

4.11   Carter, John. ABC for book-collectors. 3d ed. rev. London, [1961].
Definitions, with occasional comment, of such words and phrases as would be likely to puzzle a student facing for the first time a bookseller's or auctioneer's catalog.

4.12   The bookman's concise dictionary. London, [1956].
Useful for British terms.

4.13   Walsh, Donald D. What's what: a list of useful terms for the teachers of modern languages. 3d ed. N.Y., 1965.
Linguistic and professional terms.

4.14   Preminger, Alex, *et al.* The Princeton encyclopedia of poetry and poetics. Princeton, N.J., 1965.
About 1,000 entries on "the history, theory, technique, and criticism of poetry from earliest times to the present," with selected bibliographies.

4.15   Deutsch, Babette. Poetry handbook: a dictionary of terms. 4th ed. N.Y., [1974].
The definitions are elementary and clear. (Works on versification usually aid greatly in defining poetical terms, e.g., George R. Stewart, Jr., *The Technique of English Verse*, N.Y., [1930]; Paul F. Baum, *The Principles of English Versification*, Cambridge, Mass., 1922; Hamden, Conn., 1969. For others, see 22.27, Karl Shapiro.)

4.16   Malof, Joseph. A manual of English meters. Bloomington, Ind., [1970].

4.17   Bowman, Walter P., and Ball, Robert H. Theatre language: a dictionary of terms in English of the drama and stage from medieval to modern times. N.Y., [1961].
Over 3,000 terms and phrases, including recent jargon, cant, and slang.

See also 5.3, 35.10–11, 35.19.

5. Preparation of manuscripts for publication

5.1 On the publication of research: essays by R. B. McKerrow and Henry M. Silver. Reprinted from PMLA, v. 65 (April, 1950). N.Y., [1964].
Brief practical instructions on how to organize an article, how to prepare the manuscript, and principles to follow in reading proof. (See also *PMLA*, v. 81, September, 1966.)

5.2 The MLA style sheet. Comp. William R. Parker, *et al.* 2d ed. N.Y., [1970].
Directions for preparing manuscripts, footnotes, and bibliographies for theses. The style suggested here is used by a large number of scholarly journals. (The pamphlet may be obtained from the Modern Language Association of America.) See also Edward D. Seeber, *A Style Manual for Authors*, Bloomington, Ind., [1965].

5.3 A manual of style. By the staff of the University of Chicago press. 12th rev. ed. Chicago, [1969].
Rules for preparation of copy, suggestions for editing, specimens of type, etc. This excellent work is widely used by magazine and book publishers. Contains also a glossary of technical terms.

5.4 Hurt, Peyton, and Richmond, Mary L. Bibliography and footnotes: a style manual. 3d ed. rev. Berkeley and Los Angeles, 1968.

5.5 Von Ostermann, Georg F. Manual of foreign languages. 4th ed. rev. N.Y., 1952.
Editorial manual indicating peculiarities of capitalization, accents, abbreviations, numerals, etc., for a large and diverse list of languages.

5.6 Nicholson, Margaret. A manual of copyright practice for writers, publishers, and agents. 2d ed. N.Y., 1956.
"What to do in a specific situation involving copyright." See also the same author's *Practical Style Guide for Authors and Editors*, N.Y., [1967].

5.7 Wittenberg, Philip. The protection of literary property. Boston, [1968].
On American laws concerning copyright, libel, permissions for quotations, censorship, etc. See also Norman H. Pearson, "Problems of Literary Executorship," *Studies in Bibliography*, v. 5, pp. 3–20 (1952–1953). *Copyright Law Symposium Number Ten*, N.Y., 1959, contains essays by law students offering advice on such matters as reproducing printed works on microfilm, the amount and kind of quotation that are legally permissible, the use of manuscripts, and an author's rights in his article published in a magazine. (The history of an important phase of copyright is dealt with by Aubert J. Clark in *The Movement for International Copyright in Nineteenth Century America*, Washington, 1960; 1973.

Joseph W. Rogers, *U.S. National Bibliography and the Copyright Law,*
N.Y., [1960], is chiefly a review of the history of catalogs of copyright
entries since 1891. See also Matt Roberts, *Copyright: A Selected Bibliography of Periodical Literature Relating to Literary Property in the U.S.,*
Metuchen, N.J., 1971.)

5.8 Hogan, John C., and Cohen, Saul. An author's guide to scholarly publishing and the law. Englewood Cliffs, N.J., [1965].
Includes sample forms and discusses photoduplication problems.

5.9 Spiker, Sina. Indexing your book: a practical guide for authors. 2d ed.
Madison, Wis., 1963.

5.10 McNaughton, Harry H. Proofreading and copyediting. N.Y., 1973.
An elementary compendium useful to a beginner.

5.11 Byrd, Milton B., and Goldsmith, Arnold L. Publication guide for literary
and linguistic scholars. Detroit, 1958.
Lists 180 journals, chiefly of interest to scholars in English and American literature, with subscription data, editorial policies, and information
on the nature and handling of manuscripts.

5.12 Gerstenberger, Donna, and Hendrick, George. Third directory of periodicals publishing articles in English and American literature and language. Chicago, [1970].
List 547 periodicals, with pertinent information on each. Included are
several journals devoted to folklore and some "little" magazines that
"carry an occasional critical article." See also 7.14.

5.13 Harmon, Gary L., and Harmon, Susanna M. Scholar's market: an international directory of periodicals publishing literary scholarship. Columbus, Ohio, 1974.
The essential information is offered, and there are classifications on
"American Ethnic Minorities," "Literary Reviews," "Film," "Poetry," etc.

5.14 The literary market place. N.Y., 1940——.
Annual directory which arranges American publishers by location and
by type of books published. It also supplies lists of national associations,
literary awards, columnists, radio book programs, magazines and newspapers containing book news, etc. (Literary awards are more extensively
considered in *Literary and Library Prizes*, 8th ed., N.Y., 1973——.)

5.15 Lee, Marshall. Bookmaking: the illustrated guide to design and production. N.Y., [1965].
Provides an easily understood description of the mechanics (composition, engraving, plate-making, printing, etc.), for authors and editors,
as well as production people.

6. Library of Congress catalogs and chief registers of U.S. publications

6.1   A catalog of books represented by Library of Congress printed cards issued to July 31, 1942. 167 v. Ann Arbor, Mich., 1942–1946; Paterson, N.J., 1960.

Photographic reproduction of nearly two million cards, alphabetically arranged. Not all the books represented by the cards are in the Library of Congress. This work does not cover all the holdings of the Library of Congress—but only works for which cards were printed, even when the works were in other libraries—from August, 1898, to 1942.

6.2   ———. Supplement: cards issued August 1, 1942—December 31, 1947. 42 v. Ann Arbor, Mich., 1948; Paterson, N.J., 1960.

6.3   The Library of Congress author catalog: a cumulative list of works represented by Library of Congress printed cards 1948–1952. 24 v. Ann Arbor, Mich., 1953; Paterson, N.J., 1960.

For the years 1942–1962 this and the following appear in a master cumulation, Detroit, 1969———.

6.4   The national union catalog: a cumulative author list representing Library of Congress printed cards and titles reported by other American libraries 1953–1957. 28 v. Ann Arbor, Mich., 1958; N.Y., 1961———. Supplements are cumulated annually and then quinquennially.

Registers also music, phonorecords, motion pictures, and filmstrips. Since 1956 includes "not only Library of Congress cards but also cards representing titles with 1956 or later imprints reported to the National Union Catalog by other North American libraries, together with locations of all such titles reported to the National Union Catalog." Continued serially as *National Union Catalog*. See 1.12 for complementary subject list. The catalogs covering imprints of 1955 and earlier are in process of being reprinted, ALA, London, 1968———.

6.5   Evans, Charles. American bibliography: a chronological dictionary of all books, pamphlets and periodical publications printed in the U.S. . . . 1639–[1800]. 14 v. Chicago, and Worcester, Mass., 1903–1959. Supplement by Roger P. Bristol. Charlottesville, Va., 1962———.

V. 13, edited by Clifford K. Shipton, was published in Worcester, Mass. V. 14, likewise published in Worcester, is an index, prepared by Roger P. Bristol, who is also responsible for *Index of Printers, Publishers, and Booksellers Indicated by Charles Evans in His American Bibliography*, Charlottesville, Va., 1961. The earlier volumes were reprinted by Peter Smith, Gloucester, Mass., in 1941. A number of "ghost" titles appear, especially in the earlier volumes. (The American Antiquarian Society has reproduced in microprint all the available works listed in Evans.)

6.6 Shipton, Clifford K., and Morney, James E., eds. National index of American imprints through 1800: the short-title Evans. 2 v. Barre, Mass., 1969.

Covers the 39,000 items listed in Evans (6.5) and adds nearly 10,000 additional ones. Designed as companion to "Early American Imprint Series" started in 1955 by the American Antiquarian Society.

6.7 Waters, Willard O. American imprints, 1648–1797, in the Huntington Library, supplementing Evans' American Bibliography. [Cambridge, Mass., 1933].

Reprinted from *Huntington Library Bulletin*, no. 3 (February, 1933).

6.8 Stark, Lewis M., and Cole, Maud D. Checklist of additions to Evans' American Bibliography in the rare book room of the New York Public Library. N.Y., 1960.

6.9 Shaw, Ralph R., and Shoemaker, Richard H. American bibliography: a preliminary checklist for 1801–1819. 22 v. N.Y., 1958–1966.

Compiled entirely from secondary sources, this makes a tentative step in filling the gap in the listing of American publications for the period 1801–1819 inclusive. The entries are uneven in quality, but the locations of copies are included. The 1966 volume consists of corrections. (For this period there are also many state or regional lists of imprints.)

6.10 Growoll, Adolf. Book-trade bibliography in the U.S. in the 19th century. N.Y., 1889; [1966].

Lists the chief older sources of information on works printed in the U.S. during the century.

6.11 Sabin, Joseph. Bibliotheca Americana: a dictionary of books relating to America, from its discovery. . . . 29 v. N.Y., 1868–1936; Amsterdam, 1961–1962.

Includes works published in America and about America printed elsewhere. Arrangement is alphabetical by author, primarily. In later volumes the scope is materially reduced. Like Evans, this often mentions libraries owning copies, and hence is useful for interlibrary loans.

6.12 Roorbach, Orville A. Bibliotheca Americana, 1820–1861. 4 v. N.Y., 1852–1861; 1939.

Catalog of publications, including reprints, arranged by authors and titles, giving publisher, date, price. By no means are all American published works of the period listed. Displaced by Richard H. Shoemaker, R. H. Shaw, and M. Frances Cooper, *A Checklist of American Imprints 1820——*, N.Y., 1965——.

6.13 Kelly, James. The American catalogue of books published in the U.S. from January, 1861 to January, 1871. 2 v. N.Y., 1866–1871; 1938.

Like Roorbach, far from complete.

6.14 The American catalogue, 1876–1910. 9 v. in 13. N.Y., 1876–1910; 1941.

6. Library of Congress catalogs

(For the gap between 1872 and 1876, see *Publishers' Weekly*, 1872–1876. Lee Ash, 31 Alden Rd., New Haven 15, Conn., is planning a cumulative index for this period.)

6.15 Annual American catalogue, 1869–1872, 1886–1910. 25 v. N.Y., 1887–1911.
Inferior to, but sometimes supplementary to, *American Catalogue*.

6.16 The United States catalog: books in print. Minneapolis and N.Y., 1900–1928.
Succeeded by the following item, which has a wider coverage.

6.17 Cumulative book index, 1928/1932——. N.Y., 1933——.
Now appears monthly, except July and August. Semiannual volumes.

6.18 Publishers' weekly, 1872——. N.Y., 1872——.
Lists new publications weekly. Books are often announced in advance, in special numbers issued in January (for spring), May (for summer), and September (for fall). In September, 1974, the listing of new books was split off in a separate publication entitled *Weekly Record*.

6.19 American book publishing record. February, 1960——.
Cumulates monthly the *Publishers' Weekly* announcements, along with full Library of Congress cataloging. An annual index started for 1962, N.Y., 1963——.

6.20 Books in print: an author-title-series index to the Publishers' Trade List Annual. N.Y., 1948——.
Registers by authors and then by titles all the books listed for sale in the current catalogs of the vast majority of American publishers. (For the corresponding subject index, see 1.14.) *Forthcoming Books* (January, 1966——) appears six times per year and now includes books recently printed, prior to the annual edition of *Books in Print*.

6.21 Paperbound books in print. N.Y., 1955——.
Serially issued by the R. R. Bowker Co. Indexed by subject, author, and title. American publishers only.

7. Indexes to contents of magazines

7.1 Poole's index to periodical literature, 1802–1907. 7 v. in 6. N.Y., 1938.
Subject index only. The 479 British and American periodicals covered are thrown into one alphabet in Marion V. Bell and Jean C. Bacon, *Poole's Index: Date and Volume Key*, Chicago, 1957. C. Edward Wall, *Cumulative Author Index for Poole's* . . . , Ann Arbor, Mich., 1971, helps

to remedy the lack of information on the authors of the bulk of the items in Poole. (Poole and later indexing services are included in *Indexed Periodicals*, v. 1——, Ann Arbor, Mich., 1975——, which is a guide showing where the periodicals are indexed, etc.)

7.2 Cushing, Helen G., and Morris, Adah V. Nineteenth century readers' guide to periodical literature, 1890–1899: with supplementary indexing 1900–1922. 2 v. N.Y., 1944.

Fifty-one British and American magazines are covered for the nineties; fourteen are continued beyond 1899. Many anonymous contributors are identified.

7.3 Readers' guide to periodical literature, 1900——. Minneapolis, etc., 1905——.

7.4 International index to periodicals, devoted chiefly to the humanities and science, 1907——. N.Y., etc., 1916——.

In June, 1965 (v. 53), the title was changed to *Social Sciences and Humanities Index* from which *Humanities Index* was split, 1974——.

7.5 Annual magazine subject index, 1907–1949. 43 v. Boston, 1908–1952.

About half of the magazines covered relate to history, especially American local history. Also contains "Dramatic Index" of books and articles on drama and theater (cumulated in *Cumulated Dramatic Index, 1909–1949*, 2 v., Boston, 1955). The 43 volumes are rearranged in one alphabetical sequence in *Cumulated Magazine Subject Index, 1907–1949*, 2 v., Boston, 1964.

7.6 The book review digest, 1905——. N.Y., 1906——.

Excerpts from the early reviews of selected newly published books. The periodicals covered are largely general organs like weeklies that review books fairly soon after they appear. Helpful in obtaining a cursory view of contents of books and a sampling of the reviewers' reactions to them. Many books in English, as well as in other languages, not covered by *Book Review Digest* are included in the reviews appearing in *Bibliographie der Rezenzionen*, 77 v., Leipzig, 1900–1944.

7.7 Book review index V. 1——. Detroit, 1965——.

Covers more than 200 publications; primarily fiction, general literature, humanities, and social sciences. Presently a monthly, cumulated quarterly and annually.

7.8 Goode, Stephen H. Index to little magazines, 1900–1919: to which is added a selected list of British and Continental titles for the years 1900–1950, together with addenda and corrigenda to previous indexes. 3 v. Troy, N.Y., 1974.

7.9 Index to little magazines, 1948——. Denver and Chicago, 1949——.

Sporadic publication, for the most part annual. Covers primarily literary contents of selected "little" magazines which are not indexed in

Readers' Guide or *International Index*. A selected list is covered by Stephen H. Goode in *Index to American Little Magazines, 1920–1939*, N.Y., [1969]; *Index to Little Magazines 1940–1942*, N.Y., [1967]; and *Index to Little Magazines 1943–1947*, Denver, [1965].

7.10 Index to early American periodical literature, 1728–1870. N.Y., 1941.
Describes a card index, compiled by WPA, housed at New York University and available for the use of scholars.

7.11 The New York Times Book Review index, 1896–1970. 5 v. N.Y., 1973.
The first volume indexes by author; the fourth by subject. Letters to the editor, essays, etc. are covered as well as the books reviewed in the weekly.

7.12 O'Neill, Edward H. A description and an analysis of the bibliography of American literature. Philadelphia, 1941.
Describes a card index, compiled by WPA, housed at the University of Pennsylvania and available for the use of scholars. Like the NYU index, this is very useful in making lists of works by minor authors published in older American periodicals.

7.13 Haskell, Daniel C. A checklist of cumulative indexes to individual periodicals in the New York Public Library. N.Y., 1942.
Helps to answer questions like, "Is there a published index to the contents of the *Atlantic Monthly?*"

7.14 Ulrich's International Periodicals Directory. 15th edition. 1973–74: N.Y., [1973]——.
Annuals, monographs in series, and government publications, with a few exceptions are excluded, but may sometimes be found in *Irregular Serials Annuals: An International Directory*. N.Y., [1967]——.

7.15 Abstracts of English studies. 1958——.
Monthly publication abstracting articles in a variety of professional journals of interest to students of English and American literature and the English language.

7.16 An index to book reviews in the humanities. March 31, 1960——. Annual cumulation, 1963——.
A quarterly covering certain newspapers as well as selected magazines, all in English.

8. American studies or American civilization

8.1 Mugridge, Donald H., and McCrum Blanche P. A guide to the study of the U.S. of America: representative books reflecting the development of American life and thought. Washington, 1960.

The largest and most diversified annotated list of books concerned with the several aspects of American "civilization," this excellent compilation was supervised by Roy P. Basler. Coverage to 1955. Among the contents are entries on literature (pp. 1–175), literary history and criticism (pp. 183–223), periodicals and journalism (pp. 244–268), general history, diplomatic history, and foreign relations (pp. 300–438), science and technology (pp. 625–647), entertainment (pp. 672–684), sports and recreation (pp. 685–700), education (pp. 701–724), philosophy and psychology (pp. 725–751), religion (pp. 752–784), folklore, folk music, folk art (pp. 785–815), music (pp. 816–840), art and architecture (pp. 841–872), economic life (pp. 893–948), constitution and government (pp. 949–997), and books and libraries (pp. 1062–1080). The annotations vary in quality and were made chiefly by librarians. A supplement, covering 1956–1965, is in preparation.

8.2   American quarterly. 1949——.
Official organ of the American Studies Association. A supplementary issue lists annually dissertations in progress in the field of American Studies, articles of an interdisciplinary sort, and works on the theory and teaching of American Civilization. Hennig Cohen has gathered some of the contents in *Articles in American Studies, 1954–1968*, 2 v. Ann Arbor, Mich., [1972]. There is also a *Midcontinent American Studies Journal*, v. 1—— (Spring, 1960——).

8.3   Carman, Harry J., and Thompson, Arthur W.   A guide to the principal sources for American civilization, 1800–1900, in the city of New York. 2 v. Manuscripts. N.Y., 1960. Printed materials. N.Y., 1962.
Of far greater use than the limitation to one city might suggest. A kind of predecessor is Evarts B. Greene and Richard B. Morris, *A Guide to the Principal Sources for Early American History (1600–1800) in the City of New York*, 2d ed., N.Y., 1953.

8.4   Crick, Bernard R., and Alman, Miriam, eds.   A guide to manuscripts relating to America in Great Britain and Ireland.   London, 1961.
Manuscripts, letters, etc., of authors are also included. See also Crick's article, "A Survey of Library Resources in the United Kingdom for the Teaching of American History and Literature in the Universities," *Journal of Documentation*, v. 14, pp. 109–118 (1958). Addenda to the *Guide* have appeared in *British Association for American Studies Bulletin*.

8.5   Americana in deutschen Sammlungen.   Munich, 1968.
An indexed guide to archival and similar records pertaining to American history in West German collections.

8.6   Tate, Cecil F.   The search for a method in American Studies.   Minneapolis, [1973].
A fairly substantial discussion of certain of the attitudes underlying exponents of American studies. Four examples are examined in detail with a view to their illustrating "myth" or "holism."

8.7   Fishwick, Marshall W., ed.   American studies in transition.   Rev. ed. Philadelphia, [1968].
   A collection of essays, of uneven value, dealing with both Europe and the U.S.A., which points up the regnant confusions.

8.8   Meredith, Robert, ed.   American studies: essays on theory and method. Columbus, Ohio, [1968].
   Reprints sixteen essays, many by competent scholars, and in its introduction reports on previous publications relevant to the subject in general.

8.9   Kwiat, Joseph T., and Turpie, M. C., eds.   Studies in American culture: dominant ideas and images.   Minneapolis, 1960; N.Y., 1971.
   Includes several essays, by various hands, on methodology, along with a reprint of the following item.

8.10   Smith, Henry N.   "Can 'American Studies' develop a method?"   American quarterly, v. 9, pp. 197–208 (Summer, 1957).
   See also Robert Sklar, in the same journal, v. 27, pp. 245–262 (Aug., 1975).

8.11   den Hollander, A. N. J., and Skard, Sigmund, eds.   American civilisation: an introduction.   London, [1968].
   Sponsored by the European Association for American Studies, this textbook consists of essays by American and transatlantic scholars which offer brief surveys of various aspects of the field, such as economic structure, education, philosophy, music, the stage, American English, mass media, etc. The short bibliographies are selective but call attention to works by Europeans as well as Americans. The essay on literature is the product of Heinrich Straumann.

8.12   Walker, Robert H., ed.   American Studies abroad.   Westport, Conn., [1975].
   Articles from *American Studies* (8.14).

8.13   Skard, Sigmund.   American studies in Europe: their history and present organization.   2 v.   Philadelphia, [1958].
   Describes seminars, institutes, and programs concerned with the U.S. in various European countries. Also contains much information on the reception of American literature in Europe in days gone by. Skard's *The American Myth and the European Mind: American Studies in Europe 1776–1960*, Philadelphia, [1961], is a semi-popular redaction of the above, which only occasionally comes closer to date. See the following item for more recent activities.

8.14   American studies.   Washington, 1962——.
   An international newsletter issued irregularly by the Committee on International Exchange of Persons of the Conference Board of Associated Research Councils. Contains news of activities abroad and in the U.S. Originally called *American Studies News*.

8.15 Newsletter of the European Association for American Studies. 1955———.

Includes a curent bibliography. The association was founded in 1954 at a meeting in Salzburg. The British Association for American Studies (founded 1955) also published a *Bulletin* (1956———). The Nordic Association for American Studies (founded 1959) likewise engages in publication, as do many other foreign associations.

8.16 Journal of American studies. 1967———.

Published twice a year as the official organ of the British Association for American Studies.

8.17 Indian journal of American studies. 1968———.

Sponsored by the American Studies Research Centre in Hyderabad. The Centre, beginning with no. 9 (July, 1966), publishes checklists of studies produced in India, in a *Newsletter*.

8.18 Amerikastudien. Heidelberg, 1956———.

Publication of the German Society for American Studies, chiefly devoted to articles, some in English, on literature and history. Originally entitled *Jahrbuch für Amerikastudien*. Contains also reviews, bibliographies, and lists of dissertations. The German SAS also issued a *Mitteilungsblatt*, which contains bibliography and lists of dissertations, as well as information about the activities of the various institutes and seminars concerned with American Studies. (German dissertations on English and American literature are periodically listed also in *Zeitschrift für Anglistik und Amerikanistik*, 1953———, published in East Germany.)

8.19 Studi Americani. Rome, 1955———.

An annual devoted to the literature and art of the U.S. Some of the articles are in English.

8.20 Lubbers, Klaus. Einführung in das Studium der Amerikanistik. Tübingen, 1970.

Heavily weighted in the direction of *Sprachwissenschaft* and *Amerikanisches Englisch*, this valuable guide, intended for German students, occasionally helps to call attention to European studies of both the language and the literature of the U.S.

9. American history: general tools

9.1 Harvard guide to American history. Rev. ed. 2 v. Ed. Frank Freidel *et al*. Cambridge, Mass., 1974.

Extensive lists of works on all phases of the subject, arranged and indexed. Coverage to July, 1970. Preliminary chapters deal with the nature of the historian's task and preparation for research and writing. The revision is eccentric and sometimes inaccurate.

9.2   Beers, Henry P. Bibliographies in American history: guide to materials for research. 2d ed. N.Y., 1942; 1973.

Often outmoded by the *Harvard Guide*, but still useful because of its independent index and arrangement. *The American Historical Association's Guide to Historical Literature*, ed. George F. Howe *et al*, N.Y., 1961, of course includes selected works on all aspects of American history, pp. 711–744.

9.3   Writings on American history, 1902–1961. 1904–1976.

A series of volumes, with gaps, containing a list of books and important articles on all phases of American history. Some of the earlier volumes are available in reprints, N.Y., 1962. See item immediately following.

9.4   Index to the writings on American history 1902–1940. Compiled for the American Historical Association. Washington, [1956].

Contains references and subject classifications not to be found in the separate indexes of the individual volumes.

9.5   Writings on American history: a subject bibliography of articles. Washington and Millwood, N.Y., 1974——.

Successor to, but more limited than, item 9.3, and based on about 400 journals. Articles published in 1962–1973 have been collected in four volumes (1975). Beginning with those for 1973–74 (1974) annual publication is planned. In addition to chronological and geographical categories there are sixty other subject headings.

9.6   America: history and life. 1964——.

Sponsored by the American Bibliographical Center of Santa Barbara, Calif., this serial contains summaries of articles, including some published abroad, dealing with U.S. and Canadian history. Recently added are bibliographies, dissertations, and an index of book reviews.

9.7   American historical review. 1895——.

Official organ of the American Historical Association; largely devoted to current bibliography and reviews of books, including extensive lists of current books and articles on the history of the U.S. and its various sections.

9.8   Journal of American history. 1914——. Formerly called Mississippi Valley historical review.

The chief journal devoted solely to American history; essays, book reviews, bibliographical notices, and checklists of articles, the last not so inclusive as similar lists in *American Historical Review*. Index covering 1914–1964, by T.D. Clark, Bloomington, Ind., 1973.

9.9 Perspectives in American history. Ed. Donald Fleming and Bernard Bailyn. Cambridge, Mass., 1967——.

An annual journal emanating from the Charles Warren Center for Studies in American History, Harvard University.

9.10 Kuehl, Warren F. Dissertations in history. Lexington, Ky., 1965.

Lists doctoral dissertations completed in history departments of U.S. and Canadian universities 1873–1960 in v. 1. V 2 covers 1961 to June, 1970.

9.11 List of doctoral dissertations in history in progress or completed at colleges and universities in the U.S. since 1958. Washington, 1961.

This list is now published triennially by the American Historical Association. The 1955 listing included only dissertations in progress.

9.12 Billington, Ray A. A guide to American history manuscript collections in libraries of the U.S. N.Y., 1952.

Reprinted from *Mississippi Valley Historical Review*, v. 38, no. 3 (December, 1951). Cf. also the lists of guides to manuscript materials in *Harvard Guide*, 9.1, Hamer, 1.16, Crick and Alman, 8.4, and Carman and Thompson, 8.3.

9.13 Morris, Richard B., and Commager, Henry S., eds. The new American nation series. N.Y., 1954——.

An extensive history covering the whole range of American history and planned for 43 volumes. Each volume is written by an authority who also supplies a critical bibliography. (In progress also is the Chicago History of American Civilization, ed. Daniel J. Boorstin, Chicago, 1956——, which includes chronological and topical surveys, with less extensive bibliographies.)

9.14 Morison, Samuel E., and Commager, Henry S. The growth of the American republic. 6th ed. 2 v. N.Y., 1969.

One of the most widely used basic textbooks.

9.15 Schlesinger, Arthur M., and Fox, Dixon R., eds. A history of American life. 13 v. N.Y., 1927–1948.

An extensive social history of the U.S. The individual volumes, written by various authors, are uneven in quality and coverage. Contains critically annotated bibliographies for all chapters. See also Gerald N. Grob, *American Social History before 1860*, N.Y., 1969, a bibliography, and its sequel by Robert H. Bremmer, N.Y., [1971].

9.16 Adams, James T., ed. Dictionary of American history. 5 v. plus index. 2d rev. ed. N.Y., 1946. Supplement One. Ed. J. G. E. Hopkins and Wayne Andrews. N.Y., 1961; 7 v., 1968.

Contains no biographical sketches. The supplement extends or revises older entries and extends coverage 1940–1960.

9.17 Morris, Richard B., ed. Encyclopedia of American history. 4th ed. N.Y., [1970].

A basic chronology is followed by a topical outline, plus biographical data on notable Americans. One of the best chronological outlines of American "Civilization."

9.18 Carruth, Gorton, *et al.*, eds. The encyclopedia of American facts and dates. 6th ed. N.Y., [1972].
Includes listings through 1969 and is very fully indexed. Strong in social history.

9.19 The pageant of America: a pictorial history of the U.S. Ed. Ralph H. Gabriel *et al.* 15 v. [New Haven, Conn., 1925–1929].
The most extensive pictorial survey, from Indians to football.

9.20 Adams, James T., *et al.*, eds. Album of American history. 5 v. N.Y., 1944–1960; 6 v., 1968.
Pictures illustrating the social history of the U.S. from colonial times to 1953. (For other pictorial records see *Harvard Guide*, 9.1.)

9.21 Historical statistics of the U.S., colonial times to 1957. Continuation to 1962 and revisions. Prepared by the Bureau of the Census with the co-operation of the Social Science Research Council. Washington, [1965].
For more recent data, including revisions, see *Statistical Abstract of the U.S.*, Washington, 1963——.

9.22 U.S. national archives and records service. Guide to the national archives of the U.S. Washington, 1974.
As of June 30, 1970. Broad subjects, as well as persons and units involved, govern the index.

9.23 Paullin, Charles O. Atlas of the historical geography of the U.S. Ed. John K. Wright. [Washington and N.Y.], 1932; Westport, Conn., 1975.
Other atlases of considerable breadth include Clifford L. Lord and Elizabeth H. Lord, *Historical Atlas of the United States*, rev. ed., N.Y., 1953; 1969; James T. Adams and Roy V. Coleman, *Atlas of American History*, N.Y., [1943]; and *The American Heritage Atlas of U.S. History*, N.Y., 1968.

9.24 Peterson, Clarence S. Consolidated bibliography of county histories in fifty states in 1961, consolidated 1935–1961. Baltimore, 1961; 1973.
Privately reproduced by the compiler, this aims to list "all county histories of at least 100 pages, with few exceptions." Inaccurate.

9.25 Directory of historical societies and agencies in the U.S. and Canada 1956——. Columbus, Ohio and Nashville, Tenn., 1956——.
Names, addresses, and titles of officers to whom correspondence should be addressed. Biennial.

9.26 Whitehill, Walter M. Independent historical societies: an inquiry into their research and publication functions and their financial future. Boston, 1962.

Excellently written, provides historical background, etc., and concludes with general observations on methods, financing, etc., of such organizations. Cf. Leslie W. Dunlap, *American Historical Societies, 1790–1860*, Madison, Wis., 1944; Philadelphia, 1974.

9.27   Kiger, Joseph C.   American learned societies.   Washington, [1963]; [1975].
A workmanlike study of sixty learned societies, twenty-nine of which are devoted to the humanities and social sciences.

9.28   Loewenberg, Bert J.   American history in American thought.   N.Y., [1972].
First of a projected four-volume series "Historical Writing in American Culture," this is a history of ideas about the writing of history. Begins with European backgrounds and ends with Henry Adams.

9.29   Theory and practice in historical study: a report of the committee on historiography.   Social Science Research Council bulletin, no. 54.   N.Y., [1946].
Chapter 2 discusses "Controlling Assumptions in the Practice of American Historians," and Chapter 6 is a "Selective Reading List on Historiography and the Philosophy of History," including most of the important works by Americans. Cf. also 2.2, Howe *et al.*

9.30   Wish, Harvey.   The American historian: a social-intellectual history of the writing of the American past.   N.Y., 1960.
After two preliminary chapters the discussion centers on Sparks, Hildreth, Bancroft, Parkman, McMaster, Henry Adams, Turner, Von Holst, Phillips, Beard, Parrington, and Nevins. Bibliographical notes appear.

9.31   Kraus, Michael.   The writing of American history.   Norman, Okla., [1953]; [1968].
A pioneer work on American historiography.

9.32   Hutchinson, William T., ed.   The Marcus W. Jernegan essays in American historiography.   Chicago, [1937]; [N.Y., 1972].
Twenty-one historians of Americana are treated by various authors.

9.33   Van Tassel, David D.   Recording America's past: an interpretation of the development of historical studies in America 1607–1884.   Chicago, 1960.
A grass-roots approach to causes and trends which throws light upon many lesser-known historians and on the development of several historical societies.

9.34   Levin, David.   History as romantic art: Bancroft, Prescott, Motley, and Parkman.   Stanford, Calif., 1959; N.Y., [1963].
Disjointed but often excellent analysis of the art and background ideas of the four historians.

9.35 Hofstadter, Richard E. The progressive historians: Turner, Beard, Parrington. N.Y., 1968; 1970.
Goes beyond immediate focus on the three men, and weaves in the historical ideas both antecedent to and contemporary with them.

9.36 Cunliffe, Marcus, and Winks, Robin W., eds. Pastmasters: some essays on American historians. N.Y., [1969].
The subjects range from Parkman to the two Schlesingers and C. Van Woodward. The authors are themselves historians, and their work is sometimes excellent.

9.37 Higham, John, *et al.* History. Englewood Cliffs, N.J., [1965]; N.Y., [1973].
A survey of recent history writing in the U.S. which treats both the sociological and the ideological aspects of the subject. The most valuable element deals with the history of the writing of the history of the U.S.

9.38 Higham, John. Writing American history: essays on modern scholarship. Bloomington, Ind., 1970.
"In effect, a supplement" to 9.37, so says the author. Most of the book consists of revised articles previously published.

9.39 Billias, George H., and Grob, Gerald N. American history: retrospect and prospect. N.Y., 1971.
The ten original articles by divers hands on aspects of historiography more than suggest a trend toward the social science approach and the waning of the humanistic tradition.

9.40 Skotheim, Robert A. American intellectual histories and historians. Princeton, N.J., 1966; 1970.
Begins with several historians prior to the 20th century, especially M. C. Tyler and Edward Eggleston, but centers on "the progressive tradition" (Robinson, Beard, Parrington, *et al.*) and challengers like Morison, Miller, and Gabriel. Since World War II, Commager, Persons, Goldman, Schlesinger II, and Hofstadter are among the historians discussed.

9.41 Cirker, Hayward, and Cirker, Blanche, eds. Dictionary of American portraits: 4,045 pictures of important Americans from earliest times to the beginning of the twentieth century. N.Y., [1967].
Contains a bibliography listing, selectively, published sources of portraits and an index analyzing the portraits by the profession or occupation of the subjects.

9.42 Research catalog of maps of America to 1860 in the William L. Clements Library. 4 v. Boston, 1972.
The library is located at the University of Michigan in Ann Arbor. Arranged by cartographer and map titles and then by geographical region.

9.43   Waserman, Manfred J. Bibliography on oral history. N.Y., 1971——.
A pamphlet issued by the Oral History Association, which also sponsors *The Oral History Review*.

9.44   Shumway, Gary L. Oral history in the U.S.: a directory. N.Y., 1971.
Over 200 projects are listed with pertinent information gathered by the Oral History Association.

10. American history: some special studies

10.1   Vaughan, Alden T. The American colonies in the seventeenth century. N.Y., 1971.
A bibliography for school use.

10.2   Andrews, Charles M. The colonial period of American history. 4 v. New Haven, Conn., 1934–1938.

10.3   Nye, Russel B. The cultural life of the new nation 1776–1830. N.Y., [1960]; [1963].
Compact, with excellent bibliography, this work is especially valuable for the student of literature. One chapter deals with "The Quest for a National Literature."

10.4   A history of the South. Ed. Wendell H. Stephenson and E. Merton Coulter. 10 v. [Baton Rouge, La.], 1947–1967.
Various authorities cover the region from 1607 to 1945.

10.5   Mark, Charles, ed. Sociology of America: a guide to information sources. Detroit, [1975]
A beginner's tool.

10.6   Bernard, Luther L., and Bernard, Jessie. Origins of American sociology: the social science movement in the U.S. N.Y., [1943].
History of social-science theory in the 19th century. More contemporary developments are dealt with in *Handbook of Modern Sociology*, ed. Robert E. L. Faris, N.Y., 1964, a collection of essays by various sociologists, with bibliographies.

10.7   The economic history of the U.S. 9 v. N.Y., 1945——.
Various authorities detail economic development from colonial times to 1941. See also George R. Taylor, *American Economic History before 1860*, N.Y., 1969, a handy bibliography, and T. Orsagh *et al.*, *The Economic History of the U.S.: An Annotated Bibliography*, new ed., Santa Barbara, Calif., 1975.

10. American history: special studies

10.8   Kelly, Alfred H., and Harbison, Winfred A. The American constitution, its origins and development. 4th ed. N.Y., [1970].

    The constitution itself, annotated with cases decided by the Supreme Court to June 22, 1964, may be found in 88 Congress, 1 Session, Senate Documents, no. 39, Washington, 1964, ed. Norman Small. Dorothy C. Tompkins, *The Supreme Court of the U.S.*, Berkeley, Calif., 1959, is an annotated bibliography useful for the history of the court, its *modus operandi*, and its relationship to the other branches of the government. Edward Dumbauld, *The Constitution of the U.S.*, Norman, Okla., [1964]; [1965], gives origin, evolution, and interpretations, clause by clause. Cf. also Paul L. Rosen, *The Supreme Court and Social Science*, Urbana, Ill., 1972.

10.9   Binkley, Wilfred T. American political parties, their natural history. 4th ed. rev. N.Y., 1962.

    A standard textbook which includes bibliography. Ranging outside the discussion of political parties and elections is *Politics, Parties and Pressure Groups*, by Vladimer O. Key, 5th ed., N.Y., [1964].

10.10   Wynar, Lubomyr R. American political parties: a selective guide to parties and movements of the 20th century. Littleton, Colo., 1969.

10.11   Schlesinger, Arthur M., Jr., ed. History of U.S. political parties. 4 v. N.Y., 1973.

    Various authorities contributed in all 26 essays appended to each of which are selections from source documents.

10.12   Jones, Maldwyn A. American immigration. Chicago, 1960.

    Compactly reassembles the long-established facts, along with recent scholarship, and includes bibliographical comments which serve as a handy guide. Cf. also Marion T. Bennett, *American Immigration Policies: A History*, Washington, [1963]; and Joshua A. Fishman *et al., Language Loyalty in the U.S.: The Maintenance and Perpetuation of Non-English Mother Tongues by American Ethnic and Religious Groups*, The Hague, 1966.

10.13   Wittke, Carl F. We who built America: the saga of the immigrant. Rev. ed. Cleveland, 1964; 1967.

    Broader outlines of the entire history of immigration, plus special sections on various national groups: Irish, Germans, Orientals, Mexicans, etc.

10.14   Hansen, Marcus L. The Atlantic migration 1607–1860. Cambridge, Mass., 1940; N.Y., [1961].

    Deals with immigration from Europe.

10.15   Bowers, David F., ed. Foreign influences in American life: essays and critical bibliographies. Princeton, N.J., 1944; [1966].

    A symposium, with a cursory chapter on "The American Literary Expatriate." The bibliographies cover immigration, the pattern of assimilation, the economic impact, the political impact, the artistic and literary impact, and the religious and philosophical impact.

10.16 de Camp, L. Sprague.   The heroic age of American invention.   Garden City, N.Y., 1961.
A popular treatment of Stevens, Morse, Colt, McCormick, Ericsson, Mergenthaler, Bell, Edison, Selden, the Wright brothers, *et al.*

10.17 Bode, Carl.   The American lyceum: town meeting of the mind.   N.Y., 1956; Carbondale, Ill., 1968.
A history of the lyceum movement.

10.18 Morrison, Theodore.   Chautauqua: a center for education, religion, and the arts in America.   Chicago, 1974.
A popular account primarily of the New York institution founded in 1874 which spread its educative network all over the country and spawned scores of imitators, these last dealt with in one chapter.

10.19 Taylor, George R., ed.   The Turner thesis concerning the role of the frontier in American history.   Rev. ed.   Boston, [1956]; [1972].
Two essays by Frederick Jackson Turner are followed by discussions pro and con, in a volume included in the series *Problems in American Civilization*, edited from Amherst College. (Turner has been a vital influence on historical studies of a wide variety, including literary history. Cf. 29.11, Hazard. Ray A. Billington, *America's Frontier Heritage*, N.Y., 1966, reviews recent discussions of the frontier concept and probes origins in *The Genesis of the Frontier Thesis*, San Marino, Calif., 1971.)

10.20 Parry, Albert.   Garrets and pretenders: a history of bohemianism in America.   Rev. ed.   N.Y., [1961].
A poular but incomplete account. The revision consists largely of a new chapter, on the beatniks, by Harry T. Moore.

10.21 Filler, Louis.   Crusaders for American liberalism.   Rev. ed.   Kent, Ohio, [1964].
History of the muckraking movement 1900–1915. See also David M. Chalmers, *The Social and Political Ideas of the Muckrakers*, N.Y., [1964], for magazine journalists involved.

10.22 Herbst, Jurgen.   The history of American education.   Northbrook, Ill., [1973].
A "Goldentree Bibliography." Material on individual colleges and universities appears on pp. 32–37.

10.23 Cordasco, Francesco, and Brickman, William W., eds.   A bibliography of American educational history: an annotated and classified guide. N.Y., [1975].
The broader connections of education with history and society are also encompassed. See also Mark Beach, *A Bibliographical Guide to American Colleges and Universities*, Westport, Conn., 1975.

10. American history: special studies

10.24 Cremin, Lawrence A. A history of American education. N.Y., 1970——.
 Of the three volumes projected this, the first, covers 1607–1783 and is the best treatment thus far.

10.25 Butts, R. Freeman, and Cremin, Lawrence A. A history of education in American culture. N.Y., [1953].
 Contains bibliography. See also Barbara S. Marks, *The New York University List of Books in Education*, N.Y., 1968, which covers history as well as other aspects of the subject.

10.26 Cremin, Lawrence A. The transformation of the school: progressivism in American education, 1876–1957. N.Y., 1961.
 Puts the progressive movement in the schools in the broader context of the times.

10.27 Elson, Ruth M. Guardians of tradition: American schoolbooks of the nineteenth century. Lincoln, Nebr., [1964]; [1972].
 Intellectual history as shaped by about 1,000 elementary school textbooks of considerable popularity.

10.28 Rudolph, Frederick. The American college and university: a history. N.Y., 1962.
 A semipopular history, with excellent footnotes and an annotated bibliography.

10.29 Veysey, Laurence R. The emergence of the American university. Chicago, 1965; 1970.
 Describes and evaluates the developments in the period 1865–1910.

10.30 Friedman, Lawrence M. A history of American law. N.Y., 1973.
 A general survey that makes much of law as reflective of social history. The colonial period is skimpily treated and the coverage extends to about 1900, with illustrations drawn largely from state laws.

10.31 Krichmar, Albert. The women's rights movement in the U.S. 1848–1970: a bibliography and sourcebook. Metuchen, N.J., 1972.
 Certain manuscript collections are also included.

10.32 Flexner, Eleanor. Century of struggle: the woman's rights movement in the U.S. Rev. ed. Cambridge, Mass., 1975.
 A readable but scholarly and comprehensive account.

10.33 Spear, Dorothea N. Bibliography of American directories through 1860. Worcester, Mass., 1961; N.Y., 1968.
 Contains 1,647 items, of which the American Antiquarian Society holds 1,110.

10.34 Curti, Merle. American philanthropy abroad. New Brunswick, N.J., [1963].

Nongovernmental aid to foreign lands and peoples. The major portion, understandably, deals with the present century.

10.35 May, Ernest R.   American imperialism: a speculative essay.   N.Y., 1968.
Impact on America of expansionary policies of European nations at end of the 19th century. See also E. Berkeley Tompkins, *Anti-Imperialism in the U.S.: The Great Debate 1890–1920*, Philadelphia, 1970.

10.36 Fogel, William R., and Engerman, Stanley L.   Time on the cross.   2 v. Boston, [1974].
A sensation-making revision of the historical views on the economics of slavery in the U.S., based on computer research. V. 2 provides the evidence and explains the methods of "cliometricians." Bitterly attacked.

10.37 Hohenberg, John.   The Pulitzer prizes: a history.   N.Y., 1974.
The awards in drama, music, and journalism, as well as in the field of books, are listed, along with notes. (The author administered the program for a number of years.)

10.38 Mangione, Jerre.   The dream and the deal: the Federal Writers' Project, 1935–1943.   Boston, [1972].
The author worked with the publishers of the State Guide Series and thus his recollections and observations are prime sources.

10.39 Marken, Jack W.   The Indians and Eskimos of North America: a bibliography of books in print through 1972.   Vermillion, S. D., 1973.
Most fictional works are omitted.

10.40 Washburn, Wilcomb E.   The American Indian and the U.S.: a documentary history.   4 v.   N.Y., [1973].
The selected government records here assembled are competently introduced and will help greatly in tipping the balance in favor of historical accuracy rather than sentimental journalism. A lengthy index expedites use. Washburn's *The Indian in America*, N.Y. [1975], is compact, judicious, and useful also for its well-selected bibliography.

10.41 Encyclopedia of Indians of the Americas: volume 1, conspectus and chronology.   St. Clair Shores, Mich., [1974———].
The South Americans are slighted so far in this big venture, which promises many future volumes.

10.42 Prospects: an annual journal of American cultural studies.   N.Y., 1975———.
A considerable element deals with literature, and there are pictures to boot.

10.43 Adams, Leon D.   The wines of America.   Boston, 1973.
This is the best general study of the beginnings and history of viticulture and oenology in the various states. The research is extensive, but no bibliography is attached.

11. Biography

11.1   Hyamson, Albert W.   A dictionary of universal biography of all ages and of all peoples.   2d ed.   N.Y., 1951.
An index of names included in the chief general biographical dictionaries in English and several other European languages.

11.2   Riches, Phyllis M.   An analytical bibliography of universal collected biography, comprising books published in the English tongue in Great Britain and Ireland, America and the British dominions.   London, 1934.

11.3   Biography index: a cumulative index to biographical material in books and magazines.   N.Y., 1946——.
Quarterly index covering books and 1,500 periodicals in English, chiefly American; includes obituaries and some fictional treatments.

11.4   The new Century cyclopedia of names.   Ed. Clarence L. Barnhart *et al.*   3 v.   N.Y., [1954].
A standard reference work for names of consequence of various nationalities.

11.5   Dictionary of American biography.   20 v. plus index, plus supplement (1944).   N.Y., 1928–1937; 1946.   2d supplement, 1958.   3d supplement, 1973.
Each sketch is followed by a list of sources, often including manuscript material. The following sometimes offer sketches of individuals not represented in the *DAB: Appleton's Cyclopaedia of American Biography*, 7 v., N.Y., 1887–1900 (v. 8, 1918, is an index); *Lamb's Biographical Dictionary of the U.S.*, 7 v., Boston, 1900–1903; *The National Cyclopaedia of American Biography*, 47 v., N.Y., 1892–1965 (in progress); *White's Conspectus of American Biography*, 3d ed., N.Y., 1973; now renamed *Notable Names in American History*. For series of more specialized biographies, see *Harvard Guide*, 9.1. Cf. also Jane Kline, *Biographical Sources for the U.S.*, Washington, 1961. (*National Cyclopaedia* is the most extensive dictionary.)

11.6   Concise dictionary of American biography.   Ed. Joseph G. E. Hopkins *et al.* N.Y., [1964].
An abridgment of 11.5 in one volume. The sketches of distinguished authors are not reduced so radically as are those of most of the other subjects.

11.7   Van Doren, Charles, ed.   Webster's American biographies.   Springfield, Mass., [1974].
Includes 3,000 men and women, dead and alive. Artists and writers are weighted more heavily than in John A. Garraty, ed., *Encyclopedia of American Biography*, N.Y., 1974 (1,000 entries).

11.8   The New York Times obituaries index, 1858–1968. N.Y., 1970.
Some 350,000 obituaries that appeared in the *Times*.

11.9   James, Edward T., *et al*. Notable American women 1607–1950: a biographical dictionary. 3 v. Cambridge, Mass., 1971.
A total of 1,359 sketches, modeled after those in the *DAB*, of women who died before 1951.

11.10   O'Neill, Edward H. Biography by Americans 1658–1936: a subject bibliography. Philadelphia, 1939; Boston, 1972.
A checklist of biographies individual and collective written by Americans. In the cases of particularly famous men only the "important books" on them are recorded.

11.11   Dargan, Marion. Guide to American biography. Part 1, 1607–1815; part 2, 1815–1933. Albuquerque, N. Mex., 1949–1952, Westport, Conn., 1973.
Selective; arranged by chronological periods, subdivided by geographical regions.

11.12   Kaplan, Louis, *et al*. A bibliography of American autobiographies. Madison, Wis., 1961.
Coverage to 1946. A subject index classifies the books according to occupation, place of residence, and connection with historical events associated with the subjects. For each item one library owning a copy is indicated. See also Mary S. Carlock, "American Autobiographies, 1840–1870, a Bibliography," *Bulletin of Bibliography*, v. 23, pp. 118–120 (May–August, 1961).

11.13   Lillard, Richard G. American life in autobiography: a descriptive guide. Stanford, Calif., [1956].
Selected autobiographies are listed under headings made according to the profession or occupation of the writers, e.g., "Actors and Show People," "Journalists, Newspaper and Magazine Editors."

11.14   Brignano, Russell C. Black Americans in autobiography. Durham, N.C., 1974.
An annotated register of 400 autobiographies written since the Civil War. There is an appendix noting recent printings of ante-bellum works.

11.15   Matthews, William. American diaries in manuscript, 1580–1954: a descriptive bibliography. Athens, Georgia, [1974].
Locations of the manuscripts are also provided.

11.16   Matthews, William. American diaries. Berkeley and Los Angeles, 1945; Boston, 1959.
List of published diaries written prior to 1861.

11.17   Kunitz, Stanley J., and Haycraft, Howard, eds. American authors, 1600–1900. N.Y., 1938.
Contains 1,300 biographical sketches and 400 portraits.

11.18   Adams, Oscar F.   A dictionary of American authors.   5th ed. rev. and enlarged.   Boston, 1905; Detroit, [1969].

11.19   Burke, W. J., and Howe, Will D.   American authors and books: 1640 to the present day.   Augmented and rev. by Irving Weiss.   3d ed.   N.Y., [1973].
Brief sketches; lists many minor names which do not appear in *Oxford Companion to American Literature.*

11.20   Herzberg, Max J., ed.   The reader's encyclopedia of American literature.   N.Y., [1962].
An elaborate but erratic compilation occasionally useful chiefly for sketches of minor authors available nowhere else.

11.21   Duyckinck, Evert A., and Duyckinck, George L.   Cyclopaedia of American literature.   Rev. ed.   2 v.   Philadelphia, 1875; Detroit, [1967].
Useful only for minor earlier writers.

11.22   Wallace, W. Stewart.   A dictionary of North American authors deceased before 1950.   Toronto, [1951].
The authors may be journalists, lawyers, merchants, etc., but many literary men are listed, by field of interest, with places and dates of birth and death.

11.23   Kunitz, Stanley J., and Haycraft, Howard.   Twentieth century authors.   N.Y., 1942.   1st supplement.   N.Y., 1955.
Biographical sketches of 1,850 authors of various nationalities, but chiefly American, plus 1,700 portraits. The supplement adds about 700 new authors, usually those who have come into prominence since 1942.

11.24   Who's who in America.   Chicago, 1899——.
Biennial publication containing sketches of living individuals, who themselves supply the information. (For persons dropped because of death there is a *Who Was Who. Who's Who in the East* and other sectional compilations include many additional names. *Who's Who of American Women*, 1958–1959——, began another series.)

11.25   Contemporary authors: a bio-bibliographical guide to current authors and their works.   V. 1——.   Detroit, [1962——].
The authors—in various fields—are principally Americans.

11.26   O'Neill, Edward H.   A history of American biography, 1800–1935.   Philadelphia, 1935; N.Y., [1968].

11.27   Directory of American scholars, a biographical directory.   Ed. Jaques Cattell Press.   6th ed.   4 v.   N.Y., 1974.
Historians and scholars in the various fields of literature and the humanities. Scientists are similarly treated in *American Men of Science*, N.Y., 1965–1966——.

11.28   Doane, Gilbert H.   Searching for your ancestors.   4th ed.   Minneapolis, [1973].

A guide to genealogical investigation. Methodology of genealogical research is considered also in George B. Everton, Sr., and Gunnar Rasmuson, *The Handy Book for Genealogists*, 3d ed., Logan, Utah, [1957]; Noel C. Stevenson, *Search and Research*, rev. ed., Salt Lake City, 1964; and Jacques Barzun and Henry F. Graff, *The Modern Researcher*, 2d ed., N.Y., [1970]. Lester J. Cappon, *American Genealogical Periodicals: A Bibliography with a Chronological Finding-list*, 2d ed., N.Y., 1964, is a comprehensive listing of an "exploratory nature." Describes both national and local journals.

11.29   Greenwood, Val D.   The researcher's guide to American genealogy. Baltimore, 1973.
Methods, as well as records and sources, are considered.

11.30   The American genealogical-biographical index to American genealogical, biographical and local history materials.   Middletown, Conn., 1952———.
The first 90 volumes cover names Aabrey through Jennings.

See also 3.22–23, 13.1, 19.13–17, 19.66, 19.102–104, 21.20, and 23.60.

12. Magazines

12.1   Ditzion, Sidney.   "The history of periodical literature in the U.S.: a bibliography."   Bulletin of bibliography, v. 15, pp. 110, 129–133 (1935).
Incomplete and out of date, but occasionally useful. (Cf. bibliographies in Section 13, on Newspapers, and *Ulrich's International Periodical Directory*, 7.14.)

12.2   Titus, Edna B.   Union list of serials in libraries of the U.S. and Canada. 3d ed.   5 v.   N.Y., 1965.
157,000 titles held by 956 libraries. This standard work locates files of magazines of all sorts. For serials which commenced publication since 1949, see *New Serial Titles*, issued by the Library of Congress, 1953———. (More than a thousand American magazines 1741–1910 have been, or are in process of being, made available on microfilm, through University Microfilms, Inc., Ann Arbor, Mich. For annual lists of magazines, with circulation figures, see the N. W. Ayer annual, 13.9.)

12.3   Mott, Frank L.   A History of American magazines.   V. 1, 1741–1850; v. 2, 1850–1865; v. 3, 1865–1885; v. 4, 1885–1905.   Cambridge, Mass., 1938–1957.   V. 5, Sketches of twenty-one magazines, 1905–1930.   Cambridge, Mass., 1968.

The standard work in its field. Various aspects of magazine journalism are discussed as part of the social history of the times. Certain periodicals important in the period covered in a volume are given extended historical treatment in a supplementary section, and when such publications extend beyond the chronological limits of a volume, they are carried forward to their ends or to the date of publication of the volume. For example, in v. 4 the histories of the *Saturday Evening Post, Ladies Home Journal,* and *National Geographic* are carried down to 1957. V. 5 carries an index cumulating materials in all five volumes.

12.4 Tebbel, John W. The American magazine: a compact history. N.Y., [1969].
A quick survey that may fill in a gap once in a while.

12.5 Wood, James P. Magazines in the U.S. 3d ed. N.Y., [1971].
Suggestive for the period not treated by Mott.

12.6 Peterson, Theodore. Magazines in the twentieth century. 2d ed. Urbana, Ill., 1964.
Covers American magazines chiefly of general circulation, with special emphasis on the advertising-production-circulation complex. The first edition (1956) contained a bibliography.

12.7 Richardson, Lyon N. A history of early American magazines, 1741–1789. N.Y., 1931; Port Washington, N.Y., [1968].
(All known magazines of the 18th century published in the U.S. have been made available on microfilm through University Microfilms, Inc., Ann Arbor, Mich.)

12.8 Lewis, Benjamin M. A register of editors, printers, and publishers of American magazines, 1741–1810. N.Y., 1957.

12.9 Lewis, Benjamin M. An introduction to American magazines, 1800–1810. Ann Arbor, Mich., 1961.
Covers 130 magazines published during the decade.

12.10 Neal, Edgar L. A history and bibliography of American Magazines, 1810–1820. Metuchen, N.J., 1975.
Provides a good beginning for study of the period.

12.11 Conlin, Joseph R., ed. The American radical press, 1880–1960. 2 v. Westport, Conn., [1974].
A hundred essays on 119 periodicals originally conceived as introductions in a reprint series. Bellamy nationalism, anarchism, socialism, the I.W.W. and the theories of Debs, Upton Sinclair, etc. generated the "radicalism" portrayed.

12.12 Smyth, Albert H. The Philadelphia magazines and their contributors, 1741–1850. Philadelphia, 1892; Detroit, 1970.

12.13 Fleming, Herbert E. Magazines of a market-metropolis: being a history of the literary periodicals and literary interests of Chicago. Chicago, 1906.
Originally published in *American Journal of Sociology*, v. 11 and 12.

12.14 Gilmer, Gertrude C. Checklist of Southern periodicals to 1861. Boston, 1934; Boston, 1972.

12.15 Gohdes, Clarence. The periodicals of American transcendentalism. Durham, N.C., 1931; N.Y., 1970.
Historical account of various magazines of the 19th century conducted by people who were identified with the Transcendentalists—Emerson, Theodore Parker, *et al.*

12.16 Noel, Mary. Villains galore. N.Y., 1954.
History of popular 19th-century story weeklies like the N.Y. *Ledger*.

12.17 Ulrich, Carolyn, and Patterson, Eugenia. Little magazines: a list. N.Y., 1947.
Includes the periodicals in the N.Y. Public Library; period covered is 1890–1946.

12.18 Union list of little magazines. Chicago, 1956.
A list of 1,037 little magazines in libraries of various Middle Western universities, compiled under the auspices of Indiana University Library.

12.19 Hoffman, Frederick J., *et al.* The little magazine: a history and a bibliography. [2d ed.] Princeton, N.J., 1947; N.Y., 1966.
Partially supplemented by J. B. May, *Twigs as Varied Bent*, Corona, N.Y., 1954. Since 1952 the magazine *Trace* has reported the births and deaths of many little magazines and put out an annual *International Guide*, London, 1960——, by no means exhaustive. Cf. also *International Directory of Little Magazines*, 9th ed., Paradise, Calif., [1973——].

12.20 Janssen, G.A. The American literary review: a critical history. The Hague, [1968].
A Norwegian scholar gives an account of *Hound & Horn*, the *Dial*, *Symposium*, *Southern Review*, plus the *Kenyon*, *Sewanee*, and *Partisan* reviews. Of use largely for certain details.

12.21 Gilbert, James B. Writers and partisans: a history of literary radicalism in America. N.Y., [1968].
Centers on the history of the *Partisan Review* but slops over in the chronological basin 1920–1952.

12.22 Wilson, Harold S. McClure's Magazine and the muckrakers. Princeton, N.J., 1970.
A careful history of McClure's journalistic career and of the place of his magazine in the "muckraking movement." The literary connections are subordinated to the political and economic.

13. Newspapers

13.1   Price, Warren C.   The literature of journalism: an annotated bibliography.   Minneapolis, [1959].
Centered principally on the U.S. and Canada, this book lists histories of journalism and of individual newspapers and magazines, biographies, etc.

13.2   Price, Warren C., and Pickett, Calder M.   An annotated journalism bibliography, 1958–1968.   Minneapolis, [1970].
Supplements 13.1.

13.3   Blum, Eleanor.   Basic books in the mass media: an annotated, selected booklist covering general communications, book publishing, broadcasting, film, magazines, newspapers, advertising, indexes, and scholarly and professional periodicals.   Urbana, Ill., [1972].
An updating of a work which originally appeared with a slightly different title in 1962. The reference books listed are annotated.

13.4   Journalism quarterly.   1924——.
Since 1930 includes annotated bibliographies on various journalistic subjects.

13.5   Editor and publisher international yearbook.   N.Y., 1920——.
Includes since 1936 a selective bibliography on journalistic matters.

13.6   Gregory, Winifred.   American newspapers 1821–1936, a union list of files available in the U.S. and Canada.   N.Y., 1937; 1967.
Partially superseded by the numerous union lists covering newspaper files located in various cities, states, or regions.

13.7   Downs, Robert B., *et al.*   American library resources: a bibliographical guide.   Chicago, 1951; Boston, [1972].   Supplement, 1950–1961.   Chicago, 1962.   Supplement, 1961–1970.   Chicago, 1972.
Lists, among other materials, a limited number of published checklists of local holdings of newspapers and magazines. (There are numerous catalogs of newspapers of various states and localities as well as of holdings of individual libraries. Consult the card catalog of your library under the name of state, locality, or special library.)

13.8   Newspapers in microform U.S. 1948–1972.   Washington, 1973.
Lists 34,289 titles from holdings reported by 843 American libraries.

13.9   N. W. Ayer & Son's directory of newspapers and periodicals.   Philadelphia, 1880——.
Lists annually, by state and city, newspapers and certain other periodicals published in the U.S. and Canada and supplies relevant information, including circulation, political affiliation, etc.

13.10 Rowell's American newspaper directory . . . 1869–1908. Ed. George P. Presbury. 40 v. in 61. N.Y., 1869–1908.

A list of papers and periodicals, with circulation figures, etc.; long a rival of N. W. Ayer & Son's annual and in 1908 merged with it.

13.11 Mott, Frank L. American journalism: a history, 1690–1960. 3d ed. N.Y., [1962].

Standard work on the history of American newspapers.

13.12 Emery, Edwin, and Smith, Henry L. The press and America. 3d ed. rev. N.Y., 1972.

A comprehensive history plus an examination of current activities in the world of papers, magazines, radio, television, and newsgathering.

13.13 Rosewater, Victor. History of coöperative news-gathering in the U.S. N.Y., 1930; 1971.

13.14 Watson, Elmo S. A history of newspaper syndicates in the U.S., 1965–1935. Chicago, 1936.

13.15 Brigham, Clarence S. History and bibliography of American newspapers 1690–1820. 2 v. Worcester, Mass., 1947; Hamden, Conn., 1962.

The standard work for its period. The reprint includes also "Additions and Corrections to History and Bibliography of American Newspapers, 1690–1820," *Proceedings of the American Antiquarian Society*, v. 71, pp. 15–62 (1961).

13.16 Latham, Edward C. Chronological tables of American newspapers, 1690–1820. Barre, Mass., 1972.

In chronological tables the availability of the 86 earliest newspapers is indicated. To be used in conjunction with C. S. Brigham (13.15).

13.17 Schlesinger, Arthur M. Prelude to independence: the newspaper war on Britain 1764–1776. N.Y., 1958.

Contains much material on several papers of the times, including an appendix on their circulations.

13.18 Brayer, Herbert O. "Preliminary guide to indexed newspapers in the U.S., 1850–1900." Mississippi Valley historical review, v. 33, pp. 237–258 (September, 1946).

The indexes are often on cards. Repositories are indicated. Very incomplete.

13.19 New-York Daily Tribune index for 1875–1906. 31 v. N.Y., 1876–[1907].

13.20 The New York Times index. N.Y., 1913——.

There is also available a microfilm index of the contents of the *Times*, 1851–1855; 1860; 1863—June, 1905. An index for 1863–1874 has been published, N.Y., [1966].

13. Newspapers

13.21   The Wall Street Journal index. N.Y., December, 1957———.
Appears monthly, with yearly accumulations.

13.22   Index of the Christian Science Monitor. Boston, 1960———.

13.23   Press intelligence directory: a manual of newspaper content, local writers,
and syndicated columnists. Washington, [1957].
Part II is a list of topics—e.g., book news, theater news—followed by
selected examples of papers carrying such material and often supplying
names of the local writers of it.

13.24   Detweiler, Frederick. The Negro press in the U.S. Chicago, [1922];
Port Washington, N.Y., [1968].

13.25   Arndt, Karl J., and Olson, May E. German-American newspapers and
periodicals, 1732–1955: history and bibliography. 2d rev. ed. N.Y.,
[1965].
Addenda are included in the following.

13.26   Arndt, Karl J.R., and Olson, May E. German language press of the
Americas, 1732–1968: history and bibliography. V. 2. Totowa, N.J.,
1973.

14. Book trade and publishing

14.1   Tanselle, G. Thomas. Guide to the study of U.S. imprints. 2 v. Cambridge, Mass., 1971.
Three checklists of materials on printing and publishing, arranged according to region, genre, and author, are followed by items dealing with
copyright records, catalogs, and book-trade directories in the first volume.
The second volume covers studies of individual printers and publishers,
"general studies," a basic collection of 250 titles on U.S. printing and
publishing; plus a full index for the whole.

14.2   Tebbel, John. A history of book publishing in the U.S. 3 v. N.Y.,
[1972———].
The first two volumes cover 1630–1919 in a semipopular manner. The
documentation may be helpful in lieu of better bibliographical sources.

14.3   Trienes, Roger J. Pioneer imprints from fifty states. Washington, 1973.
Chronologically arranged, this is an index to the Library of Congress
holdings of earliest state imprints. The beginning of printing in each
state is described briefly.

14.4   Lehmann-Haupt, Hellmut, *et al.* The book in America: a history of the making and selling of books in the U.S. 2d ed. N.Y., 1951; 1964.

The standard work on its subject. Some recent books on publishing are to be found in Eleanor Blum, *Basic Books in the Mass Media: An Annotated, Selected Booklist*, Urbana, Ill., 1972. See also the annual listing in *Studies in Bibliography*; and Charles A. Madison, *Book Publishing in America*, N.Y., [1966].

14.5   Thomas, Isaiah. The history of printing in America. 2d ed. 2 v. Albany, 1874; N.Y., 1972.

Long out of date, but contains certain information not available elsewhere. (Rollo Silver is at work on a scholarly history of printing in the U.S.)

14.6   McMurtrie, Douglas C. A history of printing in the U.S.: Middle and South Atlantic States. N.Y., 1936; 1967.

Covers Pennsylvania, Maryland, New York, New Jersey, Delaware, District of Columbia, Virginia, South Carolina, North Carolina, and Georgia to 1800. (McMurtrie also edited a vast assortment of bibliographies listing the early imprints of various states and sections.) Lawrence C. Wroth, *The Colonial Printer*, 2d ed., Portland, Maine, 1938; Charlottesville, Va., [1964], surveys the presses of the colonies to 1800.

14.7   Directory of Western book publishing and related supplies and services. Los Angeles, 1973.

A "preliminary" pamphlet that is useful in rounding up obscure firms of the West Coast.

14.8   Bowker lectures on book publishing. [Collected ed.] N.Y., 1957.

A reprint of the first seventeen Bowker lectures, 1935–1956. A new lecture is given each year and is separately published.

14.9   Stern, Madeleine B. Imprints on history: book publishers and American frontiers. Bloomington, Ind., 1956; N.Y., 1975.

Chiefly concerned with various regional publishers but contains also a list of 191 firms surviving from the era prior to 1900. Walter Sutton, *The Western Book Trade*, Columbus, Ohio, 1961, views Cincinnati as a publishing and bookselling center during the 19th century. David Kaser has compiled lists of publishers in St. Louis, Nashville, etc., as has also Edwin H. Carpenter for southern California, 1850–1876.

14.10   Charvat, William. Literary publishing in America, 1790–1850. Philadelphia, 1959.

A "skimming" and a condensation of materials collected on the subject of the history of the economics of authorship. Of considerable value in explaining the careers of various prominent authors. See also Charvat's *The Profession of Authorship in America, 1800–1870*, ed. Matthew J. Bruccoli, Columbus, Ohio, [1968].

14. Book trade

14.11   Shove, Raymond H. Cheap book production in the U.S., 1870 to 1891. Urbana, Ill., 1937; N.Y., 1968.

Deals chiefly with works brought out in various series or "libraries" which were counterparts of the contemporary paperback series of reprints.

14.12   Schick, Frank L. The paperbound book in America and its European antecedents. N.Y., 1958.

14.13   Sheehan, Donald. This was publishing: a chronicle of the book trade in the Gilded Age. Bloomington, Ind., 1952.

From the Civil War to World War I; largely material on four firms: Holt, Harper, Scribner, and Dodd, Mead. (There are, of course, many individual histories of various publishing companies.)

14.14   Cheney, Orion H. Economic survey of the book industry 1930–1931. N.Y., 1931; [1960].

Reprinted also in 1949 with a statistical report for 1947–1948. The 1960 reprint contains new appendixes and an index providing opportunities for "then and now" comparisons.

14.15   Miller, William. The book industry. N.Y., 1949.

Commercial and editorial aspects of publishing, including relations with public libraries and book clubs.

14.16   Grannis, Chandler B., ed. What happens in book publishing. 2d ed. N.Y., 1967.

A group of specialists explain operations in the American book-publishing business, from securing of manuscripts and copy editing to university press, book clubs, paperback markets, and distribution of U.S. books abroad. Each chapter has a bibliography appended.

14.17   Dessauer, John P. Book publishing: what it is, what it does. N.Y., [1974].

Chiefly concerned with book manufacturing, with a final chapter on the finances of publishing.

14.18   The new dynamics of book publishing: an analysis of trends 1967 to 1980. N.Y., 1973.

An expensive effort to assist publishers in identifying "the moving forces" in the industry. Chapters on textbooks, adult trade books, etc. provide considerable insight into current practices.

14.19   American book-prices current. N.Y., 1895——.

Annual record of books, manuscripts, etc., sold at auction in N.Y., Boston, and Philadelphia, with records of prices paid. Various indexes of its contents have been published.

14.20 McKay, George L. American book auction catalogues 1713–1934: a union list. N.Y., 1937; Detroit, [1967].
  Supplements have appeared in the N.Y. Public Library *Bulletin*, v. 50 (1946) and v. 52 (1948). The reprint includes them. (The library of the American Antiquarian Society, Worcester, Mass., contains one of the largest collections of American book dealers' catalogs.)

14.21 Mott, Frank L. Golden multitudes: the story of best sellers in the U.S. N.Y., 1947; [1960].
  A standard study.

14.22 Hart, James D. The popular book: a history of America's literary taste. N.Y., 1950; Berkeley, 1961.
  Relates popular taste in reading to the "social pressures."

14.23 Nye, Russel. The unembarrassed muse: the popular arts in America. N.Y., 1971.
  Fiction, verse, drama, comics, jazz, films, radio, and television but not printing, sculpture, design, or architecture, are treated by a scholar. The volume is one in a series in progress entitled *Two Centuries of American Life: A Bicentennial History*.

14.24 Austin, James C., and Koch, Donald A., eds. Popular literature in America: a symposium in honor of Lyon H. Richardson. Bowling Green, Ohio, [1972].
  Fiction, humor, and reform enter into the subject matter along with television as a way of life.

14.25 Hackett, Alice P. 70 years of best sellers, 1895–1965. N.Y., 1967.
  Primarily lists of books; must be used with caution, for authentic figures on sales are often not available. Contains also a bibliography on "Books and Articles about Best Sellers."

14.26 Hawes, Gene R. To advance knowledge: a handbook on American university press publishing. N.Y., 1967.

14.27 Smith, Roger H., ed. The American reading public: what it reads, why it reads. N.Y., [1964].
  Various aspects of the publishing business are discussed by several contributors, including book reviewing. Some of the essays appeared earlier in a symposium in the journal *Daedalus*.

14.28 Welter, Rush. Problems of scholarly publication in the humanities and the social sciences. N.Y., [1959]; 1968.
  A factual report prepared for a committee of the American Council of Learned Societies; deals with periodicals as well as books.

See also 30.4, 32.5, 32.53.

15. Selected histories of ideas in the U.S.

15.1 Curti, Merle. The growth of American thought. 3d ed. N.Y., [1964].
A standard work on the history of ideas in the U.S. Special attention should be directed to its bibliography, which is both chronological and topical. Arthur Bestor discusses intellectual history to 1900 (pp. 133–156) and Ralph H. Gabriel ideas and culture in the 20th century (pp. 312–328) in essays included in *Interpreting and Teaching American History: 31st Yearbook of the National Council for the Social Studies*, ed. William H. Cartwright and Richard L. Watson, Jr., Washington, [1961]. Selective bibliography. See also Robert A. Skotheim, *American Intellectual Histories and Historians*, Princeton, N.J., 1966; 1970.

15.2 Gabriel, Ralph H. The course of American democratic thought. 2d ed. N.Y., [1956].
Literature is included, along with other factors in social history.

15.3 Ekirch, Arthur A., Jr. American intellectual history: the development of the discipline. Washington, 1973.
A pamphlet for teachers.

15.4 Horton, Rod W., and Edwards, Herbert W. Backgrounds of American literary thought. 3d ed. N.Y., [1974].
Elementary historical treatments of Puritanism, the Enlightenment, Transcendentalism, evolution and pragmatism, gentility and revolt, imperialism, naturalism, Freudianism, Southern sectionalism, and existentialism.

15.5 Parrington, Vernon L. Main currents in American thought. 3 v. [N.Y., 1927–1930; 1954]; [1963].
Survey of the political and social philosophy of American authors from colonial times to about 1880. Last volume unfinished. (This work is often mistaken for a history of literature.)

15.6 Welter, Rush. The mind of America 1820–1860. N.Y., 1975.
An intellectual history which centers on economic issues, the emergence of Jacksonian and Whig political ideas, and the development of free "institutions," i.e., religion, education, and land. An introductory chapter offers various suggestions for the student of methodology.

15.7 Commager, Henry S. The American mind: an interpretation of American thought and character since the 1880's. New Haven, Conn., [1950]; [1959].
Selected aspects of American thought are discussed, and a considerable portion is devoted to literature. To a certain degree this continues Parrington to the 1940's.

15.8 Wish, Harvey. Society and thought in America. 2 v. N.Y., 1950–1952; v. 2 revised, N.Y., 1962.

An intellectual history which stresses the social conditioning of American ideas. See also Alice F. Tyler, *Freedom's Ferment: Phases of American Social History to 1860*, Minneapolis, 1944; [1962].

15.9 Lerner, Max. America as a civilization: life and thought in the U.S. today. N.Y., 1957; 2 v., 1960; 1967.
An attempt to grasp "the pattern and inner meaning of contemporary American civilization and its relation to the world of today." The bibliography adds many recent works to the record.

15.10 Persons, Stow. American minds: a history of ideas. N.Y., [1958]; Huntington, N.Y., 1975.
An introduction to the history of American thought which describes "the principal focal concentrations of ideas," from the "colonial religious mind, 1620–1660" to the "contemporary neodemocratic mind." Very selective.

15.11 Beard, Charles A., and Beard, Mary R. The American spirit: a study of the idea of civilization in the U.S. N.Y., 1942; [1971].
This is v. 4 of a work entitled *The Rise of American Civilization*.

15.12 Dorfman, Joseph. The economic mind in American civilization. 5 v. N.Y., 1946–1959; 1966–1969.
History of economic ideas, popular and technical, from 1606 to 1933.

15.13 Hofstadter, Richard. Social Darwinism in American thought. Rev. ed. N.Y., 1955; 1959.

15.14 Persons, Stow, ed. Evolutionary thought in America. New Haven, Conn., 1950; Hamden, Conn., 1968.
A symposium and bibliography.

15.15 Egbert, Donald D., and Persons, Stow, eds. Socialism and American life. 2 v. Princeton, N.J., 1952.
V. 1 is a symposium, including also outlines of European backgrounds; v. 2 is an uneven bibliography.

15.16 Hofstadter, Richard. The American political tradition and the men who made it. N.Y., 1948; 1958.

15.17 Beitzinger, A. J. A history of American political thought. N.Y., 1972.
A textbook survey, with two thirds of the space devoted to the theories pervasive in the era from colonial times to the Civil War.

15.18 Hartz, Louis. The liberal tradition in America: an interpretation of American political thought since the Revolution. N.Y., [1955]; [1966].
A suggestive hypothesis is outlined.

15.19 Seidman, Joel, *et al.* Communism in the U.S.: a bibliography. Ithaca, N.Y., [1969].
Annotations indicate the contents of the books and articles listed.

15. Histories of ideas

15.20 Unger, Irwin. The movement: a history of the American New Left, 1959–1972. N.Y., 1974.

A brief and popular account useful in view of the absence of more scholarly surveys.

15.21 Rossiter, Clinton L. Conservatism in America. 2d ed. rev. N.Y., 1962.

Includes a discussion of the contemporary "New Conservatism."

15.22 Guttman, Allen. The conservative tradition in America. N.Y., 1967.

A thoughtful study which uses literary figures to great advantage in arguing its thesis.

15.23 Lora, Ronald. Conservative minds in America. Chicago, 1971.

Devotes more space to conservative literary figures of the twentieth century than does Guttman. Has a good bibliographical essay.

15.24 Berthoff, Rowland. An unsettled people: social order and disorder in American history. N.Y., 1971.

An extensive excursion in social history which interprets the balance between the social order and stability achieved in the colonial period as upset in the nineteenth century by the forces of individualism and economic progress. An epilogue looks forward to a new epoch as a reasonable possibility for the future.

15.25 Lewis, Richard W. B. The American Adam: innocence, tragedy and tradition in the nineteenth century. [Chicago, 1955; 1959].

"Tentative outlines of a native American mythology" as exhibited chiefly in certain aspects of literature.

15.26 Marx, Leo. The machine in the garden: technology and the pastoral ideal in America. N.Y., 1964; 1967.

The conflict of industrial and pastoral motifs; frequently illustrated in literary works.

15.27 Smith, Henry N. Virgin land: the American West as symbol and myth. Cambridge, Mass., 1950; [1970].

Various conceptions of the West, especially as they emanated in literature.

15.28 Slotkin, Richard. Regeneration through violence: the mythology of the American frontier, 1600–1860. Middletown, Conn., [1973].

"The myth of regeneration through violence became the structuring metaphor of the American experience." The frontier influence of Turner is given a new mythological twist of the tail. Use with caution.

15.29 Barker, Charles A. American convictions: cycles of public thought, 1600–1850. Philadelphia, [1970].

An intellectual history bearing chiefly on public affairs and policies which points out the cyclical nature of individualistic and innovative tendencies.

15.30 Sanford, Charles L. The quest for paradise: Europe and the American moral imagination. Urbana, Ill., [1961].

Explores aspects of America's "Edenic myth," in which the "cult of newness" comes in for attention, as well as Franklin's "art of virtue"; Henry James's expatriation is given a new reading.

15.31 Burns, Edward M. The American idea of mission: concepts of national purpose and destiny. New Brunswick, N.J., 1957; Westport, Conn., [1973].

15.32 Potter, David M. People of plenty: economic abundance and the American character. Chicago, [1954].

Lectures which begin with conceptual problems of establishing what a national character is and then analyze some of the effects of affluence on democracy, the mission of America, the frontier hypothesis, advertising, etc.

15.33 Lynn, Kenneth S. The dream of success: a study of the modern American imagination. Boston, [1955], Westport, Conn., [1972].

Dreiser, London, Phillips, Norris, and Herrick as affected by the "success myth." There is a chapter on Horatio Alger. Occasionally suggestive. See also Richard Weiss, *The American Myth of Success*, N.Y., 1969, which runs over the theme from the early colonial writings to Norman Vincent Peale.

15.34 Jones, Howard M. Ideas in America. Cambridge, Mass., 1944; N.Y., 1965.

Fugitive essays collected under three headings: "The Need for Literary History," "Studies in the History of Ideas in America," and "The Responsibilities of Contemporary American Literature."

15.35 Bode, Carl. The anatomy of American popular culture, 1840–1861. Berkeley, 1959.

Surveys popular taste of the period and attempts to relate it with psychological factors.

15.36 White, Morton G. Social thought in America: the revolt against formalism. N.Y., 1949; [1957].

An effort to trace "the development of the leading ideas" of Charles A. Beard, John Dewey, O. W. Holmes, Jr., James H. Robinson, and Thorstein Veblen.

15.37 Tomsich, John. A genteel endeavor: American culture and politics in the Gilded Age. Stanford, Calif., 1971.

The ideas of C.E. Norton, G. W. Curtis, T. B. Aldrich, R. W. Gilder, *et al.* are examined.

15.38 Purcell, Edward A., Jr. The crisis of democratic theory: scientific naturalism & the problem of value. Lexington, Ky., 1973.

The tensions between absolutes and relativism since the turn of the century are examined, with the searchlight falling chiefly on the academic mind. A useful background study for the historian of literary realism.

15.39 Pells, Richard H. Radical visions and American dreams: culture and social thought in the depression years. N.Y., [1973].

Deals "primarily with the ideas of writers and artists . . . generally associated with the Left" during the 1930's. Among the writers treated are Dewey and Sidney Hook as well as Steinbeck and Conroy.

15.40 May, Henry F. The end of American innocence: a study of the first years of our own time, 1912–1917. N.Y., 1959; Chicago, [1964].

Illustrates the thesis that a wholesale repudiation of past values started in this period rather than in the 1920's.

15.41 Haney, Robert W. Comstockery in America: patterns of censorship and control. Boston, [1960]; N.Y., 1974.

Sketchy, but contains a useful bibliography. Cf. also James C. N. Paul and Murray L. Schwartz, *Federal Censorship: Obscenity in the Mail*, N.Y., 1961; Paul S. Boyer, *Purity in Print: The Vice-Society Movement and Book Censorship in America*, N.Y., 1968; and Ralph E. McCoy, *Freedom of the Press: An Annotated Bibliography*, Carbondale, Ill., 1968.

15.42 Taylor, William R. Cavalier and Yankee: The Old South and American national character. N.Y., 1961; 1963.

Presents "the state of mind of the antebellum South."

15.43 Degler, Carl N. Out of our past: the forces that shaped modern America. Rev. ed. N.Y., 1970.

An "interpretation" of American history.

15.44 Persons, Stow. The decline of American gentility. N.Y., 1973.

Explores the reasons for the disappearance of an ancient ideal in its New World context and identifies the substitutes that have emerged in the present century. The arena of central focus is New England.

16. **Philosophy and psychology in the U.S.**

16.1 Schneider, Herbert W. A history of American philosophy. 2d ed. N.Y., 1963.

16.2 Passmore, John. "Philosophical scholarship in the U.S., 1930–1960." Philosophy, by Roderick M. Chisholm *et al.* Englewood Cliffs, N.J., [1964], pp. 3–124.

Occasionally suggestive.

16.3 Anderson, Paul R., and Fisch, Max H., eds. Philosophy in America from the Puritans to James, with representative selections. N.Y., [1939]; 1969.
Has useful bibliographies.

16.4 Townsend, Harvey G. Philosophical ideas in the U.S. N.Y., [1934]; 1968.
Better on more recent movements than on earlier: account slightly Hegelian.

16.5 Werkmeister, William H., A history of philosophical ideas in America. N.Y., [1949].
Contains a fairly full account of the period 1867–1939. Chapters 17 and 18, on Neo-Realism and Critical Realism, are the most valuable portions.

16.6 Riley, I. Woodbridge. American thought from Puritanism to Pragmatism and beyond. 2d ed. N.Y., 1923; 1969.

16.7 Fisch, Max H., ed. Classic American philosophers. 5th printing, rev. N.Y., [1966].
Scholarly anthology representing Peirce, James, Royce, Santayana, Dewey, and Whitehead.

16.8 Thayer, Horace S. Meaning and action: a critical history of Pragmatism. Indianapolis, [1968].
A comprehensive and scholarly treatment of the Pragmatic movement here and abroad.

16.9 Ayer, Alfred J. The origins of Pragmatism: studies in the philosophy of Charles Sanders Peirce and William James. San Francisco, [1968].
Selected topics are treated without reference to other studies.

16.10 Moore, Edward C. American Pragmatism: Peirce, James, and Dewey. N.Y., 1961.
A study of underlying doctrines.

16.11 Scheffler, Israel. Four Pragmatists: a critical introduction to Peirce, James, Mead, and Dewey. London and N.Y., [1974].
Includes bibliographical references.

16.12 Perry, Ralph B. The thought and character of William James. 2 v. Boston, 1935; Westport, Conn., [1974].
Provides the best means of getting the background for American philosophy in its most creative period. Reprinted in briefer form, Cambridge, Mass., 1948; N.Y., [1964].

16.13 White, Morton G. Science and sentiment in American philosophical thought from Jonathan Edwards to John Dewey. London and N.Y., [1973].
A philosophers' survey; includes bibliographical references. White

has also edited, with commentary, a sourcebook entitled *Documents in the History of American Philosophy*, N.Y., 1972; it also ranges from Edwards to Dewey.

16.14　Riley, I. Woodbridge.　American philosophy: the early schools.　N.Y., 1907; 1958.
Out of date but contains material not available elsewhere.

16.15　Reck, Andrew J.　Recent American philosophy.　N.Y., 1964.
"To furnish a fair sample of philosophical thinking for the period from the turn of the century to World War II," ten philosophers are discussed: Perry, Hocking, Mead, Boodin, Urban, Parker, Sellars, Lovejoy, Jordan, and Sheffield.

16.16　Reck, Andrew J.　The new American philosophers: an exploration of thought since World War II.　Baton Rouge, La., [1968]; N.Y., [1970].
A sequel to the preceding item, with discussion of Blanshard, Buchler, Feibleman, Hartshorne, Hook, Lewis, Nagel, Northrop, Pepper, Randall, Wild, and Weiss. Archie J. Bahm, *Directory of American Philosophers 1964–65———*, Albuquerque, N. Mex., [1964———], lists members of philosophy departments, periodicals in the field, etc.

16.17　Curti, Merle.　"The great Mr. Locke: America's philosopher, 1783–1861." Huntington Library bulletin, no. 11, pp. 107–157 (April, 1937).

16.18　Adams, George P., and Montague, William P., eds.　Contemporary American philosophy: personal statements.　2 v.　London and N.Y., [1930]; N.Y., [1961].
Statements of belief by thirty-four philosophers.

16.19　Kallen, Horace M., and Hook, Sidney, eds.　American philosophy today and tomorrow.　N.Y., [1935]; Freeport, N.Y., [1968].
Statements of belief by twenty-five thinkers.

16.20　Fadiman, Clifton, ed.　I believe: the personal philosophies of certain eminent men and women of our time.　N.Y., 1939.
Contains statements of belief by Pearl Buck, Ellen Glasgow, Santayana, and James Thurber and revised statements by Dreiser, Mencken, and other Americans, Europeans, and Asians.

16.21　Hook, Sidney, ed.　American philosophers at work: the philosophic scene in the U.S.　N.Y., [1956]; Westport, Conn., 1968.

16.22　Roback, Abraham A.　History of American psychology.　Rev. ed.　N.Y., [1964].
Uneven and sometimes biased. (Brief autobiographies, mentioning influences, etc., of selected prominent psychologists of Europe and the U.S. appear in *A History of Psychology in Autobiography*, ed. Carl A. Murchison *et al.*, 5 v., N.Y., [1967].)

16.23　Boring, Edwin G.　A history of experimental psychology.　2d ed.　N.Y., [1950].

A standard work containing special chapters on the establishment of "modern psychology" in America.

16.24 Hale, Nathan G., Jr. Freud and the Americans: the beginnings of psychoanalysis in the U.S., 1876–1917. N.Y., 1971.

This detailed study is the first volume in a series on Freud in America.

16.25 Oberndorf, Clarence P. A history of psychoanalysis in America. N.Y., 1953; [1964].

Written by a clinician whose personal experiences enter into his record of events.

16.26 Fay, Jay W. American psychology before William James. New Brunswick, N.J., 1939; 1966.

16.27 Davies, John D. Phrenology, fad and science: a 19th-century American crusade. New Haven, Conn., 1955; Hamden, Conn., 1971.

(Poe, Whitman, and other writers of their day were greatly influenced by phrenology.) See also Madeleine B. Stern, *Heads & Headlines: The Phrenological Fowlers*, Norman, Okla., [1971].

17. Transcendentalism in the U.S.

17.1 Hutchison, William R. The Transcendentalist ministers: church reform in the New England Renaissance. New Haven, Conn., 1959; Hamden, Conn., 1972.

A well-rounded account of Transcendentalism in its chief manifestation. The bibliography is the most adequate one on the subject.

17.2 Cooke, George W. Unitarianism in America: a history of its origin and development. Boston, 1902; N.Y., [1971].

An excellent account of 19th-century developments, with a special chapter on "Unitarianism and Literature." Provides a neat history of the emergence of Transcendentalism. See also Daniel W. Howe, *The Unitarian Conscience*, Cambridge, Mass., 1970.

17.3 Wilbur, Earl M. A history of Unitarianism in Transylvania, England, and America. 2 v. Cambridge, Mass., 1952.

17.4 Frothingham, Octavius B. Transcendentalism in New England: a history. N.Y., 1876; Gloucester, Mass., 1965.

17.5 Goddard, Harold C. Studies in New England Transcendentalism. N.Y., 1908; 1960.

17.6 Ellis, Charles M. An essay on Transcendentalism (1842). Ed. Walter Harding. Gainesville, Fla., 1954; Westport, Conn., 1970.

A reprint of one of the better treatments emanating from the 1840's.

17.7 Cameron, Kenneth W., ed. Transcendental climate: new resources for the study of Emerson, Thoreau and their contemporaries. 3 v. Hartford, Conn., 1963.

Primary source materials. Cameron has privately printed also other pertinent material, as well as the *Emerson Society Quarterly* and *American Transcendental Quarterly*.

17.8 Simon, Myron, and Parsons, Thornton H., eds. Transcendentalism and its legacy. Ann Arbor, Mich., [1966].

Ten essays, on Emerson, Thoreau, Emily Dickinson, etc., by Harry H. Clark *et al.*

17.9 Miller, Perry, ed. The American Transcendentalists, their prose and poetry. Garden City, N.Y., 1957.

An anthology with a suggestive introduction. See also *The Transcendentalists: An Anthology*, Cambridge, Mass., 1950; 1957.

17.10 Leighton, Walter L. French philosophers and New-England Transcendentalism. Charlottesville, Va., 1908; Westport, Conn., 1968.

Deals with the very important influence of Victor Cousin and other Frenchmen.

17.11 Wells, Ronald V. Three Christian Transcendentalists: James Marsh, Caleb Sprague Henry, Frederic Henry Hedge. N.Y., 1943; 1971.

17.12 Buell, Lawrence. Literary transcendentalism: style and vision in the American renaissance: Ithaca, N.Y., [1973]; [1975].

An effort to produce new evaluations which may help to rake the fires underlying ash-covered scholarship.

17.13 Persons, Stow. Free religion, an American faith. New Haven, Conn., 1947; Boston, [1963].

(Free religion eventually absorbed many of the later Transcendentalists.)

See also 12.15, 15.4, 21.19, 29.1, 32.42, 32.46, 32.11.

18. Religion in the U.S.

18.1 Burr, Nelson R. A critical bibliography of religion in America. 2 v. Princeton, N.J., 1961.

The most extensive bibliography of the subject, with profuse comment, at times excessive in both quantity and the charity bestowed upon the books and articles discussed. The first volume surveys guides, general histories, etc., and then turns to individual denominations and sects. The second volume treats religion in American life and culture, including the arts, literature, and intellectual history. This bibliography forms part of the following item. (General tendencies in recent treatments of the history of religion in the U.S. are outlined in Henry F. May, "The Recovery of American Religious History," *American Historical Review*, v. 70, pp. 79–92, October, 1964.)

18.2 Burr, Nelson. Religion in American life. N.Y., 1971.
May be used to locate many of the publications that have appeared since 1960.

18.3 Gaustad, Edwin S. Religion in America: history and historiography. Washington, 1973.
A pamphlet prepared by a competent authority and issued by the American Historical Association for the use of teachers.

18.4 Ahlstrom, Sydney E. A religious history of the American people. New Haven, Conn., 1972.
A huge survey—1158pp.—with ample notes and bibliography which updates the prevailing histories but does not supplant them altogether.

18.5 Smith, James W., and Jameson, A. Leland, eds. Religion in American life. 4 v. Princeton, N.J., 1961.
A loosely organized and uneven symposium of papers centered on two topics: "The Shaping of American Religion" and "Religious Perspectives in American Culture." Under the latter category, for example, appear exploratory or tentative discussions of religious poetry, the Bible in fiction, and religious novels as best sellers.

18.6 Hudson, Winthrop S. Religion in America. 2d ed. N.Y., [1973].
A general survey, with footnote references to many valuable treatises.

18.7 Gaustad, Edwin S. Religious history of America. N.Y., [1966]; [1974].
Describes "the role of religion" in various aspects of the national history, with a selective annotated list of "further readings."

18.8 Clebsch, William A. American religious thought: a history. Chicago, [1973].
Focuses on Edwards, Emerson, and William James. One of the brief volumes in the University of Chicago's "History of American Religion," ed. Martin E. Marty.

18.9 Smith, J. W., and Jameson, A. L., eds. The shaping of American religion. Princeton, N.J., 1961.
Essays by various authorities, including "Theology in America," by Sydney E. Ahlstrom, an important article.

18.10 Gaustad, Edwin S. Historical atlas of religion in America. N.Y., [1962].
Invaluable for its pictorial representation of the distribution of the sects at various times in the past; equipped with bibliographical and statistical information. Addenda in "America's Institutions of Faith: A Statistical Postscript," in *Religion in America*, ed. William G. McLoughlin and Robert N. Bellah, Boston, 1968.

18.11 Gaustad, Edwin S. Dissent in American religion. Chicago, [1973].
A quick survey over the whole period from the colonial era to the present. A volume in the University of Chicago's "History of American Religion" series.

18.12 Smith, H. Shelton, *et al.*, eds. American Christianity. 2 v. N.Y., 1960–1963.
An anthology of representative documents, both Catholic and Protestant, with historical introductions and extensive bibliographies classified according to various periods and movements.

18.13 Hall, David D. The faithful shepherd: a history of the New England ministry in the seventeenth century. Chapel Hill, N.C., 1972.
A detailed study; bibliographical essay appended.

18.14 Pope, Robert G. The Half-Way Covenant: church membership in Puritan New England. Princeton, N. J., 1969.
An analysis of the background for, and the circumstances attendant upon, the adoption of the Half-Way Covenant in Massachusetts and Connecticut in the later seventeenth century.

18.15 Morais, Herbert M. Deism in eighteenth century America. N.Y., 1934; 1967.

18.16 Koch, G. Adolf. Republican religion: the American Revolution and the cult of reason. N.Y., [1933]; Binghamton, N.Y., 1968.
Deism and the reaction against it. The reprint is entitled *Religion of the American Enlightenment*.

18.17 Billington, Ray A. The Protestant crusade, 1800–1860: a study of the origins of American nativism. N.Y., 1938; Gloucester, Mass., 1963.
Treats the opposition to Catholicism which was part of the Know-Nothing movement.

18.18 Post, Albert. Popular freethought in America 1825–1850. N.Y., 1943; 1974.

18.19 Warren, Sidney. American freethought, 1860–1914. N.Y., 1943; [1966].

18.20 Hopkins, Charles H. The rise of the social gospel in American protestantism 1865–1915. New Haven, Conn., 1940; [1967].
Deals with the "progressive" theology and sociological tendencies resulting from the impact of industrial society and scientific theories.

18.21 Brumm, Ursula. American thought and religious typology. New Brunswick, N.J., [1970].

Product of a leading German scholar. (A "Selective Check-List on Typology," compiled by Sacvan Bercovitch, appears in *Early American Literature*, V. 5, No. 1, Part II, Spring, 1970.)

18.22 Sandeen, Ernest R. The roots of Fundamentalism. Chicago, 1970.

The roots in both Britain and the U.S. are considered, and the Millenarians are lumped in. The period covered is 1800–1930.

18.23 Schneider, Herbert W. Religion in 20th century America. Rev. ed. N.Y., 1964.

A volume in the Library of Congress series in American Civilization; useful for suggestions.

18.24 Ellis, John T. A guide to American Catholic history. Milwaukee, 1959.

The same compiler has prepared *Documents of American Catholic History*, rev. ed., Milwaukee, [1962].

18.25 Glazer, Nathan. American Judaism. 2d. ed. Chicago, 1972.

A compact account which may be fortified by documentary materials included in Joseph L. Blau and Salo W. Baron, eds., *The Jews in the U.S. 1790–1840*, 3 v., N.Y., 1963, and Blau's *Judaism in America*, Chicago, 1976.

18.26 Mead, Frank S. Handbook of denominations in the U.S. 6th ed. N.Y., [1975]——.

Brief sketches of 200-odd sects or denominations. (Annual statistics appear in *Yearbook of the Churches*, published by the National Council of the Churches of Christ in the U.S.A.)

18.27 Mayer, Frederick E. The religious bodies of America. 2d ed. St. Louis, [1956].

Various denominations are treated from the angle of their theology; bibliographies are appended to each section; intended "primarily for the theological student and the parish minister."

18.28 Stewart, Randall. American literature and Christian doctrine. Baton Rouge, La., [1958].

A tentative exploration of several authors and literary traditions in terms of their religious ideas. American literature is in part considered also by Amos N. Wilder in *The Spiritual Aspects of the New Poetry*, N.Y., [1940]; *Modern Poetry and the Christian Tradition*, N.Y., 1952; and *Theology and Modern Literature*, Cambridge, Mass., 1958, all pretty thin.

18.29 Strong, Augustus H. American poets and their theology. Philadelphia, 1916; Freeport, N.Y., [1968].

Treats, in an old-fashioned way, Bryant, Emerson, Whittier, Poe, Longfellow, Lowell, Holmes, Lanier, and Whitman.

18.30 Luccock, Halford E.   Contemporary American literature and religion. Chicago, 1934; N.Y., 1970.
Occasionally suggestive.

18.31 Luccock, Halford E.   American mirror: social, ethical and religious aspects of American literature, 1930–1940.   N.Y., 1940; 1971.
A sequel to the preceding item.

18.32 Fairchild, Hoxie N.   Religious trends in English poetry.   6 v.   N.Y., 1939–1968.
The last two volumes include discussion of some of the American poets.

18.33 Frederick, John T.   The darkened sky: nineteenth-century novelists and religion.   Notre Dame, Ind., [1969].
Religion as bearing on the lives and works of Cooper, Hawthorne, Melville, Clemens, Howells, and James.

18.34 Boyd, George N., and Boyd, Lois A.   Religion in contemporary fiction. San Antonio, Texas, [1973].
A checklist of materials since 1945. Bellow, Hemingway, Malamud, O'Connor, and Steinbeck are among the authors selected.

18.35 Morgan, Richard E.   The supreme court and religion.   N.Y., 1972.
A brief, up-to-date analysis of scholarly discussions of the subject plus views of the authors on various court opinions and practices.

19. Arts other than literature

19.1 The art index: a cumulative author and subject index to a selected list of fine arts periodicals and museum bulletins 1929/1930———.   N.Y., 1930———.
Standard bibliography for the several fine arts. After October, 1957, the museum bulletins were dropped.

19.2 Chamberlin, Mary W.   Guide to art reference books.   Chicago, 1959.
Includes a section on the U.S.

19.3 Ehresmann, Donald L.   Fine arts: a bibliographic guide to basic reference works, histories, and handbooks.   Littleton, Colo., 1975.
The U.S. is included in the very wide coverage.

19.4 The Britannica encyclopedia of American art.   Chicago, [1973].
An illustrated work with texts written by good authorities and contain-

ing well selected bibliographies. Photography, silverware, glassware, and folk art also are covered.

19.5   Larkin, Oliver W.   Art and life in America.   Rev. ed.   N.Y., [1960].
Introductory survey of the history of architecture, sculpture, painting, and, sporadically, the minor arts; intended for the use of students of American Civilization. Bibliographies and illustrations add value. (The Archives of American Art, housed in the Detroit Institute of Arts, is collecting in one central place records of American painters, sculptors, and craftsmen, such as original and microfilm source materials, biographies, catalogs, and photographs of works of art.)

19.6   Mendelowitz, Daniel M.   A history of American art.   2d ed.   N.Y., [1970].
Visual arts of all sorts are covered, including the arts of the Indians. Heavily illustrated. The bibliography is brief but well selected.

19.7   Bio-bibliographical index of museums in the U.S. of America since colonial times.   Washington, 1956; St. Clair Shores, Mich., 1972.
A Library of Congress compilation covering both native and foreign museums.

19.8   Neil, J. Meredith.   Toward a national taste: America's quest for aesthetic independence.   Honolulu, [1975].

19.9   Garrett, Wendell D., *et al.*   The arts in America: the nineteenth century.   N. Y., 1969.
A general history of painting and architecture, including mention of the minor and decorative arts. For beginners.

19.10   Miller, Lillian B.   Patrons and patronism: the encouragement of the fine arts in the United States 1790–1860.   Chicago, [1966].
Federal commissions for paintings, etc., community efforts to organize societies and museums, patrons and their tastes, etc. The study is limited to painting and sculpture.

19.11   Pierson, William H., and Davidson, Martha, eds.   Arts of the U.S.: a pictorial survey.   N.Y., [1960].
Eighteen historical essays by a variety of experts are followed by a huge display of illustrative pictures—all of them separately available in color on slides. Stage design, photography, and costume design are included.

19.12   Mumford, Lewis.   The brown decades: a study of the arts in America, 1865–1895.   2d rev. ed.   N.Y., [1955]; Gloucester, Mass., [1960].
Useful largely as an overall interpretation of the period.

19.13   Gilbert, Dorothy B., ed.   Who's who in American art.   10th ed.   N.Y., 1970——.
Sculptors, painters, graphic artists, writers, and historians of art, mu-

seum personnel, cartoonists, illustrators of books, and educators are included, but not architects, photographers, and decorators. A regional index also appears, arranged alphabetically by state and city. New editions now appear triennially. (For architects see 19.66.) See also, for art associations, schools, magazines, and state arts councils, etc., *American Art Directory*, 45th ed., N.Y., 1974. For museums, see W. Aubrey Cartwright, *Guide to Art Museums in the U.S.*, v. 1——, N.Y., [1958] ——; and *Museums Directory of the U.S., and Canada*, ed. Erwin O. Christensen, N.Y., 1961—— (museums of all types).

19.14   Groce, George C., and Wallace, David H.   The New-York Historical Society's dictionary of artists in America, 1564–1860.   New Haven, Conn., 1957.
Biographical dictionary of painters, sculptors, engravers, etc., amateur and professional, to 1860.

19.15   Dawdy, Doris O.   Artists of the American West: a biographical dictionary.   Chicago, [1974].
Checklist of 1,300 artists and illustrators, about a fourth of whom are provided with extended sketches. The Smithsonian has sponsored a similar work in *Art of the Pacific Northwest from the 1930's to the Present*, Washington, 1974.

19.16   Fielding, Mantle.   Dictionary of American painters, sculptors, and engravers.   Rev. ed.   Bridgeport, Conn., 1974.

19.17   Cederholm, Theresa D.   Afro-American artists: a bio-bibliographical directory.   Boston, 1973.
"From the slave-craftsman of the 18th century to the present." One can derive from this book an excellent view of the publications on Negro art of the U.S., pp. 325–348.

19.18   Christensen, Erwin O.   The index of American design.   Washington, 1950; N.Y., 1950; 1967.
Describes and reproduces numerous examples of the holdings of the Index of American Design, which is a collection of WPA drawings and paintings of a vast variety of products of crafts and folk art, now housed in the National Gallery of Art in Washington.

19.19   Hornung, Clarence P.   Treasury of American design: a pictorial survey of popular folk arts based upon watercolor renderings in the Index of American Design, at the National Gallery of Art.   2 v.   N.Y., 1972.
Similar to *The Index of American Design* (19.18) but much more extensive.

19.20   Chipp, Herschel B., ed.   Theories of modern art: a source book of artists and critics.   Berkeley, 1969.
Remarks of the American artists appear on pp. 501–589.

Painting and drawing

19.21 Keaveney, Sydney S. American painting: a guide to information sources. Detroit, [1974].

In addition to bibliography of its main subject, information is also supplied on publishers, research collections, national art organizations, and museums noted for their holdings of the art of the U.S.

19.22 Barker, Virgil. American painting: history and interpretation. N.Y., 1950; 1960.

Ends about 1900 with the work of Homer, Ryder, and Eakins. (The Frick Art Reference Library, in New York, is the leading research library in its field.)

19.23 Richardson, Edgar P. Painting in America: the story of 450 years. Updated ed. N.Y., [1965].

The appended selective bibliography makes a special point of museum exhibition catalogs, which often contain reproductions of pictures.

19.24 Baigell, Matthew. A history of American painting. N.Y., 1971.

Though concise, this attempts to indicate the development of "Americanness" and brings in certain elements of the social and cultural context. It will provide a general introduction, and its 222 illustrations help.

19.25 Monro, Isabel S., and Monro, Kate M. Index to reproductions of American paintings: a guide to pictures occurring in more than eight hundred books. N.Y., 1948. 1st supplement. N.Y., 1964——.

Occasionally locates the paintings in the permanent collections which house them. Cf. 19.11.

19.26 Beall, Karen F. American prints in the Library of Congress. Baltimore, [1970].

The catalog deals with 1250 artists and almost ten times as many prints, from colonial times to the 1960's.

19.27 Cowdrey, Bartlett. National Academy of Design exhibition record, 1826–1860. 2 v. N.Y., 1943.

The Academy was a vital element in art circles of the U.S.

19.28 Naylor, Maria. The National Academy of Design exhibition record: 1861–1900. 2 v. N.Y., 1973.

Lists over 20,000 paintings from the original catalogs of the Academy.

19.29 Gerdts, William H., and Burke, Russell. American still life painting. N.Y., 1971.

The most extensive survey of this kind of painting. Contains bibliography.

19.30 Hills, Patricia. The painters' America: rural and urban life, 1810–1910. N.Y., [1974].

Published in conjunction with an exhibition held at the Whitney Museum, this small volume surveys American genre painting of the period indicated.

19.31 Quimby, Ian M. G., ed. American painting to 1776: a reappraisal. Charlottesville, Va., 1971.
A Winterthur conference collection of papers, sometimes technical.

19.32 Hoopes, Donelson F. The American impressionists. N.Y., 1972.
Cassatt, Twachtman, Glackens, *et al.*

19.33 Dunlap, William. A history of the rise and progress of the arts of design in the U.S. New ed. 3 v. Boston, 1918; N.Y., 1967.
Originally published in 1834, this is still valuable because of its first-hand accounts of artists of the late 18th and early 19th centuries.

19.34 Goodrich, Lloyd, and Baur, John I. H. American art of our century. N. Y., [1961].

19.35 Brown, Milton W. American painting from the Armory Show to the Depression. Princeton, N.J., 1955; 1970.
A history, chiefly of the realists, from the Ash Can School to the new realism, illustrated by T. H. Benton. See also Brown's *The Story of the Armory Show*, Greenwich, Conn., [1963].

19.36 Rose, Barbara. American art since 1900: a critical history. N.Y., 1967; 1975.
Begins with the Ash Can School. The same author has edited *Readings in American Art since 1900: A Documentary Survey*, N.Y., 1968 (bib., pp. 209–224).

19.37 Hunter, Sam. American art of the 20th century. N.Y., 1972.
Painting and sculpture, chiefly since 1945. A classified bibliography appears on pp. 437–470 but was compiled in 1959.

19.38 Sandler, Irving. The triumph of American painting: a history of abstract expressionism. N.Y., 1970.
The N.Y. school of the 1950's enters into the picture in strength.

19.39 Janis, Sidney. Abstract and surrealist art in America. N.Y., [1944].

19.40 Weitenkampf, Frank. American graphic art. New ed. N.Y., 1924; 1970.
Engraving and book illustration.

19.41 Murrell, William. A history of American graphic humor. 2 v. N.Y., 1933–1938; 1968.
Covers the chief cartoonists 1747–1938. See also Stephen D. Becker, *Comic Art in America: A Social History of the Funnies, the Political Cartoons, Magazine Humor, Sporting Cartoons, and Animated Cartoons,* N.Y., 1959, a popular survey.

19.42 Kempkes, Wolfgang. International bibliography of comics literature. 2d ed. N.Y., 1974.

A German product that devotes about half of its space to American productions. Cut off date is December, 1972.

19.43 Nevins, Allan, and Weitenkampf, Frank. A century of political cartoons: caricature in the U.S. from 1800 to 1900. N.Y., 1944; 1975.

An annotated list appears in Frank Weitenkampf, *Political Caricature in the U.S.*, N.Y., 1953; 1971, which originally appeared in the *Bulletin of the New York Public Library*, v. 56 (March-December, 1952).

19.44 Cummings, Paul. A dictionary of contemporary American artists. Rev. ed. N.Y., [1971].

Brief entries on several hundred painters, most of them still living.

Sculpture

19.45 Craven, Wayne. Sculpture in America. N.Y., [1968].

The chief survey, with a selected bibliography which stars the outstanding studies.

19.46 McCausland, Elizabeth. "A selected bibliography on American painting and sculpture from Colonial times to the present." Magazine of art, v. 4, pp. 329–349 (November, 1946).

An uncritical checklist; reprinted in *Who's Who in American Art*, Washington, 1947, v. 4, pp. 611–653.

19.47 Proske, Beatrice G. Brookgreen Gardens sculpture. Brookgreen, S.C., 1943, v. 2. Brookgreen, S.C., 1955; N.Y., 1968.

Contains brief sketches and bibliographies of many sculptors 1870–1940. The second volume is a kind of supplement.

19.48 Gardner, Albert T. E. Yankee stonecutters: the first American school of sculpture, 1800–1850. N.Y., 1945; Freeport, N.Y., [1968].

The biographical sketches and the bibliography are also useful. Lists the early 19th-century American sculpture in the collection of the Metropolitan Museum.

19.49 Gerdts, William H. American neo-classic sculpture. N.Y., [1973].

See also for women sculptors of the Neo-classical style the exhibition catalog issued by Vassar College, Poughkeepsie, N.Y., [1972].

19.50 Gardner, Albert T. E. American sculpture: a catalogue of the collection of the Metropolitan Museum of Art. N.Y., [1965].

Contains biographical sketches of the 176 sculptors represented. Lorado Taft, *The History of American Sculpture*, new ed., N.Y., 1930, still has value as source material.

19.51 Schnier, Jacques P. Sculpture in modern America. Berkeley, 1948; Westport, Conn., [1972].

19. Arts other than literature

19.52 Andersen, Wayne V. American sculpture in process, 1930–1970. Boston, 1975.
A history of recent developments minus the work of the realists.

Architecture

19.53 Sokol, David M. American architecture and art: a guide to information sources. Detroit, 1975.
Useful in updating older standard works.

19.54 The American Association of Architectural Bibliographers papers. Charlottesville, Va., 1965————.
An annual which specializes in checklists, chiefly on American subjects. V. XI (1974) is a cumulative index.

19.55 Burchard, John, and Bush-Brown, Albert. The architecture of America: a social and cultural history. Boston, [1961].
A popular treatise which often provides the background for, rather than, a history. Includes bibliography. Wayne Andrews, *Architecture in America*, N.Y., 1960, is a pictorial history from colonial days to the present. Andrews has also produced similar books on N.Y., Chicago, Michigan, and New England, e.g.

19.56 Wodehouse, Lawrence. American architects from the first World War to the present: a guide to information sources. Detroit, [1975].

19.57 Hitchcock, Henry-Russell. American architectural books: a list of books, portfolios, and pamphlets on architecture and related subjects published in America before 1895. 3d rev. ed. Minneapolis, [1946]; [1962]; N.Y., 1975.

19.58 Roos, Frank J. Bibliography of early American architecture: writings on architecture constructed before 1860 in the eastern and central U.S. Urbana, Ill., 1968.

19.59 Giedion, Sigfried. Space, time, and architecture: the growth of a new tradition. 5th ed. enlarged. Cambridge, Mass., 1967.
Covers the Western world from the 17th century to date, but the sections on the U.S. in the 19th and 20th centuries are valuable; discusses also city planning.

19.60 Morrison, Hugh. Early American architecture: from the first colonial settlements to the national period. N.Y., 1952.
Standard work, covering the eastern colonies to the time of the Revolutionary War, French Louisiana to 1803, and the Spanish colonies to 1848.

19.61 Hamlin, Talbot F. Greek revival architecture in America. London and N.Y., 1944; [1961].
For the earlier 19th century.

19.62 Upjohn, Everard M. Richard Upjohn, architect and churchman. N.Y., 1939; 1968.
Contains considerable background material.

19.63 Hitchcock, Henry-Russell. The architecture of H. H. Richardson and his times. N.Y., 1936; Hamden, Conn., 1961.

19.64 Scully, Vincent J. The shingle style: architectural theory and design from Richardson to the origins of Wright. Rev. ed. New Haven, Conn., 1971.

19.65 Fitch, James M. American building: the environmental forces that shape it. 2d ed. 2 v. N.Y., 1972; [1975].
Gives emphasis to recent technological improvements.

19.66 American architects directory. 2 v. N.Y., 1955–1962.
See also Henry F. Withey and Elsie R. Withey, *Biographical Dictionary of American Architects (Deceased)*, Los Angeles, 1956; 1970. Cf. 19.13.

19.67 Mumford, Lewis, ed. Roots of contemporary American architecture. N.Y., [1959]; [1972].
Thirty-seven essays by twenty-nine writers, from mid-nineteenth century to 1950, having to do with the theory and philosophy of architecture.

19.68 Wright, Frank L. Writings and buildings. Selected by Edgar Kaufman and Ben Raeburn. [N.Y., 1960].
A convenient summary of writings by or about the great innovator (1869–1959). More than 150 illustrations.

19.69 Von Eckardt, Wolf, ed. Mid-century architecture in America: honor awards of the American Institute of Architects, 1949–1961. Baltimore, [1961].
Photographs, occasionally designs also, with brief sketches of the architects or firms to whom the awards have been given.

19.70 Pierson, William H., and Jordy, W. H., eds. American buildings and their architects. Garden City, N.Y., 1970———.
Elementary but clear exposition of various phases of U.S. architecture, with numerous illustrations.

19.71 Heyer, Paul. Architects on architecture: new directions in America. N.Y., [1966].
"This book presents the design approach, the ideas and the major work of some forty leading American architects or groups of architects." Based on interviews, well illustrated, and roughly geographical in arrangement.

Music

19.72 Jackson, Richard. U.S. music: sources of bibliography and collective biography. Brooklyn, N.Y., [1973].

A well-annotated selection of the high spots, but not up to date. *Notes: The Quarterly Journal of the Music Library Association*, July, 1934—— is helpful with its reviews and other bibliographical aids. Cf. also Jackson's list in Schwann-1, catalog for July, 1975, "Bicentennial Music U.S.A." (*Recorded Tape Guide*), pp. 35–38. Rita H. Mead has prepared *Doctoral Dissertations in American Music: A Classified Bibliography*, Brooklyn, N.Y., [1974].

19.73 Duckles, V. H. Music reference and research materials: an annotated bibliography. 3d ed. N.Y., [1974].
Coverage of the U.S. is incidental.

19.74 Howard, John T. Our American music: a comprehensive history from 1620 to the present. 4th ed. rev. N.Y., [1965]; [1967].
May be generally supplemented by Chase. Contains a bibliography, by Karl Kroeger (pp. 769–845).

19.75 Chase, Gilbert. America's music: from the Pilgrims to the present. Rev. 2d ed. N.Y., [1966].
Supplements Howard from time to time, and its approach is different.

19.76 Lowens, Irving. Music and musicians in early America. N.Y., [1964].
A collection of solid essays on such topics as the *Bay Psalm Book*, "Music and American Transcendentalism (1835–50)," and "The American Tradition in Church Song."

19.77 Hixon, Donald L. Music in early America: a bibliography of music in Evans. Metuchen, N.J., 1970.
Music publications listed in Charles Evans, *American Bibliography* (6.5).

19.78 Mussulman, Joseph A. Music in the cultured generation: a social history of music in America, 1870–1900. Evanston, Ill., 1971.
Based on a dissertation, this is a thin study of the remarks on music published in the *Atlantic, Harper's, Scribner's,* and the *Century*. The lists of articles from these journals appended are the most valuable element.

19.79 Swoboda, Henry. The American symphony orchestra. N.Y., [1967].
Copland, Piston, Stokowski, *et al.* provide essays or interviews which make source material for the musicologist. Originally prepared for the Voice of America radio program.

19.80 Mueller, John H. The American symphony orchestra: a social history of musical taste. Bloomington, Ind., 1951.

19.81 Shanet, Howard. Philharmonic: a history of New York's orchestra, N.Y., 1975.
Includes bibliography.

19.82 Hipsher, Edward E. American opera and its composers. Philadelphia, [1934].

Surveys the history of serious opera and offers a "summary of the lighter forms which led up to its birth." Inaccurate.

19.83 Davis, Ronald L. A history of opera in the American West. Englewood Cliffs, N.J., 1965.

New Orleans, Chicago, Dallas, Central City, San Francisco, and Santa Fe.

19.84 Setsam, William M., ed. Metropolitan Opera annuals. N.Y., 1947. Supplement 1947–57. N.Y., 1957. Supplement 1957–1966. N.Y., 1966——.

19.85 Mates, Julian. The American musical stage before 1800. New Brunswick, N.J., [1962].

Not a history of opera.

19.86 Green, Stanley. The world of musical comedy: the story of the American musical stage as told through the careers of its foremost composers and lyricists. 2d ed. rev. N.Y., [1974].

See also 23.57 and S. Green, *Encyclopaedia of the Musical Theatre*, N.Y., 1976.

19.87 Levine, Richard, and Simon, Alfred. Encyclopedia of theatre music: a comprehensive listing of more than 4,000 songs from Broadway and Hollywood: 1900–1960. N.Y., [1961].

See also John Chipman, *Index to Top-Hit Tunes (1900–1950)*, Boston, [1962].

19.88 Mattfeld, Julius. Variety music cavalcade, 1620–1969: a chronology of vocal and instrumental music popular in the U.S. 3d ed. Englewood Cliffs, N.J., [1971].

19.89 Wilgus, Donald K. Anglo-American folksong scholarship since 1898. New Brunswick, N.J., 1959.

A survey of scholarship devoted to ballads and folksongs in English: theory, collectors, editors, etc. Eminent collections are described, and appendixes offer a discography of LP records, a bibliography, and a glossary of technical terms.

19.90 Lawless, Ray M. Folksingers and folksongs in America. Rev. ed. N.Y., [1965].

Brief biographies of over 200 singers, a short account of folk-music instruments, a richly annotated bibliography, a listing of LP records, and a selected roster of song titles make this an almost ideal handbook for the serious-minded student without professional knowledge. Chapter 17 describes folklore societies and their journals as well as various folk festivals of the U.S.

19.91 Malone, Bill C. Country music U.S.A.: a fifty-year history. Austin, Texas, 1968.

Much detail in its biographical information. A publication of the American Folklore Society.

19.92 Merriam, Alan P. A bibliography of jazz. Philadelphia, 1954; N.Y., 1970.

Publication of the American Folklore Society, with 3,324 entries and a list of 113 jazz periodicals.

19.93 Gregor, Carl. International jazz bibliography: jazz books from 1919 to 1968. Strasbourg, 1969. 1970 supplement. Graz, 1971.

Covers the U.S. also.

19.94 Kennington, Donald. The literature of jazz: a critical guide. Chicago, 1971.

Originally published in 1970 in England. Selective, but most of the important works are mentioned. There is a special section on jazz and literature.

19.95 Kinkle, Roger D. The complete encyclopedia of popular music and jazz 1900–1950. 4 v. New Rochelle, N.Y., [1974].

Two volumes are devoted to biographical sketches of pop/jazz folk, with selected discography. A host of song titles and movie musicals are also listed.

19.96 Jazzforschung. Vienna, 1969——.

Research reports appearing in the first four volumes include "Musicology and Jazz," "Problems and Methods of Jazz Historiography," and "Jazz and Musical Education." Product of the International Society for Jazz Research (Graz).

19.97 Gregor, Carl. Stilformen des Jazz. V.1——. Vienna, [1973——].

Surveys methodically the character and criteria of styles from ragtime to "Chicago."

19.98 Schuller, Gunther. Early jazz: its roots and musical development. N.Y., [1967].

First volume of a two-volume work, this is a very substantial study, covering the history down to the 1930's. For obsolete as well as current jazz terms, see Robert S. Gold, *Jazz Talk*, Indianapolis, 1975.

The acceptance of the "new art form" between the two world wars especially is considered by Neil Leonard in *Jazz and the White Americans*, Chicago, [1962]. The evolution of the phonograph is surveyed in *From Tin Foil to Stereo*, by Oliver Read and Walter L. Welch, 2d ed., Indianapolis, [1975]. (Housed at Tulane University is an Archive of New Orleans Jazz.)

19.99 Russo, William. Jazz composition and orchestration. Chicago, [1968]; [1975].

"An attempt to deal with basic musical procedure as it is to be found in jazz, to codify jazz procedures, and to reform them as well. . . ."

19.100 Stearns, Marshall W. The story of jazz. N.Y., 1956; 1970.

Includes bibliographical references. Biographies of directors and performers appear in Leonard Feather, *The Encyclopedia of Jazz*, rev. ed., N.Y., [1960] and Feather, *The Encyclopedia of Jazz in the Sixties*, N.Y., [1967].

19.101 Belz, Carl. The story of rock. 2d ed. N.Y., 1972.

A list of sources and records is added to this wide-ranging study, which gets as far from aesthetic considerations as the practice of payola and the influence of disk jockeys on public taste.

19.102 Edmunds, John, and Boelzner, Gordon. Some twentieth-century American composers: a selective bibliography. 2 v. N.Y., 1959–1960.

Consists chiefly of writings by or about selected composers.

19.103 American Society of Composers, Authors and Publishers. The ASCAP biographical dictionary of composers, authors, and publishers. 3d ed. N.Y., 1966.

19.104 Reis, Claire. Composers in America: biographical sketches of contemporary composers with a record of their works. Rev. ed. N.Y., 1947; Detroit, 1974.

19.105 Marrocco, W. Thomas, and Gleason, Harold, eds. Music in America: an anthology, from the landing of the Pilgrims to the close of the Civil War, 1620–1865. N.Y., [1964]; [1974].

Historical and explanatory notes accompany a good selection of compositions representative of the abler musicians as well as the taste of the era.

19.106 Southern, Eileen. The music of Black Americans: a history. N.Y., [1971].

Bibliography and discography, pp. 511–532.

19.107 Ewen, David. New complete book of the American musical theater. N.Y., 1970.

A popular and incomplete account.

19.108 Shapiro, Nat, ed. Popular music: an annotated index of American popular songs. 6 v. N.Y., [1964–1973].

V.1 covers 1950–1959; v.2 1940–1949; v.3 1960–1964; v.4 1930–1939; v.5 1920–1929, v.6 1965–1969. The list is quite selective.

19.109 Denisoff, R. Serge. Great day coming: folk music and the American Left. Urbana, Ill., 1971.

Traces connections between social radicalism and pseudo-folk music, from the 1930's through the sixties.

19.110 Smith, Cecil M. Worlds of music. Philadelphia, [1952].

Music as a business: concert management, touring performers, etc.

19. Arts other than literature

19.111 Krohn, Ernst C. Music publishing in the Middle Western states before the Civil War. Detroit, 1972.

A survey of sheet music printed from metal plates in Chicago, Cincinnati, Cleveland, Detroit, Louisville, and St. Louis, beginning in 1839.

19.112 Pavlakis, Christopher. The American music handbook. N.Y., [1974].

Covers present-day organizations, ensembles, stage music, performers, composers, festivals, fellowships, schools, libraries, radio and t.v., periodicals, music industries, concert managers, etc. Based on questionnaires; no bibliography.

19.113 Ewen, David. Great men of American popular song: the history of the American popular song told through the lives, careers, achievements, and personalities of its foremost composers and lyricists. Rev. ed. Englewood Cliffs, N. J., [1972].

A thin thread carries on from William Billings of Revolutionary War fame down to Bob Dylan and Johnny Cash.

Pottery

19.114 Evans, Paul. Art pottery of the U.S.: an encyclopedia of producers and their marks. N.Y., 1974.

A list of reference works appears in an appendix. See also Ralph and Terry Kovel, *The Kovels' Collector's Guide to American Art Pottery*, N.Y., 1974.

20. Chief general bibliographies of American literature

20.1 Literary history of the United States. Ed. Robert E. Spiller *et al.* 4th ed. rev. 2 v. N.Y., 1974.

The second volume is the most extensive bibliography of the subject and contains both a general section and special lists on many individual authors. It originally appeared as v. 3 of *LHUS* in 1948 and was prepared by Thomas H. Johnson. In 1959 and 1972 Richard M. Ludwig added supplements. Out of date and insufficiently indexed.

20.2 Nilon, Charles. Bibliography of bibliographies in American literature. N.Y., [1970].

Conflates items in the regular sources, and provides a generous index to subjects as well as authors. For bibliographies on American authors published as separates, see especially the bibliographies listed in the review section of *American Literature* (20.9) and works like Wynar, *American Reference Books Annual* (1.4).

20.3   Havlice, Patricia P. Index to American author bibliographies. Metuchen, N.J., 1971.

The intention is to gather under one cover "as many American author bibliographies as possible which have been published in periodicals." Supplements Nilon (20.2) considerably, though its coverage is limited to 28 periodicals.

20.4   Quinn, Arthur H., ed. The literature of the American people: an historical and critical survey. N.Y., [1951]; Folcroft, Pa., 1975.

Contains a 120-page bibliography with critical comments, prepared by the four authors of the volume. Out of date but occasionally still useful.

20.5   The Cambridge history of American literature. Ed. William P. Trent *et al.* 4 v. N.Y., 1917–1921.

Bibliographies, arranged by chapters, appear at end of v. 1, 2, and 4. Both text and bibliographies are often, but not always, outmoded, especially as they concern major figures. In 1944 the three volumes were reprinted in one, without the bibliographies.

20.6   Leary, Lewis G. Articles on American literature 1900–1950. Durham, N.C., 1954; 1970.

Conflates lists from *PMLA, American Literature*, and other sources. (For articles since 1950, see *PMLA* annual bibliography and the quarterly checklists in *American Literature.*)

20.7   Leary, Lewis, *et al.* Articles on American literature, 1950–1967. Durham, N.C., 1970.

Supplements the item above.

20.8   Clark, Harry H., American literature: Poe through Garland. N.Y., [1971].

A "Goldentree Bibliography." The material on certain individual authors may be more helpful than the rest of the book. Primarily for undergraduates.

20.9   American literature. 1929————.

The chief journal in its field, published quarterly by the Duke University Press, with the co-operation of the American Literature Section of the Modern Language Association of America. Contains articles of a historical, critical, or bibliographical sort, book reviews, lists of dissertations in progress and a checklist of current periodical articles. (The articles listed in its bibliography have been conflated in Leary.) Many volumes of the journal have been reprinted by the Kraus Reprint Corporation.

20.10   Marshall, Thomas F. An analytical index to American Literature, v. 1–30 (March, 1929—January, 1959). Durham, N.C., 1963.

Indexes by author and subject the articles published in the journal and the chief books reviewed in it.

20. General bibliographies

20.11 "American bibliography for 1921——." PMLA, v. 37——, 1922——.
Annual listing of books and articles on various modern European languages and literatures; until 1957 largely limited to works by Americans. Carries regularly a special section on American literature. In 1963 title was changed to *MLA International Bibliography*, and it was published separately in hard covers. Now appears in several sections, the first volume of which includes American literature.

20.12 MLA abstracts, 1970——. 3 v. N.Y., 1972——.
An annual companion to the *MLA International Bibliography*. Articles on American literature are abstracted in the first of the three volumes. Articles on language are covered in v. 3. Most of the abstracts have been prepared by the authors of the articles.

20.13 Resources for American literary study. Spring, 1971——.
A semiannual which specializes in checklists, evaluative bibliographical essays, descriptions of collections of research materials, edited documents, etc. Carries a short section of book reviews.

20.14 Woodress, James. Dissertations in American literature 1891–1966. Durham, N.C., 1968.
A classified list of doctoral dissertations from about 100 universities.

20.15 Howard, Patsy C. Theses in American literature, 1896–1971. Ann Arbor, Mich., 1974.
Unpublished A.B. and M.A. theses are listed, chiefly products of American schools, but the roster is very far from being complete.

20.16 Woodress, James, *et al.* American literary scholarship: an annual/ 1963——. Durham, N.C., 1965——.
The first volume covers books and articles on selected topics and authors published in 1963. More than a dozen collaborators treat such general topics as "Literature to 1800," "Poetry: 1900 to the 1930s," "Drama," "Fiction: the 1930s to the Present," along with the work done on major authors like Emerson, Thoreau, Hawthorne, Melville, Whitman, Mark Twain, Henry James, Faulkner, Hemingway, and Fitzgerald. The volume for 1964 contains index for 1963 also. A chapter on folklore began to appear in the third annual volume.

20.17 American literature abstracts: a review of current scholarship in the field of American literature. December, 1967——.

20.18 American literary realism, 1870–1910. Fall, 1967——.
Issued now four times a year, this periodical specializes in "comprehensive annotated bibliographies of secondary comment on those literary figures of the designated period who have not received adequate coverage elsewhere." In 1975 a guide to dissertations on the period began to appear.

20.19 American writers series. General editor, Harry H. Clark. N.Y., etc., [1934–1950].

A series of textbooks, most of which are devoted to individual authors, from Edwards and Franklin to Harte and James; selected writings plus carefully prepared introductions and annotated selective bibliographies. Various scholars edited the several volumes. To the date of their publication the bibliographies are exceptionally well chosen from the supply of both books and articles. Several of the books have been reprinted as part of the American Century Series of Hill and Wang, and some of these latter have substantially revised bibliographies.

20.20 Blanck, Jacob. Bibliography of American literature. New Haven, Conn., 1955——.

Descriptive bibliographies of all first editions and various other separates of about 300 authors of belles lettres who died before 1931. A most accurate work, with invaluable lists. Locates copies in selected libraries. V. 6 covers A. B. Longstreet to T. W. Parsons. (Readex Microprint Corporation has announced an intention to reproduce items in Blanck in microprint.)

20.21 Johnson, Merle D. American first editions. 4th ed. Rev. and enlarged by Jacob Blanck. N.Y., 1942; Waltham, Mass., 1965.

Lists the chief first editions of 194 American authors of the 19th and 20th centuries. The 1936 edition contained 24 authors omitted from this one, including Ray S. Baker, Zona Gale, Mary N. Murfree, D. G. Phillips, Upton Sinclair. A fifth edition is promised, ed. Joseph Katz.

20.22 Foley, Patrick K. American authors 1795–1895: a bibliography of first and notable editions chronologically arranged with notes. Boston, 1897; 1971.

Still useful for works by certain minor authors.

20.23 Gohdes, Clarence. Literature and theater of the states and regions of the U.S.A.: an historical bibliography. Durham, N.C., 1967.

A checklist with more than 6,000 items covering books and articles on local belles lettres and drama. Unpublished dissertations are not included. Appendixes list works on "Western" and regionalism.

20.24 Jones, Joseph, *et al.* American literary manuscripts: a checklist of holdings in academic, historical and public libraries in the U.S. Austin, Tex., [1960].

A calendar of the holdings of various libraries, prepared by a committee of the American Literature Section of the MLA, headed by J. Albert Robbins, Indiana University, which plans a supplement. See also Hamer, *A Guide to Archives and Manuscripts in the U.S.* (1.16); *National Union Catalog of Manuscript Collections* (1.15); Carman and Thompson, *A Guide to the Principal Sources for American Civilization, 1800–1900, in the City of New York: Manuscripts* (8.3); Crick and Alman, *A Guide to Manuscripts Relating to America in Great Britain and Ireland* (8.4); and George Hendrick, "American Literary Manuscripts in Continental Libraries," *Bulletin of Bibliography*, v. 25, pp. 49–58 ff., May-August, 1967.

20. General bibliographies

20.25 Boston Public Library. American literary manuscripts in the Boston Public Library: a checklist. Boston, 1973.

20.26 Northup, Clark S. A register of bibliographies of the English language and literature. New Haven, Conn., 1925; N.Y., 1962.
Includes various American authors and topics, such as Negro literature, printing and publishing, local literature.

20.27 Van Patten, Nathan. An index to bibliographies and bibliographical contributions relating to the work of American and British authors, 1923–1932. Stanford, Calif., 1934.
Works included were printed 1923–1932, plus a very few from 1933.

20.28 Woodress, James, ed. Eight American authors: a review of research and criticism. Rev. ed. N.Y., [1971].
Poe, Emerson, Hawthorne, Thoreau, Melville, Whitman, Clemens, and James are treated by well-known scholars, among them five who contributed to the first edition (1956).

20.29 Rees, Robert A., and Harbert, Earl N., eds. Fifteen American writers before 1900. Madison, Wis., [1971].
Substantial bibliographical essays on J. Adams, Bryant, Cooper, Crane, Dickinson, Edwards, Franklin, Holmes, Howells, Irving, Longfellow, Lowell, Norris, E. Taylor, and Whittier, plus two on the literature of the South.

20.30 Bryer, Jackson R., ed. Sixteen modern American authors: a survey of research and criticism. Durham, N.C., [1973].
Capable scholars provide a chapter each on S. Anderson, Cather, H. Crane, Dreiser, Eliot, Faulkner, Fitzgerald, Frost, Hemingway, O'Neill, Pound, Robinson, Steinbeck, Stevens, Williams, and Wolfe.

20.31 Woodress, James. American fiction, 1900–1950; a guide to information sources. Detroit, [1974].
An excellent beginner's bibliography which gives the outstanding information on the subject in general and then proceeds to treat 44 writers: S. Anderson—R. Wright. Similar guides are in progress: American Fiction to 1950 (David K. Kirby), Afro-American Fiction, 1853–1973 (Robert A. Corrigan), American Drama, 1900–1970 (Paul Hurley), American Poetry to 1900 (Bernice Slote), American Poetry, 1900–1950 (W. White and A. Lozynsky), Contemporary Poetry in America and England, 1950–1970 (Calvin Skaggs), The Literary Journal in America to 1900 (Edward E. Chielens), The Literary Journal in America, 1900–1970 (Edward E. Chielens), The Little Magazine in America and England, 1950–1970 (Jackson R. Bryer), American Prose and Criticism, 1900–1950 (John Clendenning).

20.32 The Serif series: bibliographies and checklists. Kent, Ohio, 1967——.
American authors dominate this helpful series, among them R. Chandler and E. S. Gardner as well as Edward Taylor, Dreiser, E. A. Robinson, Roethke, and Updike.

20.33 Kennedy, Arthur G., *et al.* A concise bibliography for students of English. Stanford, Calif., 1972.

W. E. Colburn's revision of this standard tool for students in English departments gives additional weight to the element dealing with American literature. It is accurate, though at times confusing because of its lack of editorial comment.

20.34 Proof: the yearbook of American bibliographical and textual studies. Columbia, S.C., 1971——.

Bibliography and texts connected with American literature are the province of this serial. A "Registry of Current Publications" in the field is also a feature.

20.35 Heard, J. Norman, and Hoover, J. H. Bookman's guide to Americana. 6th ed. Metuchen, N.J., 1971.

An alphabetically arranged dishing of out-of-print Americana and the prices asked. A couple scores of dealer's catalogs provided the grist.

20.36 Charles E. Merrill checklists. Matthew J. Bruccoli and Joseph Katz, general editors. Columbus, Ohio, 1969——.

Highly selective lists of works by and about various American authors, compiled by divers authorities and published in pamphlet form. S. Anderson, Dreiser, Emerson, Frederic, Frost, James, Melville, and Poe are among the authors covered.

21. Chief general histories and selected critical discussions of American literature

21.1 Literary history of the United States. Ed. Robert E. Spiller *et al.* 4th ed. rev. 2 v. N.Y., 1974.

Usually referred to as *LHUS*. Fifty-five authors contributed one or more chapters, which vary in quality but make up the most extensive academic history of the subject. The second volume is exclusively devoted to bibliography, for which see 20.1. Originally published in 1948 in three volumes. A one-volume edition lacking the full bibliography has been published from time to time.

21.2 Quinn, Arthur H., ed. The literature of the American people: an historical and critical survey. N.Y., [1951]; Folcroft, Pa., 1975.

Written by four scholars, this is in method the most scholarly narrative of the literature of the United States in English, but it is out of date.

21. General histories

21.3 Spiller, Robert E. The cycle of American literature. N.Y., 1955; 1967.
An excellent short history, along with a partial elaboration of a dubious theory of cycles.

21.4 Taylor, Walter F. The story of American letters. Chicago, 1956.
Revised edition of a historical survey originally (1936) entitled *A History of American Letters*. Uses the colonial period as a point of departure and ends with authors established at the time of World War II.

21.5 Howard, Leon. Literature and the American tradition. Garden City, N.Y., 1960; Staten Island, N.Y., 1972.
A short comprehensive history which, in part, undertakes to "seek out those attitudes of mind which controlled the creative imagination and helped shape the country's literature toward a recognizable national character."

21.6 Lüdeke, Henry. Geschichte der amerikanischen Literatur. 2d ed. Bern, [1963]; [1966].
Especially valuable for its references to German backgrounds.

21.7 Link, Franz H. Amerikanische Literatur-geschichts-schreibung. Stuttgart, 1963.
A survey of the historiography of American literature treating both American and European historians of the subject.

21.8 Link, Franz H., ed. Amerika, Vision und Wirklichkeit. Frankfurt a. M., 1968.
Sturdy esays by German authorities on aspects of the literature, from Franklin to T. Williams.

21.9 Arnavon, Cyrille. Histoire littéraire des États-Unis. [Paris, 1953].
Best general history of the subject written by a Frenchman. The standard history in Italian is Carlo Izzo, *Storia della Letteratura Nord-Americana*, Milan, 1957.

21.10 Cunliffe, Marcus. The literature of the United States. 3d ed. Baltimore, 1967; 1976.
A brief account, written by an Englishman, useful for occasional criticisms.

21.11 Brooks, Van Wyck. Makers and finders: a history of the writer in America, 1800–1915.
A series of five volumes containing a well-written, impressionistic history in which many minor writers are interwoven. The scholar usually finds the treatment of the minor authors more rewarding factually than the discussion of the major figures. As a venture in criticism in the broader sense, the series is the most extensive as well as the most brilliantly written survey of its subject ever produced by a single author. The five volumes in the order of coverage are: *The World of Washington Irving* N.Y., [1944]; *The Flowering of New England, 1815–1865*, new and rev. ed., N.Y., 1937; *The Times of Melville and Whitman*, N.Y., 1947; *New*

England: Indian Summer, 1865–1915, N.Y., 1940; *The Confident Years: 1885–1915*, N.Y., 1952. All of these have been reprinted, e.g., in Everyman's Library.

21.12   Nye, Russel B.   American literary history: 1607–1830.   N.Y., 1970.
A short but excellent survey.

21.13   Martin, Jay.   Harvests of change: American literature, 1865–1914. Englewood Cliffs, N.J., [1967]; [1969].
Well documented information, with inaccuracies in the footnotes. The treatment is largely thematic.

21.14   Berthoff, Warner.   The ferment of realism: American literature 1884–1919.   N.Y., [1965].
Described by Robert Spiller as a "thoroughly provocative book of impressionistic and analytical criticism in a loosely historical context." Commentators on the social scene, like Veblen, Lloyd, and Henry George, are discussed as well as regnant figures like James, Howells, Cather, Dreiser, and Robinson.

21.15   Pattee, Fred L.   A history of American literature since 1870.   N.Y., 1915; 1969.
Still very helpful, though it must be used in connection with the following item.

21.16   Pattee, Fred L.   The new American literature, 1890–1930.   N.Y., [1930]; 1968.
A vigorous critical and historical account. In certain cases this reassesses authors and works published prior to 1890.

21.17   Essays on American literature in honor of Jay B. Hubbell.   Ed. Clarence Gohdes.   Durham, N.C., 1967.
Twenty-three essays by eminent scholars on subjects or authors ranging from the 17th century to the present, including several "neglected" writers like Mrs. Stowe, Kate Chopin, Hearn, London, O. Henry, and Thornton Wilder. Contains also an important article on American Studies, by H. M. Jones.

21.18   Foerster, Norman, ed.   The reinterpretation of American literature. N.Y., 1928; 1959.
Contains essays on the influence of Puritanism, the frontier, etc. This work was very influential on the academic study of American literature for a number of years.

21.19   Clark, Harry H., ed.   Transitions in American literary history.   Durham, N.C., 1953; N.Y., 1967.
A symposium of seven exploratory essays, by various scholars, on "The Decline of Puritanism," "The Late Eighteenth Century," "The Decline of Neoclassicism," "The Rise of Romanticism," "The Rise of Transcendentalism," "The Decline of Romantic Idealism," and "The Rise of Realism 1871–1891."

21.20 Hart, James D. The Oxford companion to American literature. 4th ed. N.Y., 1965.

The standard handbook; includes sketches of authors and magazines, outlines of plots, explanations of movements, and terminology.

21.21 Bradbury, Malcolm, *et al.*, eds. The Penguin companion to American literature. N.Y., [1971].

Chiefly biographical sketches of authors. The final third of the volume covers Latin American literature.

21.22 Herzberg, Max J., *et al.*, eds. The reader's encyclopedia of American literature. N.Y., [1962].

An exceedingly uneven collection of entries, chiefly biographical, a few by capable authorities. Many of the authors listed have little or nothing to do with belles lettres. Occasionally useful in supplementing Hart's *Oxford Companion*. See also 11.19.

21.23 Wilson, Edmund, ed. The shock of recognition: the development of literature in the U.S. recorded by the men who made it. 2 v. N.Y., [1955]; [1974].

A collection of literary documents by distinguished American authors commenting on other authors. V. 1 covers 1845–1900; v. 2 the 20th century.

21.24 Howells, William D. Literary friends and acquaintance: a personal retrospect of American authorship. N.Y., 1900; Bloomington, Ind., 1968.

Contains much firsthand material on Boston and New York as literary centers 1860–1900 and presents invaluable portraits of Holmes, Longfellow, and Lowell in old age.

21.25 Garland, Hamlin. Roadside meetings. N.Y., 1930; Companions on the trail. N.Y., 1931; My friendly contemporaries. N.Y., 1932; Afternoon neighbors. N.Y., 1934.

A series of recollections of authors and literary history covering "the purely literary side" of Garland's experiences during the period 1885–1930. See also *Hamlin Garland's Diaries*, ed. Donald Pizer, San Marino, Calif., 1968.

21.26 Knight, Grant C. The critical period in American literature. Chapel Hill, N.C., [1951]; Cos Cob, Conn., 1968.

Literary history of the decade 1890–1900. (For a sequel covering the folowing decade, see 28.10.)

21.27 Ziff, Larzer. The American 1890's: life and times of a lost generation. N.Y., 1966.

Correlates political, social, and other trends with the productions of the chief authors and a number of the minor ones.

21.28 Macy, John, ed. American writers on American literature. N.Y., [1931]; Westport, Conn., [1974].

Thirty-seven writers contributed a chapter each, on an important author or topic like colonial historians or contemporary poetry. One of the better ventures of the sort.

21.29 Matthiessen, Francis O. American renaissance. N.Y., [1941]; [1968].
A standard critical study concerned with Emerson, Hawthorne, Melville, Thoreau, and Whitman.

21.30 Brownell, William C. American prose masters. N.Y., 1909; Cambridge, Mass., 1963.
Discriminating essays on Cooper, Hawthorne, Emerson, Poe, Lowell, and Henry James.

21.31 Miller, Perry. The raven and the whale: the war of words and wits in the era of Poe and Melville. N.Y., [1956]; Westport, Conn., [1973].

21.32 Ringe, Donald A. The pictorial mode: space & time in the art of Bryant, Irving & Cooper. Lexington, Ky., [1971].
Points out parallels between the literature and the landscape painting of the early Romantics.

21.33 Browne, Ray B., and Pizer, Donald, eds. Themes and directions in American literature: essays in honor of Leon Howard. Lafayette, Ind., 1969.
A distinguished offering with essays ranging from a discussion of Puritan devotion to a screed on Randall Jarrell's poetry.

21.34 Bruccoli, Matthew J., ed. The chief glory of every people. Carbondale, Ill., [1973].
A clutch of essays by various professors on the authors represented in the editions helped by the Center for Editions of American Authors.

21.35 Deakin, Motley, and Lisca, Peter, eds. From Irving to Steinbeck: studies in American literature in honor of Harry Warfel. Gainesville, Fla., 1972.
A miscellaneous collection of considerable value.

21.36 DeMott, Robert, and Marovitz, Sanford, eds. Artful Thunder: versions of the romantic tradition in American literature. Kent, Ohio, 1975.
A collection of essays of superior quality by divers hands honoring Howard P. Vincent. Five deal with Melville.

21.37 Falk, Robert, ed. Literature and ideas in America: essays in memory of Harry H. Clark. Athens, Ohio, 1975.
Better than average in the quality of its constituent essays.

21.38 Aaron, Daniel. The unwritten war: American writers and the Civil War. N.Y., 1973; 1975.
From Emerson to Stephen Crane, the reaction of the authors to the war.

21.39 Wilson, Edmund. Patriotic gore: studies in the literature of the American Civil War. N.Y., 1962; 1966.

For ideology emanating from the war, see also Robert P. Warren, *The Legacy of the Civil War: Meditations on the Centennial*, N.Y., [1961].

21.40 Hubbell, Jay B. Who are the major American writers? Durham, N.C., 1972.

A splendid account of the shifting of literary reputations, based on polls, anthologies, prizes, etc., as well as on the ranking by historians and critics.

21.41 Gross, Theodore L. The heroic ideal in American literature. N.Y., [1971].

This dissertation considers "some of the representative heroes of American literature and their struggle with a conflict central to the moral life of our country—the conflict between idealism and authority." Begins with Emerson and Melville and tops off with Mailer. The Southern hero, as well as the Black, comes in for a chapter.

21.42 University of Minnesota pamphlets on American writers. Ed. William V. O'Connor *et al.* Minneapolis, 1959———.

A series of brief pamphlets, each dealing with a single author or genre and containing biography, "simple, easily got at critical introductions," and bibliography of the author's books and of articles and books about him. The pamphlets are prepared by various critics, chiefly college professors. Several groups of the pamphlets have been published as books.

21.43 The American authors and critics series. Ed. Foster Provost and John Mahoney. N.Y., 1961———.

Each volume, of about 150 pages, is aimed to provide an "introduction and interpretation" and is equipped with selective bibliographical material. Various college teachers are the authors.

21.44 Twayne's United States authors series. Ed. Sylvia E. Bowman. N.Y., 1961———.

More than 350 volumes are planned, each of about 150 to 200 pages, largely critical and interpretative and equipped with notes and selective bibliography. The authors are college teachers, who vary considerably in capacity. Steinbeck, Eudora Welty, Zona Gale, and Joseph Kirkland appear as subjects side by side with Franklin, Cooper, Poe, and Whitman. Works on general topics or genres are also planned.

21.45 Chandler facsimile series in American literature. Ed. Hamlin Hill. San Francisco, 1968———.

First editions of various important works are reproduced, with critical introductions by various hands. Such titles as Whitman's *Leaves of Grass* (1855), Crane's *Maggie*, Clemens's *Huckleberry Finn*, and Emerson's *Nature* (1836) appear in the series.

See also 8.1, 15.3, 20.5, 20.9, 20.19.

22. Poetry

22.1 Granger's index to poetry. 6th ed. N.Y., 1973———.
An old work with inception in 1904 is revamped and enlarged to the point of covering 514 anthologies. The new editor is William J. Smith.

22.2 Cline, Gloria S., and Baker, Jeffrey A. An index to criticisms of British and American poetry. Metuchen, N.J., 1973.
Criticisms of 1510 poems by 285 poets, up to 1970.

22.3 Stauffer, Donald B. A short history of American poetry. N.Y., 1974.
An objective survey of the poets, Bryant to Williams, with a minimum of deference to the "isms."

22.4 Stedman, Edmund C. Poets of America. Boston and N.Y., 1885; N.Y., 1970.
Old but still useful, both as history and commentary, especially on Bryant, Whittier, Emerson, Longfellow, Poe, Holmes, Lowell, Whitman, and Bayard Taylor.

22.5 Kreymborg, Alfred. A history of American poetry: our singing strength. N.Y., 1934.
In 1929 this book appeared under the title *Our Singing Strength*. To be used with caution.

22.6 Pearce, Roy H. The continuity of American poetry. Princeton, N.J., 1961.
A purposefully unhistorical discussion of the tradition of American poetry in relation to the national culture. More valuable for certain parts than for the whole.

22.7 Allen, Gay W. American prosody. N.Y., [1935]; 1966.
Versification of eleven poets, from Freneau to Emily Dickinson.

22.8 Sutton, Walter. American free verse: the modern revolution in poetry. N.Y., 1973.
A compressed survey of practitioners from Emerson and Whitman as precursors through Pound, Williams, *et al.*

22.9 Wells, Henry W. The American way of poetry. N.Y., 1943; 1964.
Uneven survey of the "indigenous and unique," with good critical chapters on Freneau, Whitman, Emerson, Emily Dickinson, *et al.*

22.10 Kuntz, Joseph M. Poetry explication: a checklist of interpretations since 1925 of British and American poems past and present. Rev. ed. Denver, 1962; [1963].
(A periodical entitled the *Explicator*, 1942———, is especially devoted to "explication"; a considerable portion of the poems treated is American. The June issues contain an annual checklist of "explication." The material is reassembled in *Explicator Cyclopedia*, Chicago, 1966———.)

22. Poetry

22.11 Hastings, Henry C. Spoken poetry on records and tapes: an index of currently available recordings. Chicago, 1957.
See also Helen Roach, *Spoken Records*, 3d ed., Metuchen, N.J., 1970.

22.12 Literary recordings: a checklist of the archive of recorded poetry and literature in the Library of Congress. Washington, 1966.
Brings the inventory up through June, 1965.

22.13 Conner, Frederick W. Cosmic optimism: a study of the interpretation of evolution by American poets from Emerson to Robinson. Gainesville, Fla., 1949; N.Y., 1973.

22.14 Lenhart, Charmenz S. Musical influence on American poetry. Athens, Ga., [1956].

22.15 Wegelin, Oscar. Early American poetry. 2d ed. rev. and enlarged. 2 v. N.Y., 1930; Gloucester, Mass., 1962.
Incomplete list of volumes of verse, 1650–1820.

22.16 Lemay, J. A. Leo. A calendar of American poetry in the colonial newspapers and magazines and in the major English magazines through 1765. Worcester, Mass., 1972.
Notes on the authors are among the features of this valuable tool.

22.17 Arms, George. The fields were green: a new view of Bryant, Whittier, Holmes, Lowell, and Longfellow, with a selection of their poems. Stanford, Calif., [1953].

22.18 Kindilien, Carlin T. American poetry in the eighteen nineties. Providence, R.I., 1956.
Based on the Harris Collection at Brown University, which is one of the largest special collections of poetry in the U.S.

22.19 Walker, Robert H. The poet and the Gilded Age: social themes in late nineteenth century American verse. Philadelphia, [1963]; N.Y., 1969.
Covers poets of the period 1876–1901.

Poetry, 20th century

22.20 Irish, Wynot R. The modern American muse . . . 1900–1925. [Syracuse, N.Y., 1950]; Boston, 1972.
Lists chronologically by year of publication 6,906 books of verse.

22.21 "American poetry: 1930–1940." Accent, v. 1, pp. 213–228 (Summer, 1941).
Records "notable books of poetry and about poetry" published year by year in the U.S.

22.22 Tate, Allen. Sixty American poets 1896–1944. Rev. ed. Washington, 1954; Detroit, 1969.
Lists selected books by and about the poets.

22.23 Murphy, Rosalie, ed. Contemporary poets of the English language. Chicago, [1970].
> Bio-bibliographies.

22.24 Zulauf, Sander W., and Weiser, Irwin H. Index of American periodical verse: 1971——. Metuchen, N.J., 1973——.
> The periodicals selected for coverage range from the academic through the popular to the weird.

22.25 Malkoff, Karl. Crowell's handbook of contemporary American poetry. N.Y., [1973]; [1974].
> A concise but rapid survey of American verse since 1940 is followed by material on 70 poets, plus various schools and movements.

22.26 Braithwaite, William S. B., ed. Anthology of magazine verse for 1913–1929, and yearbook of American poetry. N.Y., [1913]–1929.
> Reprints have been announced for 1976.

22.27 Shapiro, Karl. A bibliography of modern prosody. Baltimore, 1948; Folcroft, Pa., 1973.
> English and American books and articles are listed with brief comments on their contents. Only a few items are earlier than the 20th century.

22.28 Gregory, Horace, and Zaturenska, Marya. A history of American poetry, 1900–1940. N.Y., [1946]; [1969].
> Written by poets, not scholars.

22.29 Untermeyer, Louis. American poetry since 1900. N.Y., 1923; Philadelphia, 1976.

22.30 Rittenhouse, Jessie B. The younger American poets. Boston, 1906; Freeport, N.Y., [1968].

22.31 Bogan, Louise. Achievement in American poetry, 1900–1950. Chicago, 1951; [1962].
> A sketch padded out with selections from the poets.

22.32 Lowell, Amy. Tendencies in modern American poetry. Boston, [1927]; N.Y., 1971.
> Robinson, Frost, Masters, Sandburg, H. D., and Fletcher.

22.33 Coffman, Stanley K. Imagism: a chapter for the history of modern poetry. Norman, Okla., [1951]; N.Y., 1972.

22.34 Hughes, Glenn. Imagism and the imagists. Stanford, Calif., 1931; N.Y., 1973.

22.35 Wells, Henry W. New poets from old. N.Y., 1940; 1964.
> The relationship of 20th-century poets, chiefly American, with older traditions in English verse.

22. Poetry

22.36   Kenner, Hugh. The Pound era. Berkeley and Los Angeles, 1971.
Eliot, Williams, and Marianne Moore are brought into the Pound vortex and the critical insights of the ingenious author.

22.37   Cook, Bruce. The Beat generation. N.Y., [1971].
An account of the turmoil makers of the 1950's—Ginsberg, Ferlinghetti, *et al.*

22.38   Rexroth, Kenneth. American poetry in the twentieth century. N.Y., [1971].
An unsatisfactory summary, of value only for individual glimpses based on the author's own participation in the turmoils of American verse since the 1920's.

22.39   Waggoner, Hyatt H. The heel of Elohim: science and values in modern American poetry. Norman, Okla., [1950].
Attention is given largely to thematic discussion and to the following poets: Robinson, Frost, Eliot, Jeffers, MacLeish, and Hart Crane.

22.40   Stepanchev, Stephen. American poetry since 1945: a critical survey. N.Y., [1965]; [1967].
Elementary but clearheaded.

22.41   Dembo, L. S. Conceptions of reality in modern American poetry. Berkeley and Los Angeles, 1966.
Principally Fletcher, H. D., Amy Lowell, W. C. Williams, Stevens, Marianne Moore, Cummings, Hart Crane, Pound, and Eliot.

22.42   Rosenthal, Macha L., ed. The new poets: American and English poetry since World War II. N.Y., 1967.
Focuses primarily on the Americans. The attempt to find general themes results in a loss of perspective, but many neglected poets are included.

22.43   A directory of American poets: including names and addresses of 1300 ... N.Y., 1973.
The poets and poetasters are listed, with addresses, by state. There are also a list of organizations sponsoring verse and a miscellaneous welter of anthologies, films, tapes, little magazines, and awards.

See also 18.32 and 32.73.

23. Drama and theater

23.1   Baker, Blanch M. Theatre and allied arts: a guide to books dealing with the history, criticism, and technic of the drama and theatre and related arts and crafts. N.Y., 1952, [1967].

Entries are annotated; treats U.S. and Canada on pp. 163–190 and includes regional studies as well as works on individual actors and playwrights.

23.2 Veinstein, André, *et al.* Performing arts collections: an international handbook. N.Y., 1960.
Lists the chief collections, libraries, etc., in various countries, including the U.S. (The card catalog of the N.Y. Public Library's theater collection has been printed in offset by G. S. Hall.)

23.3 Young, William C. American theatrical arts: a guide to manuscripts and special collections in the U.S. and Canada. Chicago, 1971.
Primary source materials on persons, playbills, theatrical histories, posters, etc. The contents of the special collections of 138 institutions, many not previously listed, are covered.

23.4 Keller, Dean H. Index to plays in periodicals. Metuchen, N.J., 1971. Supplement. 1973——.
The supplement adds 37 magazines to the 16 originally covered. Translations are also registered.

23.5 Santaniello, A. E. Theatre books in print. 2d ed. N.Y., 1966.
An annotated guide to books on drama, theater, movies, television, and radio available in the U.S. and their prices. U.S. theater is covered on pp. 120–128. See also *Chicorel Index to Drama Literature*, N.Y., 1975.

23.6 Ryan, Pat M. American drama bibliography: a checklist of publications in English. Fort Wayne, Ind., 1969.
Covers colonial times to the present. The first section, "History and Reference," offers 60 items; the second section deals with "General Background." The third section offers selective items on almost 200 individual dramatists. Drama, rather than theater, is the fundamental criterion.

23.7 Litto, Frederic M. American dissertations on the drama and the theatre: a bibliography. Kent, Ohio [1969].
Products of foreign language as well as English, speech, history, and music departments, to the number of 4500 or so, are computerized. Supplements are planned for five-year intervals.

23.8 Long, E. Hudson. American drama from its beginnings to the present. N.Y., [1970].
A "Goldentree Bibliography," designed for collegiate classes. The "major" dramatists chosen for individual checklists number 25; the "lesser" (among them Belasco, Daly, and Thomas), 26.

23.9 Stratman, Carl J. Bibliography of the American theatre: excluding New York City. Chicago, [1965].
Arranged by state and city, this covers college and school dramatics

along with professional activities. Includes a limited number of unpublished theses as well as published articles but does not include chapters or sections of local histories.

23.10 Gohdes, Clarence. Literature and theater of the states and regions of the U.S.A.: an historical bibliography. Durham, N.C., 1967.

Includes materials on New York and other cities and items published in books of local history, as well as magazine articles. Stratman is fuller on children's and collegiate theaters.

23.11 A bibliography of theatre arts publications in English, 1963——. Washington, 1965——.

This annual is compiled by the American Educational Theatre Association, Bernard F. Dukore, ed.

23.12 Moody, Richard. Dramas from the American theatre 1762–1909. Cleveland and N.Y., [1966]; [1969].

An anthology which contains excellent selective bibliographies not only on the individual plays and authors represented but on basic sources of historical or critical value, etc.

23.13 Firkins, Ina T. E. Index to plays 1800–1926. N.Y., 1927; 1971. Supplement, 1927–1934. N.Y., 1935.

Lists published plays written chiefly by British and American authors. (*Play Index: 1949–1952*, comp. Dorothy H. West and Dorothy M. Peake, N.Y., 1953, is a kind of sequel, as is also *Play Index, 1953–1960*, comp. Estelle A. Fidell and Dorothy M. Peake, N.Y., 1963——.)

23.14 Hill, Frank P. American plays printed 1714–1830: a bibliographical record. Stanford, Calif., [1934]; N.Y., [1968].

23.15 Wegelin, Oscar. Early American plays, 1714–1830. 2d rev. ed. N.Y., 1905; 1970.

A list of titles of plays and dramatic poems.

23.16 Roden, Robert F. Later American plays, 1831–1900. N.Y., 1900; 1965.

Very incomplete catalog.

23.17 Dramatic compositions copyrighted in the U.S., 1870 to 1916. 2 v. Washington, 1918; N.Y., 1968.

About 60,000 plays registered for copyright. (For titles of plays, etc., copyrighted since 1916, see U.S. Copyright Office catalog of copyright entries.)

23.18 America's lost plays. 20 v. Princeton, N.J., 1940–1942; Bloomington, Ind., [1963–1965].

A series of previously unpublished plays by a variety of authors. New volumes are now being added, 1969——, by Indiana University Press.

23.19 The best plays of 1894–1899. Ed. John Chapman and Garrison P. Sherwood. N.Y., 1955; Plainview, N.Y., 1975.

A brief listing to bridge the gap between 23.32 (Odell) and the following.

23.20   The best plays of 1899–1909 and the year book of the drama in America. Ed. Burns Mantle and Garrison P. Sherwood. N.Y., 1944; Plainview, N.Y., 1975.

23.21   The best plays of 1909——. N.Y., 1910——.
Has been continued to date in a series, variously edited, of annual supplements. These contain abridged texts of selected plays, lists of others performed or published, and a variety of other information.

23.22   Guernsey, Otis L. Directory of the American theater, 1894–1971: indexed to the complete series of Best Plays theater yearbooks. N.Y., [1971].
A general index for all the "Best Plays" series of books.

23.23   Lovell, John. Digests of great American plays. N.Y., 1961.
More than a hundred plots are digested, from the 18th century to the 1950's. See also Theodore J. Shank, *A Digest of 500 Plays*, N.Y., [1963]; [1966], pp. 309–393.

23.24   Hartnoll, Phyllis, ed. The Oxford companion to the theatre. 3d ed. London, 1967.
Contains many entries on American theaters, playwrights, producers, etc.

23.25   "A bibliography on theatre and drama in American colleges and universities 1937–1947." Speech monographs, v. 16, no. 3 (November, 1949).
Includes books, articles, dissertations, and master's essays. *Speech Monographs* carries an annual bibliography.

23.26   Stratman, Carl J. American theatrical periodicals, 1798–1967: a bibliographical guide. Durham, N.C., 1970.
Almost 700 periodicals are listed, 85 of which have never been located in any library.

23.27   The drama. 21 v. Chicago, 1911–1931.

23.28   Theatre magazine. 53 v. N.Y., 1900–1931.
There is *A Selective Index to Theatre Magazine*, by Stan Cornyn, N.Y., 1964.

23.29   Theatre arts monthly: a magazine for the world theatre. 48 v. 1916—January, 1964.

23.30   Quinn, Arthur H. A history of American drama from the beginning to the Civil War. 2d ed. N.Y., 1943; 1975.
This, with the following item, is the standard work in the field.

23.31   Quinn, Arthur H. A history of the American drama from the Civil War to the present day. Rev. ed. N.Y., 1939; 1945; 1975.

23.32 Odell, George C. D. Annals of the New York stage. 15 v. N.Y., 1927–1949; 1970.

Covers greater New York City plays, operas, etc. from the beginnings through the season of 1894: first performances, original casts, criticisms. (Since many of these plays went on the road, Odell is valuable also for theatrical history outside the N.Y. area.) The N.Y. Public Library has in scrapbooks a dramatic index covering new plays and important revivals produced in the city between August 20, 1896, and January 1, 1923.

23.33 Hornblow, Arthur. A history of the theatre in America from its beginnings to the present time. 2 v. Philadelphia, 1919; N.Y., [1965].

Contains some material not in Quinn.

23.34 Hughes, Glenn. A history of the American theatre, 1700–1950. N.Y., [1951].

A satisfactory general account, marred by inaccuracies in detail.

23.35 Seilhamer, George O. History of the American theatre. 3 v. Philadelphia, 1888–1891; N.Y., 1969.

Covers the period 1749–1797.

23.36 Hewitt, Barnard. Theatre U.S.A., 1668 to 1957. N.Y., 1959.

Surveys the professional theater primarily through contemporary accounts. Most of the book is source material, chiefly reviews of plays.

23.37 Meserve, Walter J. An outline history of American drama. Totowa, N.J., [1965].

A "'cram book," sensible and clearheaded, which gives considerable space to the present century.

23.38 Wilson, Garff B. Three hundred years of American drama and theatre. Englewood Cliffs, N.J., 1973.

A book for the "general reader."

23.39 Brockett, Oscar G., and Findlay, Robert R. Century of innovation: a history of European and American theater and drama since 1870. Englewood Cliffs, N.J., 1973.

A reference manual rather than a history. Contains pictures.

23.40 Wilson, Garff. A history of American acting. Bloomington, Ind., [1966].

A pioneer study climaxed by a whole chapter on Minnie Maddern Fiske.

23.41 Moody, Richard. America takes the stage: romanticism in American drama and theatre, 1750–1900. Bloomington, Ind., [1955].

Contains a treatment of native themes and characters and attempts to relate stage material to contemporary painting, architecture, etc.

23.42 Grimstead, David. Melodrama unveiled: American theatre and culture 1800–1850. Chicago, [1968].

The melodramas of the period are yoked to intellectual history. Based on primary sources. The bibliography includes unpublished theses and is one of the best available for the theater of the period.

23.43   Rankin, Hugh F.   The theater in colonial America.   Chapel Hill, N.C., [1965].
Based largely on newspaper sources, this offers full-scale treatment to 1764.

23.44   McNamara, Brooks.   The American playhouse in the eighteenth century. Cambridge, Mass., 1969.
An architectural account.

23.45   Havens, Daniel F.   The Columbian muse of comedy: the development of a native tradition in early American social comedy, 1787–1845.   Carbondale, Ill., [1973].
Fourteen plays are discussed.

23.46   Dormon, James H.   Theater in the antebellum South: 1815–1861. Chapel Hill, N.C., 1967.
The best treatment of the topic; foci for the history are the theaters in Richmond, Charleston, New Orleans, and St. Louis. The bibliography is noteworthy.

23.47   Felheim, Marvin.   The theater of Augustin Daly: an account of the late nineteenth century American stage.   Cambridge, Mass., 1956; Westport, Conn., [1975].
Daly was a key figure in his day.

23.48   Pollock, Thomas C.   The Philadelphia theatre in the eighteenth century. Philadelphia, 1933; N.Y., 1968.

23.49   James, Reese D.   Old Drury of Philadelphia: a history of the Philadelphia stage, 1800–1835.   Philadelphia, 1932; N.Y., 1968.

23.50   Wilson, Arthur H.   A history of the Philadelphia theatre: 1835 to 1855. Philadelphia, 1935; N.Y., 1969.

23.51   Gagey, Edmond M.   The San Francisco stage, a history.   N.Y., 1950; Westport, Conn., [1975].

23.52   Reed, Perley I.   The realistic presentation of American characters in native American plays prior to 1870.   Columbus, Ohio, [1918].

23.53   Wittke, Carl F.   Tambo and bones: a history of the American minstrel stage.   Durham, N.C., 1930; N.Y., 1968.

23.54   Toll, Robert C.   Blacking up: the minstrel show in nineteenth-century America.   N.Y., 1974.
Needs to be compared with Wittke (23.53).

23.55   Slout, William L.   Theatre in a tent.   Bowling Green, Ohio, [1972].
A survey of the history of the tent show in the U.S.

23.56 Graham, Philip. Showboats: the history of an American institution. Austin, Tex., 1951; 1970.

23.57 Smith, Cecil M. Musical comedy in America. N.Y., [1950]; [1962].
Plots as well as information on actors and songs are given in David Ewen, *The New Complete Book of the American Musical Theater: A Guide to More than 300 Productions*, N.Y., [1970], a popular account beginning with *The Black Crook* (1866). See also 19.86.

23.58 Laufe, Abe. Broadway's greatest musicals. N.Y., [1973].
Deals with 101 musicals that had a run of at least 500 performances as of May, 1972. The most stellar, like *Show Boat* and *Oklahoma!*, are given separate chapters each.

23.59 Gilbert, Douglas. American vaudeville: its life and times. N.Y., [1940]; [1963].
A sketchy history which can be often fortified by Joe Laurie, Jr., *Vaudeville*, N.Y., [1953]. Albert F. McLean, *American Vaudeville as Ritual*, Lexington, Ky., [1965], mixes history with theories concerning "myth."

Drama and theater, 20th century

23.60 Rigdon, Walter. The biographical encyclopaedia and who's who of the American theatre. N.Y., [1966].
In addition to biographical sketches, this contains a list of New York City productions January 1, 1900—May 31, 1964; complete playbills of same, 1959–1964, as well as accounts of theater groups and buildings. A list of biographies and autobiographies of leading persons in the theater, living and dead, appears on pp. 983–993.

23.61 Gagey, Edmond M. Revolution in American drama. N.Y., 1947; Plainview, N.Y., 1975.
A kind of descriptive catalog covering the thirty years prior to publication.

23.62 Weingarten, Joseph A. Modern American playwrights, 1918–1948. 2 v. N.Y., 1946–1957; 1967.
A list of plays, arranged alphabetically by authors, plus occasional information on publication or availability of scripts.

23.63 Downer, Alan S. Fifty years of American drama 1900–1950. Chicago, 1951; 1966.
A brief survey which covers the earlier years in a rather selective way.

23.64 Nathan, George J. The theatre book of the year, 1942–1950. N.Y., 1943–1951.
Comments on various plays by a popular journalist and critic. Some-

what similar commentary for the seasons 1952–1956 may be found in Eric Bentley, *The Dramatic Event*, N.Y., 1954; and *What is Theatre*, Boston, [1956]. Cf. also John Gassner, *Theatre at the Crossroads: Plays and Playwrights on the Mid-century American Stage*, N.Y., [1960].

23.65 Weales, Gerald. American drama since World War II. N.Y., [1962]. More recent dramatists are discussed by Weales in *The Jumping-Off Place*, N.Y., 1969.

23.66 Lewis, Allan. American plays and playwrights of the contemporary theatre. Rev. ed. N.Y., [1970]. Brief comments on practically every playwright of the period following 1957.

23.67 Price, Julia S. The off-Broadway theater. N.Y., 1962; Westport, Conn., [1974]. Covers the 1920's to 1960; loaded with lists.

23.68 Timberlake, Craig. The bishop of Broadway: the life and work of David Belasco. N.Y., [1954]. Belasco was a key figure at the beginning of the century.

23.69 Kinne, Wisner P. George Pierce Baker and the American theatre. Cambridge, Mass., 1954; Westport, Conn., [1968]. Much detailed information on the background of theatrical history 1900–1940.

23.70 Macgowan, Kenneth. Footlights across America. N.Y., [1929]; Millwood, N.Y., 1975. Discusses the "little theater" movement.

23.71 Novick, Julius. Beyond Broadway: the quest for permanent theatres. N.Y., 1968. Helpful for theaters outside of New York City, but not a scholarly production.

23.72 Mathews, Jane D. The federal theatre, 1935–1939: plays, relief, and politics. Princeton, N.J., [1967]. Supplants the previous study by Hallie Flanagan, *Arena*, N.Y., 1940; 1967.

23.73 Knox, George A., and Stahl, Herbert M. Dos Passos and "The Revolting Playwrights." Uppsala and Copenhagen, 1964. A carefully documented account of the attempt to establish a workers' theater.

23.74 Sper, Felix. From native roots: a panorama of our regional drama. Caldwell, Idaho, 1948; Deer Park, N.Y., [1975]. The bibliography is supplanted by Gohdes (23.10).

23.75 Sievers, W. David. Freud on Broadway: a history of psychoanalysis and the American drama. N.Y., 1955.
Gives separate chapters to O'Neill and Philip Barry only.

23.76 Himelstein, Morgan G. Drama was a weapon: the left-wing theatre in New York, 1929–1941. New Brunswick, N.J., [1963].
See also Caspar H. Nannes, *Politics in the American Drama: Broadway Plays 1890–1959*, Washington, 1960, on plays revolving around a political theme; and Gerald Rabkin, *Drama and Commitment: Politics in the American Theatre of the Thirties*, Bloomington, Ind., 1964; N.Y., 1972. The latter deals with organizations like the Theatre Union, the Group Theatre, and the Federal Theatre and then turns to a survey and criticism of the works of Lawson, Odets, Behrman, Rice, and Anderson.

23.77 Goldstein, Malcolm. The political stage: American drama and theater of the Great Depression. N.Y., 1974.
Adds to previous accounts a discussion of the amateur leftist groups.

23.78 Broussard, Louis. American drama: contemporary allegory from Eugene O'Neill to Tennessee Williams. Norman, Okla., [1962].
Among other matters, proposes to "establish the attitude of American drama toward contemporary man and his problems": O'Neill, Lawson, Barry, Eliot, Wilder, *et al.*

23.79 Cohn, Ruby. Dialogue in American drama. Bloomington, Ind., [1971].
The cream is in the chapters on O'Neill, Miller, Williams, and Albee, but much is subjective "analysis."

23.80 Moore, Thomas G. The economics of the American theater. Durham, N.C., 1968.
A professional economist concentrates on the producers and the playwrights. A final chapter offers remedies and suggestions.

23.81 The performing arts: problems and prospects: Rockefeller Panel report on the future of theatre, dance, music in America. N.Y., [1965].
A thoughtful assessment of the status and financial backing of the performing arts. In an appendix appear lists of "Permanent Professional Theatres" and "Major and Metropolitan Productions" existing in the season 1964–1965.

23.82 Baumol, William J., and Bowen, William G. Performing arts: the economic dilemma. N.Y., 1966; Millwood, N.Y., 1975.
A careful analysis covering theater, opera, concert music, and the dance which points out the losing battle against the "income gap."

23.83 Taubman, Joseph. Financing a theatrical production. N.Y., [1964].
A symposium dealing with regulations of theaters as business organizations which incidentally reveals the huge costs of mounting plays on Broadway.

23.84 Toohey, John L. History of the Pulitzer Prize plays. N.Y., [1967].
Casts and other details are supplied.

23.85 Bonin, Jane F. Prize-winning American drama: a bibliographical & descriptive guide. Metuchen, N.J., 1973.
Pulitzer, Critics' Circle, and other awards 1917–1971, with a summary of each play and an account of its stage history and critical reception.

23.86 Coleman, Arthur, and Tyler, Gary R. Drama criticism. V. 1. Denver, [1966].
A checklist of comment beginning 1940 on English and American plays.

23.87 Salem, James M. A guide to critical reviews. N.Y., 1966———.
The first installment covers American dramas from O'Neill to Albee, with indexes of reviews of plays by fifty-two playwrights for the period beginning about 1920. The plan is to widen the coverage to include musicals, European drama, and screenplays in subsequent installments. Part I, which covers American drama, has been revised in a second edition, Metuchen, N.J., 1973.

23.88 Palmer, Helen H., and Dyson, Anne J. American drama criticism: interpretations, 1890–1965 inclusive. Hamden, Conn., 1967. Supplements. 1970———.
Bibliography of selected critical reactions to American plays and playwrights beginning with 18th century. Books and periodicals, including scholarly journals, are covered. More comprehensive than Salem (23.87).

23.89 Gottesman, Ronald, and Geduld, Harry M., eds. Guidebook to film: an eleven-in-one reference. N.Y., 1972.
Bibliographies add to the usefulness of this work covering varied aspects of the study of the film.

23.90 Dyment, Alan G., ed. Literature of the film; a bibliographical guide to the film as art and entertainment. Detroit, 1975.

23.91 The American Film Institute catalog of motion pictures produced in the U.S. N.Y., 1971———.

23.92 Gerlach, John C., and Gerlach, Lana. The critical index: a bibliography of articles on film in English, 1946–1973. N.Y., [1974].

23.93 Sklar, Robert. Movie-made America: a cultural history of the American movies. N.Y., 1975.
An effort to survey the subject from an American Studies point of view.

See also 1.22, 7.5, 19.82–88, 25.16, 29.10, 32.49–50, 32.64–67, 32.107.

24. Fiction

24.1 Fiction catalog. Ed. Estelle A. Fidell. N.Y., etc., 1908——.
An annotated list, of novels chiefly; covers works in the English language only. The 8th ed. (1971) includes 4,315 titles selected by staffs of public libraries. The annotations are helpful in determining plot outlines.

24.2 Cotton, Gerald B., *et al*. Fiction index. London, 1953——.
Covers novels, short story collections, anthologies, etc., mainly available since 1945, arranged under numerous subject headings.

24.3 Cook, Dorothy E., *et al*. Short story index. N.Y., 1953——.
Stories in English or translated into English are listed by author, title, and, often, subject. Supersedes a similar index compiled by Ina T. E. Firkins, 1923 plus supplements.

24.4 Wright, Lyle H. American fiction 1774–1850: a contribution toward a bibliography. Rev. ed. San Marino, Calif., 1969.

24.5 Wright, Lyle H. American fiction 1851–1875: a contribution toward a bibliography. Enlarged ed. San Marino, Calif., 1965; 1968.

24.6 Wright, Lyle H. American fiction 1876–1900: a contribution toward a bibliography. San Marino, Calif., 1966.
The books listed in this and the other two volumes in Wright's series are available in microfilm (Research Publications, New Haven, Conn.) and on microcards (Lost Cause Press, Louisville, Ky.).

24.7 Coan, Otis W., and Lillard, Richard G. America in fiction: an annotated list of novels that interpret aspects of life in the U.S., Canada, and Mexico. 5th ed. Palo Alto, Calif., 1967.

24.8 Griswold, William M. Descriptive list of novels and tales. 10 parts in 2 v. Cambridge, Mass., 1890–1892; N.Y., 1968.
Part 1 lists fiction dealing with American country life; part 2, with American city life.

24.9 Kirby, David K. American fiction to 1900. Detroit, 1975.
A selective companion bibliography to Woodress (20.31), its sequel.

24.10 Studies in American fiction. Spring, 1973——.
Chiefly critical essays and shorter notes; carries reviews also.

24.11 Holman, C. Hugh. The American novel through Henry James. 2d ed. Northbrook, Ill., [1976].
A bibliography in which general categories are followed by lists of books and articles on twenty-one "major" novelists and twenty-one "lesser ones."

24.12 Gerstenberger, Donna, and Hendrick, George. The American novel 1789–1959: a checklist of twentieth-century criticism. Denver, [1961]; [1962]. Supplement, 1960–1968. Chicago, [1970].

Lists materials in books and articles on about 230 individual novelists from all periods and follows with a checklist of general studies of the American novel.

24.13 Eichelberger, Clayton L. A guide to critical reviews of U.S. fiction, 1870–1910. 2 v. Metuchen, N.J., 1971–1974.

Thirty British or American periodicals are covered; arrangement is by author. Volume 2 adds ten more to the coverage.

24.14 Perkins, George, ed. The theory of the American novel. N.Y., [1970].

An intelligently conceived anthology which gathers specimens of our novelists' comments on their own craft, from Brackenridge and Brown to Bellow and Nabokov.

24.15 Petter, Henry. The early American novel. Columbus, Ohio, 1971.

Some 90 novels are examined and discussed in detail. Synopses of 60 in an appendix and an excellent bibliography gild the lily.

24.16 Smith, Frank R. "Periodical articles on the American short story: a selected, annotated bibliography." Bulletin of bibliography, v. 23, pp. 9–13, 46–48, 69–72, 95–96 (January–April, 1960—January–April, 1961).

Deals with the short story in general, not with individual authors or stories.

24.17 Bungert, Hans. Die amerikanische Short Story. Darmstadt, 1972.

An anthology of remarks on the theory and nature of the short story by American novelists or critics and German scholars.

24.18 Walker, Warren S. Twentieth-century short story explication: interpretations, 1900–1966, inclusive, of short fiction since 1800. 2d ed. Hamden, Conn., 1967. Supplements. 1970 and 1973———.

Few items included were published before 1920, and most are representative of the "New Criticism." The second supplement continues through the year 1972. Many of the authors represented are Americans.

24.19 Thurston, Jarvis, *et al.* Short fiction criticism: a checklist of interpretation since 1925 of stories and novelettes (American, British, Continental) 1800–1958. Denver, [1960]; [1963].

24.20 Cowie, Alexander. The rise of the American novel. N.Y., [1949]; [1951].

An impartial treatment ending in the 1890's.

24.21 Quinn, Arthur H. American fiction: an historical and critical survey. N.Y., [1936].

Discusses also the short stories by the chief authors. Factually very reliable. For Cooper, Poe, Hawthorne, Melville, and James, see also Joel Porte, *The Romance in America*, Middletown, Conn., 1969.

24.22 Van Doren, Carl. The American novel, 1789–1939. Rev. ed. N.Y., 1940.
For the most part, outmoded by Quinn and Cowie, but still valuable for its illuminating criticism.

24.23 Wagenknecht, Edward. Cavalcade of the American novel. N.Y., [1952].
From the beginnings to 1940; heavily weighted with 20th-century novelists.

24.24 Cady, Edwin H. The light of common day. Bloomington, Ind., [1971].
Ten essays on realism in American fiction which are topped off by a much needed corrective to the nonsense on the novel perpetrated by Richard Chase and Leslie Fiedler.

24.25 Hoyt, Charles A. ed. Minor American novelists. Carbondale, Ill., [1970].
A variety of critics provide more or less mediocre essays on C. B. Brown, DeForest, Chesnutt, Cabell, Carr, West, O'Connor, and Wallant.

24.26 Pattee, Fred L. The development of the American short story. N.Y., 1923; 1966.
Though out of date, still the most consequential general survey.

24.27 Voss, Arthur. The American short story: a critical survey. Norman, Okla., [1973].
Ranges over the entire history, topping off with Roth and Updike. The balance is good, and the plot summaries are numerous.

24.28 Peden, William. The American short story: continuity and change 1940–1975. Boston, [1975].
Primarily historical and bibliographical treatment. Contains as an appendix a checklist of "notable" authors.

24.29 Leisy, Ernest E. The American historical novel. Norman, Okla., [1950]; [1970].

24.30 Dunlap, George A. The city in the American novel, 1789–1900: a study of American novels portraying contemporary conditions in New York, Philadelphia, and Boston. Philadelphia, 1934; N.Y., 1965.

24.31 Brown, Herbert R. The sentimental novel in America 1789–1860. Durham, N.C., 1940; N.Y., 1959.

24.32 Papashvily, Helen. All the happy endings: a study of the domestic novel in America, the women who wrote it, the women who read it, in the nineteenth century. N.Y., [1956]; Port Washington, N.Y., [1972].
A popular study which helps to fill the gap following Brown.

24.33 Miller, Wayne C. An armed America: its face in fiction. N.Y., 1970.
A survey of military novels from *The Spy* to *Dr. Strangelove*. Of lesser

amplitude are such studies as Stanley Cooperman, *World War I and the American Novel*, Baltimore, [1967] and Joseph J. Waldmeir, *American Novels of the Second World War*, The Hague, 1969.

24.34 Lively, Robert A. Fiction fights the Civil War. Chapel Hill, N.C., [1957]; Westport, Conn., [1973].
Contains a list of about 500 novels on the war. (Cf. also a catalog of "chief novels and short stories," 1861–1899, by Americans and dealing with the war or its effects, by Rebecca W. Smith, *Bulletin of Bibliography*, v. 16 and 17, September–December, 1939—January–April, 1941.)

24.35 Falk, Robert. The Victorian mode in American fiction 1865–1885. East Lansing, Mich., 1965.
Treats the novelists, chiefly DeForest, Howells, James, and Mark Twain, as seeking an "equilibrium of conflicting forces."

24.36 Milne, Gordon. The American political novel. N.Y., [1966].
A general study, written for a semipopular audience, with a limited number of novels listed as primary sources and a useful roster of secondary works. Cf. 24.64 for later political novels.

24.37 Flory, Claude R. Economic criticism in American fiction, 1792 to 1900. Philadelphia, 1936.

24.38 Taylor, Walter F. The economic novel in America. Chapel Hill, N.C., 1942; N.Y., [1964].
Period covered is 1865–1900. (The bibliography is considerably amplified by Lisle A. Rose, "A Bibliographical Survey of Economic and Political Writings, 1865–1900," *American Literature*, v. 15, pp. 381–410, January, 1944.)

24.39 Blake, Fay M. The strike in the American novel. Metuchen, N.J., 1972.
About 250 novels, 1855–1945, are considered. The annotated bibliography is a redeeming feature.

24.40 Hoffman, Daniel G. Form and fable in American fiction. N.Y., 1961; 1973.
A thematic treatment of ten works, by Irving, Hawthorne, Melville, and Mark Twain.

24.41 Lyons, John O. The college novel in America. Carbondale Ill., 1962.
Begins with Hawthorne but is chiefly concerned with 20th-century novels dealing with college or university life.

24.42 Jones, Arthur E. Darwinism and its relationship to realism and naturalism in American fiction, 1860–1900. [Madison, N.J.], 1950.

24.43 Fiske, Horace S. Provincial types in American fiction. N.Y., [1903]; Port Washington, N.Y., [1968].

24.44 Åhnebrink, Lars. The beginnings of naturalism in American fiction: a study of the works of Hamlin Garland, Stephen Crane, and Frank Norris, with special reference to some European influences, 1891–1903. Uppsala, [1950]; N.Y., [1961].

24.45 McMahon, Helen. Criticism of fiction: a study of trends in the Atlantic Monthly, 1857–1898. N.Y., [1952]; [1975].

24.46 Parrington, Vernon L., Jr. American dreams: a study of American Utopias. 2d ed. N.Y., 1964.

24.47 Gérard, Albert. Les tambours du néant: le problème existentiel dans le roman américain. Brussels, [1969].
Tracks the American novelists' consciousness of "antinomies fondamental de la condition humaine." James, Melville, Wright and on to the present.

Fiction, 20th century

24.48 Nevius, Blake. The American novel: Sinclair Lewis to the present. N.Y., [1970].
A "Goldentree Bibliography," designed for collegiate classes and better than average.

24.49 Best American short stories of 1915——, and the yearbook of the American short story. Ed. Edward J. O'Brien (1915–1941) and Martha Foley (1942——). Boston, 1915——.
Annual compilation containing texts of selected short stories plus other bibliographical material.

24.50 Hoffman, Frederick J. The modern novel in America, 1900–1950. 2d ed. Chicago, [1964].
Criticism rather than history.

24.51 West, Ray B., Jr. The short story in America, 1900–1950. Chicago, 1952; Freeport, N.Y., [1968].
A survey tempered by analytical criticism, rather than historical perspective, and centered on the 1940's. Cf. 24.28.

24.52 Hartwick, Harry. The foreground of American fiction. N.Y., etc., [1934]; 1967.
The novel 1890–1930 treated from a New Humanist point of view.

24.53 Simon, Jean. Le roman Américain au XXᵉ siècle. Paris, [1950].

24.54 Rose, Lisle A. A survey of American economic fiction, 1902–1909. [Chicago], 1938.

24.55 Geismar, Maxwell. Rebels and ancestors: the American novel, 1890–1915. Boston, 1953; N.Y., [1963].
Norris, Crane, London, Ellen Glasgow, Dreiser.

24.56 Geismar, Maxwell. The last of the provincials: the American novel, 1915–1925. Boston, 1947; N.Y., [1959].
Mencken, Lewis, Cather, Anderson, Fitzgerald.

24.57 Bradbury, Malcolm, and Palmer, David, eds. The American novel and the nineteen twenties. N.Y., [1971].
Essays by divers hands, some good.

24.58 Wright, Austin M. The American short story in the twenties. Chicago, [1961].
Especially Anderson, Fitzgerald, Hemingway, Faulkner, and Katherine Porter; more analytical than critical.

24.59 Beach, Joseph W. American fiction, 1920–1940. N.Y., 1941; [1964].
Caldwell, Dos Passos, Farrell, Faulkner, Hemingway, Marquand, Steinbeck, and Wolfe.

24.60 Adelman, Irving, and Dworkin, Rita. The contemporary novel: a checklist of critical literature on the British and American novel since 1945. Metuchen, N.J., 1972.
Items are derived from certain scholarly journals, principally from 1950–1970. Works of novelists who wrote before 1945 are considered if they continued to produce after that date.

24.61 Geismar, Maxwell. Writers in crisis: the American novel between two wars. Boston, 1942; N.Y., [1961].
Lardner, Hemingway, Dos Passos, Faulkner, Wolfe, Steinbeck.

24.62 Aldridge, John W. After the lost generation: a critical study of the writers of two wars. N.Y., [1951]; [1958].
A somewhat personal treatment of changes in taste and fashion during the 1940's, plus discussion of novelists like Mailer, Shaw, Vidal, Capote, *et al.*

24.63 Geismar, Maxwell. American moderns: from rebellion to conformity. N.Y., [1958].
The central focus is on the "transitional decade" from World War II to the 1950's.

24.64 Blotner, Joseph. The modern American political novel: 1900–1960. Austin Tex., [1966].
The aim is to "discover the image of American politics" as presented in the novels. Critical assessments are limited.

24.65 Rideout, Walter B. The radical novel in the U.S., 1900–1954. Cambridge, Mass., 1956; N.Y., 1966.
"Radical" means socially or politically radical. Cf. also *Proletarian Writers of the Thirties*, ed. David Madden, Carbondale, Ill., [1968].

24.66 Bernard, Harry. Le roman régionaliste aux États-Unis, 1913–1940. Montreal, 1949.

24.67 Gelfant, Blanche H. The American city novel. Norman, Okla., [1954]; [1970].

Dreiser, Anderson, Edith Wharton, Wolfe, Dos Passos, Farrell, Algren, Betty Smith.

24.68 VanDerhoof, Jack. A bibliography of novels related to American frontier and colonial history. Troy, N.Y., 1971.

About 6500 novels, colonial up to 1790. The frontier ranges to the present. The listing is by author only.

24.69 Warfel, Harry R. American novelists of today. N.Y., [1951]; Westport, Conn., [1975].

Sketches of 575 writers "who have published one or more serious novels, one of them in the last ten years."

24.70 Dickinson, A. T., Jr. American historical fiction. 3d ed. Metuchen, N.J., 1971.

Chiefly a list of novels, published 1917–1969, classified according to the historical events dealt with.

24.71 Frohock, Wilbur M. The novel of violence in America. 2d ed. Dallas, [1957]; Boston, [1964].

Chiefly Dos Passos, Wolfe, Farrell, Warren, Caldwell, Steinbeck, Faulkner, Hemingway, Agee. The first edition announces the limits of coverage 1920–1950. Louise Y. Gossett, *Violence in Recent Southern Fiction*, Durham, N.C., 1965; 1973, treats Warren, O'Connor, Welty, Styron, Capote, McCullers, and Grau.

24.72 Malin, Irving. New American Gothic. Carbondale, Ill., [1962].

A consideration of "Gothic" elements in Capote, McCullers, O'Connor, Purdy, and Salinger.

24.73 Klein, Marcus. After alienation: American novels in mid-century. N.Y., 1964.

Critical interpretations of Bellow, Ellison, Baldwin, Morris, and Malamud.

24.74 Freese, Peter. Die amerikanische Kurzgeschichte nach 1947. Frankfurt a M., 1974.

Salinger, Malamud, Baldwin, Purdy, and Barth.

24.75 Olderman, Raymond M. Beyond the Wasteland: a study of the American novel in the 1960's. New Haven, Conn., 1972.

In and out of the Wasteland with novels by Kesey, Elkin, Barth, Heller, Pynchon, Hawkes, Vonnegut, and Blagle affording the fabric for the critical weaving.

24.76 Eisinger, Chester E. Fiction of the forties. Chicago, [1963].

Discusses selected works under headings such as "The War Novel," "Naturalism," "The Conservative Imagination."

24.77 Stuckey, William J. The Pulitzer Prize novels: a critical backward look. Norman, Okla., [1966]; [1968].

24.78 Hassan, Ihab. Radical innocence: studies in the contemporary American novel. Princeton, N.J., [1961]; N.Y., [1966].

Styron, Swados, Mailer, Buechner, *et al.* are dealt with slantingly, and McCullers, Capote, Salinger, and Bellow are treated more substantially.

24.79 Bryant, Jerry H. The open decision: the contemporary American novel and its intellectual background. N.Y., 1970.

A wide-ranging study which seeks to demonstrate that our fiction since World War II is largely existentialist. War novels, business novels, and the "hip" variety of Kerouac and Burroughs form aspects of the examination, along with Barth, Bellow, Updike, Malamud, Vonnegut, and Mailer.

24.80 Harris, Charles B. Contemporary American novelists of the absurd. New Haven, Conn., [1972].

The bibliographical material may help more than the text of this superficial study of Heller, Vonnegut, Pynchon, and Barth.

24.81 Galloway, David D. The absurd hero in American fiction: Updike, Styron, Bellow, and Salinger. Rev. ed. Austin, Texas, [1970].

Critical interpretation—not a systematic study.

24.82 Bellamy, Joe D. The new fiction: interviews with innovative American writers. Urbana, Ill., 1975.

The writers are Barth, Barthelme, Gass, Gardner, Hawkes, Kosinski, Oates, Reed, Sontag, Sukenick, Vonnegut, and Wolfe.

24.83 Klinkowitz, Jerome. Literary disruptions: the making of a post-contemporary American fiction. Urbana, Ill., 1975.

The fabulous post-contemporaries are Vonnegut, Barthelme, LeRoi Jones, Sukenick, Federman, and Sorrentino. Bibliographies are included.

See also 30.47, 32.37, 32.53, 32.68, 32.74, 32.85, 32.104–105, 35.25.

25. Criticism

25.1 Brown, Clarence A., ed. The achievement of American criticism: representative selections from three hundred years of American criticism. N.Y., [1954].

Contains also historical introductions and full bibliographies.

25. Criticism

25.2   Journal of aesthetics and art criticism.   1941——.

Since 1945 contains in June issues a selective bibliography of current books and articles on aesthetics and related fields, including a section on literature. (For earlier material, see William A. Hammond, *A Bibliography of Aesthetics and of the Philosophy of the Fine Arts*, rev. ed., N.Y., 1934; [1967].)

25.3   Baym, Max I.   A history of literary aesthetics in America.   N.Y., [1973].

From Jonathan Edwards to Wallace Stevens, this opus surveys the subject, or relatives of the subject, by summarizing the theories of eighty-odd individuals. See also 19.8.

25.4   Wiener, Philip P., ed.   Dictionary of the history of ideas: studies of selected pivotal ideas.   4 v.   N.Y., [1973–1974].

Literature, criticism, and aesthetic theory loom large in the materials herein. Bibliographies follow each of the articles, about 300 in all. The fourth volume is an index, and it needs to be used.

25.5   Pritchard, John P.   Criticism in America.   Norman, Okla., [1956]; [1967].

A historical survey from the early 19th century to the "New Critics" and "Chicago School"; bibliographical notes, pp. 287–316.

25.6   Stovall, Floyd, ed.   The development of American literary criticism. Chapel Hill, N.C., 1955; New Haven, Conn., [1964].

Five professors discuss five different aspects of the subject, 1800–1950.

25.7   Foerster, Norman.   American criticism.   Boston and N.Y., 1928; N.Y., 1962.

Poe, Emerson, Lowell, Whitman; one chapter on the 20th century.

25.8   Wellek, René.   A history of modern criticism: 1750–1950.   V. 3–4. New Haven, Conn., 1965——.

The Americans treated in these two volumes, covering the 19th century, are Poe, Emerson, Jones Very, Thoreau, Margaret Fuller (v. 3, pp. 150–181), and Whitman, Lowell, Howells (v. 4, pp. 191–213), and Henry James (v. 4, pp. 213–237). There are other references to Poe in the section on the French Symbolists.

25.9   DeMille, George E.   Literary criticism in America: a preliminary survey. N.Y., [1931]; [1967].

25.10   Smith, Bernard.   Forces in American criticism.   N.Y., [1939].

Critics and critical movements are viewed from a Marxist angle as economically determined.

25.11   Charvat, William.   The origins of American critical thought, 1810–1835. Philadelphia, 1936; N.Y., [1968].

Particularly valuable for its treatment of the influence of the Scottish philosophers and critics.

25.12 Pritchard, John P. Literary wise men of Gotham: criticism in New York, 1815–1860. Baton Rouge, La., [1963].

25.13 Stafford, John. The literary criticism of "Young America": a study in the relationship of politics and literature, 1837–1850. Berkeley, 1952; N.Y., [1967].

25.14 Parks, Edd W. Ante-bellum Southern literary critics. Athens, Ga., [1962].
Covers the field 1785–1861 but omits Poe.

25.15 Clark, Harry H. "The influence of science on American literary criticism, 1860–1910, including the vogue of Taine." Transactions of the Wisconsin Academy of Sciences, Arts and Letters, v. 44, pp. 109–164 (1955).

25.16 Johnson, Albert E., and Crain, W. H., Jr. "Dictionary of American dramatic critics, 1850–1910." Theatre annual, v. 18, pp. 65–89 (1955).

25.17 Lang, Hans-Joachim. Studien zur Entstehung der neueren amerikanischen Literaturkritik. Hamburg, 1961.
A comprehensive analysis of the period from 1880 to about 1940. Occasionally critics are discussed who are seldom treated elsewhere.

25.18 Ruland, Richard, ed. The native muse: theories of American literature. V. 1. N.Y., 1972.
An anthology, with thoughtful comments, of selections from writers, ranging in time from colonials to Whitman, that deal with the debate over the "existence of native literature." A promised second volume presumably will carry on from Whitman to the present.

See also 32.122.

Criticism, 20th century

25.19 Zabel, Morton D., ed. Literary opinion in America. 3d ed. 2 v. N.Y., [1962]; Gloucester, Mass., [1968].
Copious selections, historical outline, lists of recent works in criticism, collections, and names of chief magazines publishing critical articles. Good bibliography of 20th-century American criticism.

25.20 Stallman, Robert W. The critic's note book. Minneapolis, [1950].
Three hundred quotations from British and American critics 1920–1950 are organized into eight chapters "dealing systematically with central concepts and problems of modern criticism." An extensive bibliography consists of checklists of books and articles topically arranged and includes a section on "Scholarship and Literary Criticism."

25.21 Stallman, Robert W., ed. Critiques and essays in criticism 1920–1948. N.Y., [1949]; 1975.

An anthology of British and American critical essays plus an extensive selected bibliography of "modern criticism" 1920–1948.

25.22 O'Connor, William V. An age of criticism 1900–1950. Chicago, 1952; N.Y., 1966.
Well planned but uneven in treatment.

25.23 Sutton, Walter. Modern American criticism. Englewood Cliffs, N.J., 1963.
Repeats material in various works listed above but offers summaries of books or articles which are helpful.

25.24 Ruland, Richard. The rediscovery of American literature. Cambridge, Mass., 1967.
Treats especially the New Humanists, Mencken, and Matthiessen, though V. W. Brooks, the Southern Agrarians, the Marxists, and others enter into the record.

25.25 Wellek, René. "American criticism of the last ten years." Yearbook of comparative and general literature, No. 20, pp. 5–14 (1971).

25.26 Santayana, George. The genteel tradition at bay. N.Y., 1931.
Contains unfavorable criticism of the New Humanism. This work was in part responsible for the vogue of the expression "genteel tradition." Reprinted in *The Genteel Tradition: Nine Essays by George Santayana*, Cambridge, Mass., 1967.

25.27 McKean, Keith F. The moral measure of literature. Denver, [1961]; Westport, Conn., [1973].
Contains chapters on Babbitt, More, and Y. Winters.

25.28 Zhuralev, I. K. Ocherki po istorii Marksistkoi literaturnoi kritiki S. Sh. A., 1900–1956. Saratov, 1963.
A history of Marxist literary criticism in the U.S., well documented but firmly biased by the viewpoint of conservative socialist realism.

25.29 Weimann, Robert. "New Criticism" und die Entwicklung bürgerlicher Literaturwissenschaft. Halle, 1962.
A systematic treatment, both historical and critical, not confined to Americans altogether and touched by socialist realism.

25.30 Elton, William. A guide to the new criticism. Chicago, [1951].
Explains sources as well as points of view and meaning of terms.

25.31 Hyman, Stanley E. The armed vision: a study in the methods of modern literary criticism. N.Y., 1948; 1955, abridged.
Conveys a fair amount of information, with a vast deal of waspish bias, on Wilson, Brooks, Winters, Eliot, Blackmur, Burke, and other American and British critics.

25.32 Fraiberg, Louis. Psychoanalysis and American literary criticism. Detroit, 1960.

Individual critics discussed at length are V. W. Brooks, Krutch, Lewisohn, Wilson, Burke, and Trilling. See also Claudia C. Morrison, *Freud and the Critic: The Early Use of Depth Psychology in Literary Criticism*, Chapel Hill, N.C., [1968].

25.33 Morris, Wesley. Toward a new historicism. Princeton, N.J., 1972.
A dissertation which, very selectively, offers bright ideas on Parrington, American Marxian literary postulates, Van Wyck Brooks, Ransom, and a scattering of more recent literary critics, especially Murray Krieger.

25.34 Ostendorf, Bernhard. Der Mythos in der neuen Welt: eine Untersuchung zum amerikanischen Myth Criticism. Frankfurt a. M., 1971.
A dissertation that opens up many of the necessary approaches to the full investigation that is much needed.

26. Essay, humor, and other minor types

26.1 Christadler, Martin. Der amerikanische Essay, 1720–1820. Heidelberg, 1968.
A comprehensive survey. A second volume covering 1820–1860 is promised.

26.2 Hicks, Philip M. The development of the natural history essay in American literature. Philadelphia, 1924.

26.3 Brodbeck, May, *et al.* American non-fiction: 1900–1950. Chicago, 1952; Westport, Conn., [1970].
Uneven and partial discussion of writing in philosophy, journalism, and social theory.

26.4 American humor: an interdisciplinary newsletter. Spring, 1974———.
From time to time offers bibliographical information. One of the editors, Thomas Inge, is preparing a guide to the subject.

26.5 Studies in American humor. April, 1974———.
Plans to become a "major outlet" for scholarship in its field.

26.6 Blair, Walter, ed. Native American humor. [2d ed.] San Francisco, [1960].
The selections cover the 19th century but the introduction and the very useful bibliography venture closer to date.

26.7   Rourke, Constance. American humor: a study of the national character.
        N.Y., [1931]; [1971].
        Popular work which often goes beyond its title. See also 32.9, 32.11,
        and 19.42.

26.8   Bier, Jesse. The rise and fall of American humor. N.Y., [1968].
        A critical study, described by the author as "selective," but covering
        humorists from the time of Franklin to that of Faulkner. An extensive,
        but incomplete, bibliography is appended. Valuable chiefly in that it
        complements earlier studies, especially for the period following 1920. It
        pays attention also to the local colorists.

26.9   Yates, Norris W. The American humorist: conscience of the twentieth
        century. Ames, Iowa, [1964]; N.Y., [1965].
        Begins with era of J. K. Bangs and Mr. Dooley and tops off with
        Cuppy, Perelman, Thurber, and their contemporaries. A substantial and
        very useful study.

26.10   Rubin, Louis D., Jr., ed. The comic imagination in American humor.
        New Brunswick, N.J., [1973].
        Thirty-two niblets on humor of various sorts and times in the U.S.,
        designed for broadcasting over the Voice of America.

26.11   Blair, Walter. Horse sense in American humor, from Benjamin Frank-
        lin to Ogden Nash. Chicago, [1942]; N.Y., [1962].

26.12   Tandy, Jennette R. Crackerbox philosophers in American humor and
        satire. N.Y., 1925; Port Washington, N.Y., [1965].

26.13   Levin, Harry, ed. Veins of humor. Cambridge, Mass., 1972.
        Seven of the essays, by various authors, deal with the American
        product.

26.14   Hall, Wade. The smiling phoenix: Southern humor from 1865 to 1914.
        Gainesvile, Fla., 1965.
        A dissertation with an extensive bibliography of primary sources, more
        or less mechanically arranged.

26.15   Yates, Norris W. William T. Porter and the *Spirit of the Times:* a study
        of the big bear school of humor. Baton Rouge, La., 1957.
        For a generation following 1830, Porter and the *Spirit* shaped the
        course of the mainstream of journalistic humor.

26.16   Schechter, William. The history of Negro humor in America. N.Y.,
        [1970].
        A superficial survey which centers chiefly on the stage and screen, and
        ranges from minstrel shows to the Flip Wilson t.v. serial.

26.17   Inge, M. Thomas, ed. Frontier humorists: critical views. Hamden,
        Conn., 1975.
        Critical reactions to the work of the Old Southwest humorists are

anthologized. There is also a critical checklist of this humor, by C. E. Davis and M. B. Hudson.

26.18 Falk, Robert P., ed. American literature in parody: a collection of parody, satire, and literary burlesque of American writers past and present. N.Y., [1955].

26.19 Bragin, Charles. Dime novels: bibliography, 1860–1928. Brooklyn, N.Y., 1938.

26.20 Johannsen, Albert. The house of Beadle and Adams and its dime and nickel novels. 2 v. Norman, Okla., [1950]. Supplement. [1962].
　　Contains a list of the authors and their novels. The Beadle firm was one of the chief publishers of "dime novels."

26.21 Hagen, Ordean A. Who done it?: a guide to detective, mystery, and suspense fiction. N.Y., 1969.
　　Coverage 1841–1967, chiefly of American novels. "Writings on the Mystery Novel" appear on pp. 605–619.

26.22 Mundell, E. H., and Rausch, G. Jay. The detective short story: a bibliography and index. Manhattan, Kansas, 1974.
　　Chiefly a checklist of volumes of tales by individual authors. Special sections on Sherlockeana & Poeiana, Problems-Puzzles, etc., and a list of sleuths. No title index provided.

26.23 Haycraft, Howard. Murder for pleasure: the life and times of the detective story. N.Y., 1941; enlarged, 1968.
　　A popular historical survey covering England and the U.S. 1841–1940. See also Ellery Queen, *The Detective Short Story: A Bibliography*, Boston, 1942.

26.24 Wölcken, Fritz. Der literarische Mord: eine Untersuchung über die englische und amerikanische Detektivliteratur. Nuremberg, [1953].
　　The foreign slant adds slightly to the picture.

26.25 Vogt, Jochen, ed. Der Kriminalroman: zur Theorie und Geschichte einer Gattung. 2 v. Munich, 1971.
　　Thirty-nine articles by writers of various nationalities on detective fiction, principally British and American. Most of the selections are reprints and date from the 1960's.

26.26 Buchloch, Paul E., and Becker, Jens P. Der Detektivroman: Studien zur Geschichte und Form der englischen und amerikanischen Detektivliteratur. Darmstadt, 1973.

26.27 Tuck, Donald H. The encyclopedia of science fiction and fantasy through 1968: a bibliographic survey. 3 v. Chicago, 1974——.
　　The first volume of the projected three is a "Who's Who, A-L" and a listing of their productions. The second volume will continue the biographical sketches, and the third, due in 1977, promises to be a check-

list of magazines and a separate listing of paperbacks and of subjects such as ghosts and utopias. Supplements are then to be put out every five years. Predecessors were entitled *A Handbook of Science Fiction.*

26.28   Siemon, Frederick.   Science fiction story index, 1850–1968.   Chicago, 1971.
   The stories are listed from anthologies.

26.29   Day, Donald B.   Index to the science-fiction magazines 1926–1950. Portland, Ore., 1952.
   Day has issued two supplementary lists of "fantastic literature," Denver and N.Y., 1963 and 1965 (mimeographed).

26.30   Strauss, Erwin S.   Index to the science-fiction magazines, 1951–1965. Cambridge, Mass., [1966].

26.31   Index to the science fiction magazines 1966–1970.   Cambridge, Mass., 1971——.
   A publication of the New England Science Fiction Association, which issues supplements.

26.32   Foote, Henry W.   Three centuries of American hymnody.   Cambridge, Mass., 1940; Hamden, Conn., 1968.
   Traces the story of hymns and their writers, from colonial times. Supplemented by the same author's pamphlet, *Recent American Hymnody*, N.Y., 1952.

26.33   Thompson, Ralph.   American literary annuals and gift books, 1825–1865.   N.Y., 1936; Hamden, Conn., 1967.
   Supplemented by forty-six new titles in Alan E. James, "Literary Annuals and Gift Books," *Journal of the Rutgers University Library*, v. 1, pp. 14–21 (June, 1938). Works listed in Thompson are microfilmed by Research Publications, Inc., New Haven, Conn.

26.34   Stowell, Marion B.   Early American almanacs.   N.Y., 1975.

26.35   Welch, d'Alté A.   A bibliography of American children's books printed prior to 1821.   Barre, Mass., 1972.
   Chiefly concerned with narratives in English designed for children under the age of fifteen; arrangement by authors. Originally serialized in *Proceedings of the American Antiquarian Society*, 1963–1967.

26.36   Georgiou, Constantine.   Children and their literature.   Englewood Cliffs, N.J., [1969].
   A general textbook which includes selective bibliographies.

26.37   Meigs, Cornelia, *et al.*.   A critical history of children's literature.   Rev. ed.   N.Y., [1969].
   Surveys English and American writers. (Helpful also are Elva S. Smith, *The History of Children's Literature: A Syllabus with Selected Bibliographies*, Chicago, 1937; and *Peter Parley to Penrod*, ed. Jacob Blanck,

3d printing, Cambridge, Mass., 1961; and Monica Kiefer, *American Children Through Their Books*, Philadelphia, 1969.)

26.38 Brockett, Oscar G., *et al.* A bibliographical guide to research in speech and dramatic art. Chicago, etc., [1963].

A practical compilation which covers also the "context of relevant materials both in related fields and in the broad category of general reference works."

26.39 Auer, J. Jeffery. An introduction to research in speech. N.Y., [1959].

A handbook on methodology of research in the various areas included in speech and also a bibliographical guide to professional writing in these fields.

26.40 Speech monographs. 1934————.

Includes bibliographies and an annual record of graduate theses in speech.

26.41 Kitzhaber, Albert R. A bibliography on rhetoric in American colleges, 1850–1900. Denver, 1954.

26.42 Cleary, James W., and Haberman, Frederick W. Rhetoric and public address: a bibliography, 1947–1961. Madison, Wis., [1964].

The checklists published serially in the *Quarterly Journal of Speech*, 1947–1951, and since then in *Speech Monographs* are here assembled. The coverage is international.

26.43 Brigance, William N., and Hochmuth, Marie K., eds. A history and criticism of American public address. 3 v. N.Y., 1943–1955; 1960; 2 v. 1964.

On American oratory. Contains also a chapter on rhetoric as taught in colleges in the earlier 19th century. Sponsored by the Speech Association of America.

26.44 Cox, Edward G. A reference guide to the literature of travel: v. 2, the new world. Seattle, 1938; 1950.

27. Studies of 17th and 18th centuries

27.1 Emerson, Everett, ed. Major writers of early American literature. Madison, Wis., 1972.

Essays by capable hands on Bradford, Bradstreet, Taylor, Cotton Mather, Edwards, Byrd, Franklin, Freneau, and C. B. Brown.

27.2 Stillwell, Margaret B. Incunabula and Americana, 1450–1800. N.Y., 1931; 1968.
Lists on pp. 341–440 about 550 bibliographies of, and monographs on, Americana before 1800.

27.3 Davis, Richard B. American literature through Bryant, 1585–1830. N.Y., [1969].
A "Goldentree Bibliography" which is perforce very selective in both the sections dealing with general topics and the lists of works by and about the authors chosen for inclusion.

27.4 Books about early America: a selection for non-professional readers. Williamsburg, Va., 1965.
Selected by the staff of the Institute of Early American History and Culture. Section XII deals with "Art, Architecture, and Literature"; Section XIII with "Books, Journalism, and Printing." Out of print books are not included.

27.5 Early American literature. Winter, 1966———.
Sponsored by an affiliate of the MLA; publishes reviews and bibliographies, as well as articles. With v. 3, no. 1 (Spring, 1968), the word *newsletter* was dropped from the title.

27.6 Tyler, Moses C. A history of American literature during the colonial time. [New rev. ed.] 2 v. N.Y., 1897; Ithaca, N.Y., 1949; Gloucester, Mass., [1963]. Abridged, Chicago, 1967.
Covers 1607–1765. Though originally written in the 1870's, it is still of considerable use, in view of the paucity of general studies dealing with the period surveyed.

27.7 Tyler, Moses C. The literary history of the American Revolution, 1763–1783. 2 v. N.Y., 1897; [1970].
Still the standard work on its subject.

27.8 Stearns, Raymond S. Science in the British colonies of America. Urbana, Ill., 1970.
Natural history of the colonists is admirably treated; medicine and technology are rather slighted.

27.9 Clark, Harry H. "The influence of science on American ideas, from 1775 to 1809." Transactions of the Wisconsin Academy of Sciences, Arts, and Letters, v. 35, pp. 305–349 (1943).

27.10 Hornberger, Theodore. Scientific thought in the American colleges, 1638–1800. Austin, Tex., [1946]; N.Y., 1968.

27.11 Wright, Louis B. The cultural life of the American colonies 1607–1763. N.Y., [1957]; [1962].
A social history which establishes close connections with the literary output.

27.12 Piercy, Josephine K. Studies in literary types in seventeenth century America (1607–1710). New Haven, Conn., 1939; Hamden, Conn., 1969.

An elementary critical analysis of prose writings to determine what forms of literature were established in America before 1710.

27.13 Cook, Elizabeth C. Literary influences in colonial newspapers, 1704–1750. N.Y., 1912; Port Washington, N.Y., 1966.

27.14 Gummere, Richard M. The American colonial mind and the classical tradition. Cambridge, Mass., 1963.

Deals with the general aspects of the subject as well as with the specific indebtedness of writers like Byrd, Sewall, and Logan.

27.15 Granger, Bruce I. Political satire in the American revolution. Ithaca, N.Y., 1960; 1971.

A survey and an analysis, 1763–1783.

27.16 Wright, Thomas G. Literary culture in early New England, 1620–1730. New Haven, Conn., 1920; N.Y., 1966.

Not altogether replaced by later studies.

27.17 Miller, Perry, and Johnson, Thomas H., eds. The Puritans. 2d ed. 2 v. N.Y., [1963].

An anthology containing important critical material by the editors on the intellectual background of 17th-century writing in New England. Studies since Miller's are surveyed in *William and Mary Quarterly* for January, 1970.

27.18 Miller, Perry. The New England mind: the seventeenth century. N.Y., 1939; Cambridge, Mass., 1954; Boston, 1961.

A standard intellectual history, continued in the following item.

27.19 Miller, Perry. The New England mind: from colony to province. Cambridge, Mass., 1953; Boston, 1961.

27.20 Murdock, Kenneth B. Literature and theology in colonial New England. Cambridge, Mass., [1949]; Westport, Conn., [1970].

Strikes a happy balance between "erudition and popular interpretation."

27.21 Middlekauf, Robert. The Mathers: three generations of Puritan intellectuals, 1596–1728. N.Y., 1972.

To a degree this work helps to correct the strabismus of Perry Miller.

27.22 Bercovitch, Sacvan. The Puritan origins of the American self. New Haven, Conn., 1975.

Attempts to explore the development of the American "identity" but ranges over a very broad panorama of the Puritan cultural context.

27.23 Levy, Babette M. Preaching in the first half century of New England history. Hartford, Conn., 1945, N.Y., 1967.

See also A. W. Plumstead, ed., *The Wall and the Garden: Selected Massachusetts Election Sermons, 1670–1775*, Minneapolis, [1968].

27.24 Jantz, Harold S. The first century of New England verse. Worcester, Mass., 1944; N.Y., 1962.
Corrects many previous misconceptions about the nature and amount of verse produced in the period.

27.25 Howard, Leon. The Connecticut wits. Chicago, [1943].
Trumbull, Dwight, Humphreys, and Barlow; a standard study.

27.26 Lemay, J. A. Leo. Men of letters in colonial Maryland. Knoxville, Tenn., 1972.
A sound pioneering study of belles-lettrists usually neglected in surveys of colonial accomplishments.

27.27 Forbes, Harriette. New England diaries 1602–1800: a descriptive catalogue. [Topsfield, Mass.], 1923; N.Y., 1967.

27.28 Raesly, Ellis L. Portrait of New Netherland. N.Y., 1945; Port Washington, N.Y., [1965].
Discusses, among other matters, the literary productions of the Dutch settlers.

27.29 Tolles, Frederick B. Quakers and the Atlantic culture. N.Y., 1960.
The role of the Quakers in the 17th and 18th centuries. One chapter appears on "The Quaker Esthetic," and there is another on "The Culture of Early Pennsylvania."

27.30 Jones, Howard M. The literature of Virginia in the seventeenth century, 2d ed. Charlottesville, Va., [1968].

27.31 Davis, Richard B. Intellectual life in Jefferson's Virginia 1790–1830. Chapel Hill, N.C., [1964]; [1973].
Considers such topics as education, reading and libraries, arts, literature, oratory, religion, and social theory.

See also 22.15, 26.1, 32.7, 32.16, 32.42, 32.55, 32.58, 32.64–65, 32.95.

28. Studies of 20th-century literature

28.1 Jones, Howard M., and Ludwig, Richard M. Guide to American literature and its backgrounds since 1890. 4th ed. rev. Cambridge, Mass., 1972.

This outline, accompanied by lists of books, is both a bibliography and an attempt to impose order upon the literature as well as the backgrounds.

28.2 Millett, Fred B. Contemporary American authors: a critical survey and 219 bio-bibliographies. N.Y., 1940; [1970].
A bibliographical handbook, out of date but still helpful.

28.3 The American year book, 1910–1950. N.Y. and London, 1911–1951.
Annual surveys of accomplishments and events; the arts and literature are included.

28.4 Literature and language bibliographies from the American Year Book, 1910–1919. Ann Arbor, Mich., 1970.
E. E. Hale and A. H. Quinn surveyed the field of American literature year by year. Their work, along with that of others, is reprinted.

28.5 Thorp, Willard. American writing in the twentieth century. Cambridge, Mass., 1960.
A useful brief survey prepared for the Library of Congress series on American Studies; selective bibliography, pp. 325–332.

28.6 Spiller, Robert E., ed. A time of harvest: American literature 1910–1960. N.Y., [1962].
A series of historical or critical essays by various hands, apparently originally conceived for broadcasting in Europe, which treat briefly criticism, poetry, drama, fiction, humor, and folklore. Has a special chapter on the "New Criticism," by David Daiches.

28.7 Straumann, Heinrich. American literature in the twentieth century. 3d rev. ed. N.Y., [1965]; [1968].
A systematic survey by a Swiss professor.

28.8 Weber, Alfred, and Haack, Dietmar, eds. Amerikanische Literatur im 20. Yahrhundert. Göttingen, [1971].
Papers representing lectures delivered at Tübingen in 1969, including one by René Wellek on fairly recent criticism.

28.9 Kazin, Alfred. On native grounds. N.Y., [1942]; [1972]; [1956], abridged.
Uneven criticism of prose writers only, from Howells to the authors of the 1930's.

28.10 Fishman, Solomon. The disinherited of art: writer and background. Berkeley, 1953.
Speculation on the "impact of culture" on 20th-century American literature: alienation of writers in the 1920's, Naturalism, Marxism, and Agrarianism in the 1930's, the rise of the "New Criticism," attitudes toward Europe, etc.

28.11 Knight, Grant C. The strenuous age in American literature, 1900–1910. Chapel Hill, N.C., [1954]; N.Y., [1971].
A literary history of the decade.

28. 20th century literature

28.12   Cowley, Malcolm, ed.   After the genteel tradition.   N.Y., [1937]; Carbondale, Ill., [1965].
Various critics discuss a variety of authors or topics treating the period 1910–1930.

28.13   Brooks, Van Wyck.   Opinions of Oliver Allston.   N.Y., 1941.
A vigorous arraignment of much of the literature produced 1915–1940.

28.14   Kenner, Hugh.   A homemade world: the American modernist writers. N.Y., 1975.
Faulkner, Fitzgerald, Hemingway, M. Moore, Stevens, and Williams are scrutinized by a critic of considerable experience.

28.15   Cowley, Malcolm.   A second flowering: works and days of the Lost Generation.   N.Y., 1973.
With much warmed-over material the comments center mainly on Fitzgerald, Hemingway, Dos Passos, Cummings, Wilder, Faulkner, Wolfe, and Hart Crane.

28.16   Stevenson, Elisabeth.   Babbitts and bohemians: the American 1920's. N.Y., [1967].
A popular work, like Allen (28.17), which it often supplements.

28.17   Allen, Frederick L.   Only yesterday: an informal history of the nineteen-twenties.   N.Y., 1931; [1964].
Very useful for its portrayal of fashions and attitudes of the intellectuals.

28.18   Langford, Richard E., and Taylor, W. E., eds.   The twenties: poetry and prose: twenty critical essays.   Deland, Florida, [1966].
Various aspects of the decade are touched upon by divers hands.

28.19   Cowley, Malcolm.   Exile's return: a narrative of ideas.   N.Y., [1934]; 1959.
Deals with "ideas that dominated the literary world of the 1920's." The original edition has been considerably revised in the reprints.

28.20   Krutch, Joseph W.   The modern temper: a study and a confession.   N.Y., [1929]; [1956].
Tendencies in thought in the 1920's and the mood induced by the tendencies.

28.21   Hoffman, Frederick J.   The twenties: American writing in the postwar decade.   New ed. rev.   N.Y., [1962]; [1965].
A systematic study centered on eight themes or trends, with accompanying analyses of eight illustrative literary texts.

28.22   Whipple, T. K.   Spokesmen: modern writers and American life.   N.Y., 1928; Freeport, N.Y., [1971].
Adams, Robinson, Dreiser, Frost, Anderson, Cather, Sandburg, Lind-

say, Lewis, O'Neill. A contemporary appraisal which still has considerable value because of its critical insights.

28.23 Allen, Frederick L.   Since yesterday: the nineteen-thirties in America. N.Y., 1940; [1972].
Not as consequential as Allen's similar work on the twenties.

28.24 French, Warren, ed.   The thirties: fiction, poetry, drama.   Rev. ed.   Deland, Fla., [1975].
French provides the continuity for a collection of essays, historical and critical, by various collaborators, and Jackson R. Bryer provides a bibliography which is briefly annotated.

28.25 Hassan, Ihab.   Contemporary American literature, 1945–1972.   N.Y., [1973].
A brief "introduction" with quick surveys of fiction, poetry, and drama following a chapter on generalities.

28.26 Christadler, Martin.   Amerikanische Literatur der Gegenwart in Einzeldarstellung.   Stuttgart, 1973.
Twenty-six essayists survey a number of contemporary fiction writers, dramatists, and poets.

28.27 Lepper, Gary.   Bibliographical checklist of 75 postwar American authors. San Diego, Calif., 1975.
Lists separates of authors: Nelson Algren to John Wieners, identifying first printings, points, etc.   Includes broadcasts.

28.28 Cowley, Malcolm.   The literary situation.   N.Y., 1954; 1958; [Gloucester, Mass., 1960].
"A social history of literature in our times"—war novels, paperback books, how authors earn their living, etc. Cf. also William J. Lord, *How Authors Make a Living: An Analysis of Free Lance Writers' Income*, 1953–1957, N.Y., 1962, largely statistical.

28.29 Hoffman, Frederick J.   Freudianism and the literary mind.   2d ed. Baton Rouge, La., 1957; [1967].
Indicates the impact of Freud on certain writers from the U.S. and abroad. Cf. Norman Kiell, *Psychoanalysis, Psychology, and Literature: A Bibliography*, Madison, Wis., 1963.

28.30 Duffey, Bernard.   The Chicago renaissance in American letters: a critical history. [East Lansing, Mich.], 1954; Westport, Conn., [1972].
Covers the period 1890–1930.

28.31 Kramer, Dale.   Chicago renaissance: the literary life in the Midwest, 1900–1930.   N.Y., [1966].
Often supplements Duffey (28.30).

28.32 Bradbury, John M.   The Fugitives: a critical account.   Chapel Hill, N.C., [1958]; New Haven, Conn., [1965].

Attempts "to set the Fugitive group as a whole in its proper historical place" and to indicate the nature of the literary work of each member—especially Ransom, Tate, and Warren. See also Louise Cowan, *The Fugitive Group: A Literary History*, Baton Rouge, [1959]; Rob R. Purdy, ed., *Fugitives' Reunion: Conversations at Vanderbilt*, Nashville, 1959; and John L. Stewart, *The Burden of Time*, Princeton, N.J., 1965.

28.33 Writers at work: the Paris Review interviews. Ed. Malcolm Cowley. N.Y., 1958; 1959.

A collection of discriminating interviews with sixteen contemporary authors, chiefly Americans, including Dorothy Parker, Thurber, Wilder, Faulkner, R. P. Warren, Algren, Styron, and Capote. A 2d series, N.Y., [1963], carries on, with an introduction by Van Wyck Brooks. A 3d series, N.Y., [1967], is introduced by Alfred Kazin.

28.34 Aaron, Daniel. Writers on the left: episodes in American literary communism. N.Y., 1961; 1974.

"A social chronicle of the Left Wing writer" from 1912 to the early 1940's. Part of a series called "Communism in American Life," of which Clinton L. Rossiter is the general editor.

See also the subsections on the 20th century under Poetry, Drama and Theater, Fiction, and Criticism, and **15.7, 15.33–34, 15.40–41, 16.20, 21.16, 21.23, 21.28, 30.19.**

29. Special topics or themes in American literature

29.1 Spencer, Benjamin T. The quest for nationality. [Syracuse, N.Y.], 1957.

A history of the nationalistic element in American literature from colonial times to 1892, with emphasis on the period 1830–1860, and a special chapter on Whitman. Contains also chapters on the Transcendentalists and on local-color literature.

29.2 Foerster, Norman. Nature in American literature. N.Y., 1923; [1958]. Chiefly concerned with the 19th century.

29.3 Kaplan, Harold. Democratic humanism and American literature. Chicago, [1972].

An intelligent effort to point out a major theme underlying the work of Emerson, Thoreau, Melville, Hawthorne, Whitman, Mark Twain, and Henry James.

29.4 Stovall, Floyd. American idealism. Norman, Okla., 1943; Port Washington, N.Y., [1965].

Illustrates the rise and fall of idealism in literature from the colonial period to the 1940's.

29.5 Feidelson, Charles, Jr. Symbolism and American literature. [Chicago, 1953]; [1959], abridged.

Suggests the belief that "the concept of symbolism" is not only a key to the "situation" of Hawthorne, Whitman, Melville, and Poe but also "a link between their literature and our own."

29.6 Pizer, Donald. Realism and naturalism in 19th-century American literature. Carbondale, Ill., [1966].

A reprint of articles, but the notes are updated.

29.7 Krause, Sydney J., ed. Essays on determinism in American literature. Kent, Ohio, 1964; [1966].

Melville, Clemens, William James, Dos Passos, and Farrell figure most prominently. For a broader study, see Charles C. Walcutt, *American Naturalism: A Divided Stream*, Minneapolis, 1956; Westport, Conn., [1973].

29.8 Hicks, Granville. The great tradition: an interpretation of American literature since the Civil War. Rev. ed. N.Y., 1935; 1968.

Undertakes to show the approximations to Marxism in the literature of the period; strongly Marxist in its criticism.

29.9 Wasserstrom, William. Heiress of all the ages: sex and sentiment in the genteel tradition. Minneapolis, [1959].

A cursory essay that "undertakes to study the genteel tradition, its place in American social history, its effect on literature," especially the novel.

29.10 Herron, Ima H. The small town in American literature. Durham, N.C., 1939; N.Y., 1971.

This work is complemented by Miss Herron in *The Small Town in American Drama*, Dallas, [1969].

29.11 Hazard, Lucy L. The frontier in American literature. N.Y., [1927]; [1961].

Exhibits the excess with which the frontier hypothesis was applied.

29.12 Boynton, Percy H. The rediscovery of the frontier. Chicago, [1931].

A semipopular discussion of the frontier or frontiersmen in criticism and in fiction. See also Edwin Fussell, *Frontier: American Literature and the American West*, Princeton, N.J., 1965, which treats Cooper, Thoreau, Hawthorne, Melville, and Whitman.

29.13 Boger, Louise C. The Southern mountaineer in literature: an annotated bibliography. Morgantown, W. Va., 1964.

Novels, short stories, and a few plays (496 items all told) are listed by the author, with succinct annotations on plots.

29. Special topics

29.14 Cady, Edwin H. The gentleman in America: a literary study in American culture. Syracuse, N.Y., [1949]; Westport, Conn., [1970].
The concept of the "gentleman" as reflected in literature.

29.15 Basler, Roy P. The Lincoln legend: a study in changing conceptions. Boston and N.Y., 1935; 1969.
Abraham Lincoln in poetry, fiction, drama, etc.

29.16 Bryan, William A. George Washington in American literature, 1775–1865. N.Y., 1952; Westport, Conn., [1970].
Record very incomplete.

29.17 Hintz, Howard W. The Quaker influence in American literature. N.Y., [1940]; Westport, Conn., [1970].
Discusses Penn, Paine, Woolman, C. B. Brown, Cooper, Emerson, Whitman, and "further lines of influence." See also Tolles, 27.29.

29.18 Turner, Lorenzo D. Anti-slavery sentiment in American literature prior to 1865. Washington, [1929]; Port Washington, N.Y., [1966].

29.19 Cawelti, John G. Apostles of the self-made man. Chicago, [1965]; [1968].
Shows that attitudes toward success as illustrated by writers from Franklin to Faulkner are not so uniform as popular myth would indicate.

29.20 Hilfer, Anthony C. The revolt from the village, 1915–1930. Chapel Hill, N.C., [1969].
Begins with Eggleston, Frederic, and Mark Twain and has a chapter on the 1930's and after.

29.21 Holder, Alan. Three voyagers in search of Europe. Philadelphia, [1966].
H. James, Pound, and Eliot as expatriates. An effort is made to put all three on the same string.

29.22 Kerr, Howard. Mediums, and spirit-rappers, and roaring radicals: spiritualism in American literature, 1850–1900. Urbana, Ill., 1972.
A witty and authentic survey of the impact of the extra-sensory phenomena that engaged the interest of Hawthorne, Lowell, Mark Twain, Howells, and Henry James, among others.

30. Selected studies of regional literature

30.1 Gohdes, Clarence. Literature and theater of the states and regions of the U.S.A.: an historical bibliography. Durham, N.C., 1967.

Under the names of the fifty states, the dependencies, and principal regions, this book lists monographs, anthologies, pamphlets, chapters of books, and periodical articles which provide materials for the study of the local belles lettres and theater, from earliest times to 1965. (A few more recent items have been included.) In the appendix appear lists of works on regionalism, especially in its literary aspects, and on the "Western."

30.2 Logasa, Hannah. Regional U.S.: a subject list. Boston, 1942.
Lists of selected books on the various regions, including fiction, travel, biography, poetry, essays, short stories, etc., chosen from material usually found in middle-sized libraries. (A number of the journals sponsored by the state historical societies publish regularly lists of works by or on the authors of their states.)

30.3 American guide series. 1937–1949.
Travel guidebooks for each of the states, a number of larger cities, etc., containing materials originally compiled by the WPA. Various publishers have sponsored them, and a number have been more recently revised. (The original editions have recently been reprinted, by Somerset Press, St. Clair Shores, Mich.) Many of these volumes in their introductory matter contain brief sketches of the literary and other artistic contributions of the localities or states.

30.4 McMurtrie, Douglas C. "Locating the printed source materials for U.S. history: with a bibliography of lists of regional imprints." Mississippi Valley historical review, v. 31, pp. 369–406, (December, 1944).
The WPA sponsored an American Imprints Inventory—listings of the imprints of various states, etc. McMurtrie records these listings to 1943. (More recently, many additions have been made to the recording of local printing.)

30.5 Burke, John G., ed. Regional perspectives: an examination of America's literary heritage. Chicago, 1973.
Creative writers supply long essays on their native regions, personal in tone. The bibliography appended helps to update previous studies.

30.6 New England quarterly. 1928——.
Contains annually a bibliography of books and articles dealing with the section, including works on literature. (Many items on New England literature of the colonial period appear in Section 27 of this guide.)

30.7 Western American literature. 1966——.
Quarterly journal of the Western Literature Association; runs a bibliography and announcements of research in progress in each issue.

30.8 Southern literary journal. 1968——.
Semiannual, with essays on the literature and culture of the section and review-essays covering current books in the field. (Beginning in 1969, the *Mississippi Quarterly* publishes an annual checklist of scholarship dealing with Southern literature.)

30.9 Rubin, Louis D., ed. A bibliographical guide to the study of Southern literature. Baton Rouge, La., 1969.

The most extensive bibliography, compiled by numerous scholars. The first section is devoted to general topics; the second consists of checklists of the works of 134 authors, from John Smith to Walker Percy. An appendix includes notes on 68 additional colonial authors.

30.10 Cantrell, Clyde H., and Patrick, Walton R. Southern literary culture: a bibliography of master's and doctor's theses. [Tuscaloosa, Ala.], 1955.

Coverage to 1948.

30.11 Hubbell, Jay B. The South in American literature, 1607–1900. Durham, N.C., 1954.

Covers not only the Southern authors but other writers who treated the region. Replaces all preceding studies in thoroughness, especially for the period to the Civil War. Its extensive bibliography is filled with valuable comment.

30.12 Library of Southern literature. 17 v. New Orleans, Atlanta, Dallas, [1908–1923]; N.Y., [1967].

An extensive amateurish anthology of selections from numerous authors. V. 15 is devoted solely to biographical sketches of the writers; very inaccurate.

30.13 Harwell, Richard B. Confederate belles-lettres, a bibliography and a finding list of the fiction, poetry, songsters, and miscellaneous literature published in the Confederate States of America. Hattiesburg, Miss., 1941.

30.14 Gaines, Francis P. The Southern plantation: a study in the development and the accuracy of a tradition. N.Y., 1924; Gloucester, Mass., 1962.

Old South plantation life as treated in literature.

30.15 McIlwaine, Shields. The Southern poor-white from Lubberland to Tobacco Road. Norman, Okla., 1939.

The social history of the poor whites and their treatment in literature of various periods. See also 29.13.

30.16 Skaggs, Merrill M. The folk of Southern fiction. Athens, Georgia, [1972].

The ordinary, plain Southerner as treated in the work of major and minor authors from the time of A. B. Longstreet to that of Eudora Welty. The heaviest weight is on the later nineteenth century and the earliest decades of the twentieth.

30.17 Agnew, Janet M. A Southern bibliography: Louisiana State University bulletin: Fiction 1929–1938; Historical fiction 1929–1938; Poetry 1929–1938; Biography 1929–1941. LSU Library School bibliographical series, nos. 1–4. Baton Rouge, La., 1939–1942.

The poets represented in no. 2 were all Southern born; the other lists include also works on the section written by Northerners. In all cases the records are incomplete.

30.18 Rubin, Louis D., Jr., and Holman, C. Hugh, eds. Southern literary study. Chapel Hill, N.C., 1975.
Papers by various professors discussing problems and suggesting areas in need of investigation.

30.19 Rubin, Louis D., Jr., and Jacobs, Robert D., eds. South: modern Southern literature in its cultural setting. Garden City, N.Y., [1961]; Westport, Conn., [1974].
Essays on various authors and themes, followed by a valuable checklist on thirty-six writers, compiled by James B. Meriwether. (For material on the Fugitives, see 28.32.)

30.20 Rubin, Louis D., ed. Southern renascence: the literature of the modern South. Baltimore, [1953]; [1966].
Collects articles by divers hands on a variety of 20th-century writers of the region.

30.21 Bradbury, John M. Renaissance in the South: a critical history of the literature, 1920–1960. Chapel Hill, N.C., [1963].

30.22 Rusk, Ralph L. The literature of the Middle Western frontier. 2 v. N.Y., 1925; Westport, Conn., [1975].
The standard history and bibliography, to 1840.

30.23 Midamerica: the yearbook of the Society for the Study of Midwestern Literature. East Lansing, Mich., 1974———.
The 1975 number began publishing an annual bibliography of studies in the field, 1973———, under the editorship of Donald S. Pady.

30.24 Dondore, Dorothy. The prairie and the making of middle America. Cedar Rapids, Iowa, 1926; N.Y., 1961.
History of literature of the Middle West. See also 28.30–31.

30.25 Hansen, Harry. Midwest portraits: a book of memories and friendships. N.Y., [1923].
Sandburg, Anderson, Herrick, Masters, Sarett, *et al.*

30.26 Flanagan, John T., ed. America is West: an anthology of Middlewestern life and literature. Minneapolis, [1945]; Westport, Conn., [1971].
Contains biographical notes.

30.27 Meyer, Roy W. The Middle Western farm novel in the twentieth century. Lincoln, Nebr., [1965]; [1974].
Contains also a background chapter on "The Farm in Nineteenth Century Fiction."

30.28 Lee, Robert E. From West to East: studies in the literature of the American West. Urbana, Ill., 1966.
Essays on Lewis and Clark, Timothy Flint and James Hall, Irving and Parkman, Mark Twain, Willa Cather, and Bernard De Voto. The criterion of realism is applied to their writings.

30.29 Etulain, Richard W. Western American literature: a bibliography of interpretative books and articles. Vermillion, S.D., 1972.
Included in this somewhat amateurish work are more than two thousand items, chiefly lists on about 225 individual authors.

30.30 Haslam, Gerald W. Western writing. Albuquerque, New Mexico, 1974.
Reprints selected essays on literary and historical productions, especially fiction written by DeVoto, Dobie, Guthrie, Vardis Fisher, David Lavender, *et al.* "The Regional Approach to Literature," by George R. Stewart is especially rewarding. (See also the interviews with various contemporary writers conducted by John R. Milton for *The South Dakota Review* (1964), reprinted in J. Golden Taylor, *The Literature of the American West*, Boston, [1971], an excellent anthology.)

30.31 Folsom, James K. The American Western novel. New Haven, Conn., [1966].
Begins with Cooper and goes on to the time of A. B. Guthrie and Conrad Richter.

30.32 Dobie, J. Frank. Guide to life and literature of the Southwest. Rev. ed. Dallas, 1952.
A bibliography with critical comment.

30.33 Major, Mabel, *et al.* Southwest heritage: a literary history with bibliography. 3d ed. Albuquerque, New Mexico, 1972.
See also Kenneth Kurtz, *Literature of the American Southwest: A Selective Bibliography*, Los Angeles. 1956, an interesting though inaccurate "reading list of a thousand books which express the American Southwest"; Edwin J. Gaston, Jr., *The Early Novel of the Southwest*, Albuquerque, 1961; and "Southwest Writers Series," pamphlets on various authors of the region, Austin, Tex., 1967———.

30.34 Powell, Lawrence C. Heart of the Southwest: a selective bibliography of novels, stories, and tales laid in Arizona and New Mexico . . . . Los Angeles, 1955.
See also Powell's essays on the creative writers in *Southwest Classics*, Los Angeles, 1974.

30.35 West, Ray B., Jr. Writing in the Rocky Mountains. Lincoln, Nebr., 1947.
Essays on various authors of the section, with a slight bibliography by Nellie Cliff.

30.36 Davidson, Levette J., and Bostwick, Prudence, eds. The literature of the Rocky Mountain West, 1803–1903. Caldwell, Idaho, 1939; Port Washington, N.Y., [1970].
Anthology with a bibliography.

30.37 Western writers series. Ed. Wayne Chatterton and James H. Maguire. Boise, Idaho, 1972———.

Pamphlets containing information and bibliographies dealing with both older authors like Bret Harte, Mary H. Foote, and Owen Wister and contemporaries like Vardis Fisher and G. F. Ruxton. The tenth number is devoted to "Plains Indians Autobiographies."

30.38 [Coleman, Rufus A., ed.] Northwest books. [2d ed.] Portland, Ore., [1942]. Supplement, 1942–1947. Lincoln, Nebr., 1949.
Co-operative descriptive lists of works by authors of the region and works on it. One of the lists classifies titles according to the state or area treated.

30.39 Wright, Frances U. Who's Who among Pacific Northwest authors. 2d ed. Missoula, Montana, 1969.
Biobibliographical information on selected contemporary authors of Idaho, Montana, Oregon, and Washington.

30.40 Hinkle, Edgar J., ed. Bibliography of California fiction, poetry, drama. Criticism of California literature, a digest and bibliography; Biographies of California authors and indexes of California literature. 8 v. Oakland, 1938–1942.
Mimeographed material gathered by a WPA project.

30.41 Kherdian, David. Six poets of the San Francisco Renaissance: portraits and checklists. Fresno, Calif., 1965.
Ferlinghetti, Snyder, Whalen, Melzer, McClure, and Brother Antonius. Biographical notes plus checklists of primary works.

30.42 Baird, Newton D., and Greenwood, Robert. An annotated bibliography of California fiction, 1664–1970. Georgetown, Calif., [1971].
Novels and short stories of all sorts except juveniles.

30.43 Walker, Franklin D. A literary history of Southern California. Berkeley, 1950.

30.44 Walker, Franklin D. San Francisco's literary frontier. N.Y., 1939; Seattle, [1969]. Period covered is 1848–1875, with emphasis upon the 1860's.

30.45 Powell, Lawrence C. California classics: the creative literature of the Golden State. Los Angeles, [1972].
A selective and impressionistic treatment.

30.46 Walker, Franklin D. The seacoast of Bohemia. New ed. Santa Barbara, Calif., 1973.
The best history of early Carmel as a literary oasis.

30.47 Wilson, Edmund. The boys in the backroom: notes on California novelists. San Francisco, 1941.
Reprinted in *A Literary Chronicle: 1920–1950*, Garden City, N.Y., 1956. Cain, O'Hara, Saroyan, Steinbeck, *et al.*

See also 2.16, 3.7, 23.74, 29.1, 34.1.

31. Literature on or by racial and other minorities

31.1   Barksdale, Richard, and Kinnamon, Keneth, eds. Black writers of America. N.Y., 1972.

An anthology which ranges from the 18th century to date in its selections and offers unusually well selected bibliographical aids, useful both to beginning and advanced students. Folklore is given a section by itself.

31.2   Turner, Darwin T. Afro-American writers, N.Y., [1970].

A "Goldentree Bibliography" which lists general studies (articles as well as books) and then a roster of selected Negro authors with their chief books and a selection of the writings dealing with them.

31.3   Matthews, Geraldine O. Black American writers, 1773–1949: a bibliography and union list. Boston, 1975.

Needs to be supplemented by other sources.

31.4   No crystal stair: a bibliography of Black literature, 1971. N.Y., 1971——.

A pamphlet issued by the N.Y. Public Library representing the tenth edition of a checklist formerly entitled *The Negro in the U.S.* Lists about 500 titles published since 1965, along with certain sturdier works from prior years.

31.5   McPherson, James M., *et al.* Blacks in America: bibliographical essays. N.Y., 1971.

The various essays are organized both thematically and chronologically and range from poor to good. Listings on literature and art, pp. 14–17, are followed by a substantial roster of "current and recent" periodicals that deal with "Black life" and race relations.

31.6   Fisher, Mary L. The Negro in America: a bibliography. 2d ed. Cambridge, Mass., 1970.

The first edition was compiled by Elizabeth W. Miller. Contains sections on folklore and literature.

31.7   Whitlow, Roger. Black American literature: a critical history with a 1,520-title bibliography of works written by and about black Americans. Chicago, [1973].

To the serious student the bibliography is often more useful than the text.

31.8   The Negro in print. 1965——.

Bimonthly which lists principally current publications on the Negro, and, to a lesser extent, on other minority groups.

31.9   Baker, Houston A., Jr. Long Black song: essays in Black American literature. Charlottesville, Va., [1972].

The thesis of this work is that the major elements of Black "culture" today spring from the oral tradition of days of yore. Special attention is afforded Walker, Douglass, Washington, DuBois, and Richard Wright.

31.10 Olsson, Martin. A selected bibliography of Black literature: the Harlem Renaissance. Exeter, England, [1973].
A publication of the American Arts Documentation Centre of the University of Exeter, which provides for the European public audiovisual materials for American studies.

31.11 Young, James O. Black writers of the thirties. Baton Rouge, La., [1973].
Writers of all sorts are meant; the result is more emphasis on social science and less on belles lettres. There is, however, a chapter on poets, with chief consideration, naturally, of their political, economic, and sociological ideas.

31.12 Gross, Seymour L., and Hardy, John E. Images of the Negro in American literature. Chicago and London, [1966].
Contains reprints plus a valuable introduction and an excellent checklist of critical and scholarly studies.

31.13 Nelson, John H. The Negro character in American literature. Lawrence, Kans., 1926; College Park, Md., [1968].

31.14 Butcher, Margaret J. The Negro in American culture. 2d ed. N.Y., 1972.
Surveys contribution to the arts.

31.15 Loggins, Vernon. The Negro author: his development in America. N.Y., 1931; Port Washington, N.Y., [1964].
A basic survey ending about 1900.

31.16 Davis, Arthur P. From the dark tower: Afro-American writers 1900–1960. Washington, 1974.
Intended as a text book, with a score of authors figuring in the design. A bibliography at the end is helpful.

31.17 Boitani, Piero. Prosatori Negri Americani del novecento. Rome, 1973.
Picking up from B. Washington and DuBois, with separate chapters on Wright, Ellison, Baldwin, and the Harlem Renaissance, briefer treatment is afforded Malcolm X, Jones, Cleaver, and Jackson.

31.18 Shockley, Ann A., and Chandler, Sue, eds. Living Black American authors: a biographical directory. N.Y., [1973].
Helpful chiefly for minor figures.

31.19 Porter, Dorothy B. North American Negro poets, a bibliographical checklist of their writings, 1760–1944. Hattiesburg, Miss., 1945.
Originally published in *Papers of the Bibliographical Society of America*, v. 39, pp. 192–268 (January, 1945).

31.20 Deodene, Frank, and French, William P. Black American poetry since 1944: a preliminary checklist. Chatham, N.J., 1971.
An effort to update Porter (31.19).

31.21 Schomburg, Arthur A. A bibliographical checklist of American Negro poetry. N.Y., 1916.
The Schomburg Collection, in the N.Y. Public Library, is one of the chief collections of works by Negroes. G. K. Hall has reproduced the library cards for it, as well as for several similar collections.

31.22 Redding, J. Saunders. To make a poet black. Chapel Hill, N.C., 1939; Port Washington, N.Y., [1968].
Critical survey of Negro poets, from the 18th century to the 1930's.

31.23 Wagner, Jean. Les poètes nègres des États Unis. Paris, 1963.
Treats the religious and racial sentiment 1890–1940, but goes wider in its excellent bibliography. A translation has been published, Urbana, Ill., 1973, with the bibliography updated by Keneth Kinnanon.

31.24 Bontemps, Arna, ed. The Harlem renaissance remembered. N.Y., [1972].
A collection of poor to midling essays by various hands related to the topic. Nathan I. Huggins, *Harlem Renaissance*, N.Y., 1971, may help to add to the fragments. See also 31.10.

31.25 O'Brien, John, ed. Interviews with Black authors. N.Y., [1973].
Reprints confabs with Bontemps, Colter, Demby, Dodson, Ellison, Gaines, Harper, Hayden, Major, Mayfield, Petry, Reed, Walker, Wideman, John Williams, Charles Wright, and Al Young. Chiefly from *Studies in Black Literature*.

31.26 Whiteman, Maxwell. A century of fiction by American Negroes, 1853–1952: a descriptive bibliography. Philadelphia, 1955; 1969.

31.27 Bone, Robert A. The Negro novel in America. Rev. ed. New Haven, Conn., 1965; [1970].
Attempts to "measure the contribution of the Negro novelist to American letters"—since 1853. See also Carl M. Hughes. *The Negro Novelist: A Discussion of the Writings of American Negro Novelists 1940–1950*, N.Y., 1953.

31.28 Gloster, Hugh M. Negro voices in American fiction. Chapel Hill, N.C., 1948; Secaucus, N.J., [1970].

31.29 Isaacs, Edith J. R. The Negro in the American theatre. N.Y., 1947.
Six of the eight chapters deal with the period 1917–1946.

31.30 Abramson, Doris E. Negro playwrights in the American theatre, 1925–1959. N.Y., 1969.
The social context is kept in mind. In an introductory chapter W. W. Brown and Joseph Cotter are briefly discussed, and certain works of the 1960's are touched upon in an epilogue.

31.31 Studies in American Jewish literature. 1975——.
Devoted to fiction, drama, and poetry in English dealing with the subject "Jews in the American experience."

31.32 Liptzin, Sol. The Jew in American literature. N.Y., [1966].
The "image" of the Jew as well as his role as author, from colonial times to the present.

31.33 Mersand, Joseph. Traditions in American literature: a study of Jewish characters and authors. N.Y., 1939; Port Washington, N.Y., [1968].
Incomplete account of Jewish authors in 20th-century U.S. (Many earlier works in Yiddish, German, and French are listed in the bibliography of v. 4 of *The Cambridge History of American Literature*.)

31.34 Bryer, Jackson R. "American-Jewish literature: a selected checklist of criticism." Contemporary American-Jewish literature: critical essays. Ed. Irving Malin. Bloomington, Ind., [1973].
A handy selection with a section on general studies, both books and articles, and another on individual writers, including Bellow, Fiedler, Friedman, Howe, Kazin, Mailer, Malamud, Roth, Schwartz, Shapiro, Singer, Trilling, and Wallant. (Malin seems to be the most prolific anthologist of American-Jewish writing.)

31.35 Malin, Irving. Jews and Americans. Carbondale, Ill., [1965]; [1966].
Chiefly on Shapiro, Schwartz, Rosenfeld, Fiedler, Bellow, Malamud, and Roth, who are viewed as concerned with traditional concepts of the Jewish experience. See also Robert Alter, *After the Tradition: Essays on Modern Jewish Writing*, N.Y., 1969.

31.36 Guttman, Allen. The Jewish writer in America. N.Y., 1971.
A quick history and a spotlighting of a few selected novelists and poets plus a bit of sociological psychologizing.

31.37 Harap, Louis. The image of the Jew in American literature: from early republic to mass immigration. Philadelphia, [1974].
Includes bibliographical references.

31.38 Adler, Sidney. "The Image of the Jew in the American novel: a selected checklist." Bulletin of bibliography, v. 23, pp. 211–213 (1962).
Covers novels published 1930–1961.

31.39 Fisch, Harold. The dual image: the figure of the Jew in English and American literature. N.Y., [1971].
A revision of a 1959 opus, weighted heavily with the American element.

31.40 Pinsker, Sanford. The Schlemiel as metaphor: studies in the Yiddish and American Jewish novel. Carbondale, Ill., 1971.
Uneven in quality and importance.

31.41 Gross, Theodore L., ed. The literature of American Jews. N.Y., 1973.
Forty authors are anthologized, chiefly more recent ones.

31. Racial and other minorities

31.42 Lifson, David S. The Yiddish theatre in America. N.Y., 1965.
A poorly organized work containing much material for the locating of which the index is needed.

31.43 Coleman, Edward D. The Jew in English drama: an annotated bibliography. Rev. ed. N.Y., 1969.
Includes American plays.

31.44 Stensland, Anna L. Literature by and about the American Indian: an annotated bibliography. Urbana, Ill., 1973.
A product of the National Council of Teachers of English. Cf. also *Bulletin of Bibliography* for January–March, 1973, "Indians in American Literature."

31.45 Hirschfelder, Arlene B. American Indian and Eskimo authors: a representative bibliography. N.Y., [1973].
About 400 titles by almost 300 authors of varied sorts, not solely literary folk. See also the bibliography in Barry T. Klein and Daniel Icolari, *Reference Encyclopedia of the American Indian*, 2d ed. 2 v. Rye, N.Y., 1974.

31.46 Keiser, Albert. The Indian in American literature. N.Y., 1933; 1970.

31.47 Pearce, Roy H. The savages of America: a study of the Indian and the idea of civilization. Baltimore, 1953; revised with title Savages and civilization. Baltimore, 1965; 1967.

31.48 Day, A. Grove. The sky clears: poetry of the American Indians. N.Y., 1951; Lincoln, Nebr., [1964].
Contains bibliography on North American Indian poetry.

31.49 Levitas, Gloria B., ed. American Indian prose and poetry. N.Y., [1974].
An anthology with a fair bibliography.

31.50 Witt, Shirley H., and Steiner, Stan, eds. The way: an anthology of American Indian literature. N.Y., 1972.

31.51 Chin, Frank, *et al.* eds. Aiiieeeee!: an anthology of Asian-American writers. Washington, 1974.

31.52 Robacker, Earl F. Pennsylvania German literature: changing trends from 1683 to 1942. Philadelphia, 1943.

31.53 Fenn, William P. Ah Sin and his brethren in American literature. Peiping, [1933].
Chinese characters.

31.54 Konnyu, Leslie. A history of American Hungarian literature: presentation of American Hungarian authors of the last 100 years and selections from their writings. St. Louis, 1962.

31.55 Balakian, Nona. The Armenian-American writer: a new accent in American fiction. N.Y., 1959.

See also 13.24–26.

32. American literature in relations with other countries and literatures

32.1   Books abroad. 1927———.

A quarterly especially devoted to foreign literature: articles, reviews, lists of periodical articles.

32.2   Denny, Margaret, and Gilman, William H., eds. The American writer and the European tradition. Minneapolis, [1950]; N.Y., [1964].

A symposium covering the colonial period to the present. Two of the twelve essays deal with the impact of American literature in Europe; the others, with the reverse.

32.3   Comparative literature: proceedings of the second congress of the International Comparative Literature Association. Ed. Werner P. Friederich. 2 v. Chapel Hill, N.C., 1959; N.Y., 1967.

V. 2 contains many papers on European-American literary relations.

32.4   Koht, Halvdan. The American spirit in Europe: a survey of transatlantic influences. Philadelphia, 1949; Stockholm, 1950, with an additional chapter; N.Y., 1970.

A "preliminary survey," containing sections on a variety of matters, including literature. See also 8.13 (Skard).

32.5   Brussel, Isidore R. Anglo-American first editions. 2 v. N.Y., 1935–1936.

Part I, East to West [1826–1900], describes first editions of English authors whose books were published in the U.S. prior to appearing in England. Part II, West to East [1786–1930], similarly treats books by Americans first published in England.

32.6   Gordon, George S. Anglo-American literary relations. [London], 1942; N.Y., [1972].

A sketchy account.

32.7   Cairns, William B. British criticisms of American writings, 1783–1815. Madison, Wis., 1918; St. Clair Shores, Mich., 1970.

32.8   Cairns, William B. British criticisms of American writings, 1815–1833. Madison, Wis., 1922; Folcroft, Penna., 1972.

32.9   Gohdes, Clarence. American literature in nineteenth-century England. N.Y., 1944; Carbondale, Ill., [1963].

Begins where Cairns leaves off and contains chapters on the book trade, periodicals, humor, the vogue of Longfellow, and on critics and influences. An appendix lists representative articles on American literature which appeared in British periodicals, 1833–1901.

32. Relations with other countries

32.10 The American writer in England. Charlottesville, Va., [1969].
An extensive exhibition catalog with an introduction by C. Waller Barrett, the noted collector of literary Americana.

32.11 Enkvist, Nils E. American humour in England before Mark Twain. Åbo, Finland, 1953.

32.12 Dickason, David H. The daring young men: the story of the American Pre-Raphaelites. Bloomington, Ind., 1953. N.Y., 1969.

32.13 Boyd, Alice K. The interchange of plays between London and New York, 1910–1939. N.Y., 1948.
Valuable chiefly for statistics.

32.14 Spiller, Robert E. The American in England during the first half century of independence. N.Y., [1926]; Philadelphia, 1975.
Includes certain authors like Irving, Cooper, and N. P. Willis.

32.15 Le Clair, Robert C. Three American travellers in England: James Russell Lowell, Henry Adams, Henry James. Philadelphia, 1945.

32.16 Sibley, Agnes M. Alexander Pope's prestige in America, 1725–1835. N.Y., 1949; Folcroft, Penna., 1974.

32.17 Sensebaugh, George. Milton in early America. Princeton, N.J., 1964; Staten Island, N.Y., 1975.

32.18 Leonard, William E. Byron and Byronism in America. N.Y., 1907; [1969].

32.19 Rollins, Hyder E. Keats' reputation in America to 1848. Cambridge, Mass., [1946].

32.20 Rollins, Hyder E., and Parrish, Stephen M. Keats and the Bostonians. Cambridge, Mass., 1951; N.Y., [1972].

32.21 Power, Julia. Shelley in America in the nineteenth century. [Lincoln, Nebr., 1940]; N.Y., 1969.

32.22 Nethery, Wallace. Charles Lamb in America to 1848. Worcester, Mass., 1963.

32.23 Stein, Roger B. John Ruskin and aesthetic thought in America 1840– 1900. Cambridge, Mass., 1967.
Ruskin's impact on aesthetic and critical ideas. See also 32.12.

32.24 Greer, Louise. Browning and America. Chapel Hill, N.C., [1952]; Westport, Conn., [1973].
(There are many other studies of the reputations and influence of individual British authors in the U.S.)

32.25 Raleigh, John H. Matthew Arnold and American culture. Berkeley, 1957; Gloucester, Mass., [1962].

32.26 Pochmann, Henry A., and Schultz, Arthur R. Bibliography of German culture in America to 1940. Madison, Wis., 1953; 1954.
Supplemented since 1941 by annual bibliographies listed below.

32.27 Journal of English and Germanic philology. 1897———.
July issues contain special bibliography on Anglo-German and American-German literary relations.

32.28 American-German review. 1934———.
April–May issues contain annual bibliography of Americana Germanica of all sorts, including literature.

32.29 Frenz, Horst, and Lang, H. J., eds. Nordamerikanische Literatur im deutschen Sprachraum seit 1945. Munich, 1973.
Covers German-speaking Europe's reception of American literature.

32.30 Mummendey, Richard. Belles lettres of the U.S. of America in German translations: a bibliography. Charlottesville, Va., 1961.
Originally published in Bonn, this useful book lists only works published in separate volumes—no periodical items or collections. (A list of the latter is promised.) Coverage: from Benjamin Franklin's day to 1957.

32.31 Price, Lawrence M. The reception of United States literature in Germany. Chapel Hill, N.C., 1966.
A compact survey from the colonial period to the days of Thornton Wilder and Tennessee Williams, followed by a forty-page list of bibliographies and surveys.

32.32 Nirenberg, Morton. The reception of American literature in German periodicals, 1820–1850. Heidelberg, 1970.

32.33 Timpe, Eugene F. American literature in Germany 1861–1872. Chapel Hill, N.C., 1964.

32.34 Zuther, Gerhard H. W. Eine Bibliographie der Aufnahme amerikanischer Literatur in deutschen Zeitschriften 1945–1960. Munich, 1965.

32.35 Kopp, W. Lamarr. German literature in the United States 1945–1960. Chapel Hill, N.C., 1967.
A list of translations and a selected bibliography are appended. This work constitutes the third volume of item 32.47.

32.36 Jantz, Harold S. "Amerika im deutschen Dichten und Denken." Deutsche Philologie im Aufriss. Ed. Wolfgang Stammler. V. 3, pp. 146–205. Berlin, [1957].
A quick survey covering the subject from earliest times to the present, with selected bibliography.

32.37 Springer, Anne M. The American novel in Germany: a study of the critical reception of eight American novelists between the two world wars. Hamburg, 1960.

The novelists are London, Sinclair, Lewis, Dreiser, Dos Passos, Hemingway, Faulkner. and Wolfe.

32.38 Morgan, Bayard Q. A critical bibliography of German literature in English translation. 2 v. N.Y. and London, 1965.
Covers the period 1481–1927 in the first volume (a reprint of a work published in 1938) and 1928–1955 in the second. A large proportion of the translations listed is of American origin.

32.39 Smith, Murray F. A selected bibliography of German literature in English translation 1956–1960. Metuchen, N.J., 1972.
A supplement to Morgan (32.38).

32.40 Mönnig, Richard. Amerika und England im deutschen, österreichischen und schweizerischen Schrifttum der Jahre 1945–1949: eine Bibliographie. Stuttgart, 1951.
Lists British and American works translated into German.

32.41 Locher, Kaspar T. German histories of American literature: a chronological and critical description . . . 1800–1950. Chicago, 1955.
Printed on microcards.

32.42 Pochmann, Henry A. German culture in America . . . 1600–1900. Madison, Wis., 1957; 1961.
The most extensive treatment of the influence of German philosophy and literature in the U.S.

32.43 Thomas J. Wesley. Amerikanische Dichter und die deutsche Literatur. Goslar, [1950].
A brief survey of the entire range of literary influences from Germany on authors from the time of Cotton Mather to O'Neill.

32.44 Galinsky, Hans. Wegbereiter moderner amerikanischer Lyrik. Heidelberg, 1968.
Contains material dealing with the reception of W. C. Williams and Emily Dickinson in Germany.

32.45 Long, Orie W. Literary pioneers: early American explorers of European culture. Cambridge, Mass., 1935; N.Y., 1963.
Ticknor, Everett, Bancroft, Longfellow, Motley, *et al.* as students in Germany.

32.46 Vogel, Stanley M. German literary influences on the American Transcendentalists. New Haven, Conn., 1955; Hamden, Conn., 1970.
On this topic see also the extensive treatment in Pochmann, whose conclusions are more authoritative; and René Wellek, *Confrontations*, Princeton, N.J., 1965.

32.47 Shelley, Philip A., *et al.* Anglo-German and American-German crosscurrents. 2 v. Chapel Hill, N.C., 1957–1962; N.Y., 1969, v. 1 only.
German literature as sources for Simms, Lanier, Howells, and others.

32.48 Bridgwater, Patrick. Nietzsche in Anglosaxony. Leicester, England, 1972.
A compact but excellent survey of Nietzsche's impact on English and American literature. London, Dreiser, J. G. Fletcher, O'Neill, and Wallace Stevens are given more extended treatment than Huneker, Mencken, *et al.*

32.49 Leuchs, Fritz A. H. The early German theatre in New York, 1840–1872. N.Y., 1928; 1966.

32.50 Bauland, Peter. The hooded eagle: modern German drama on the New York stage. Syracuse, N.Y., [1968].
Covers the period 1894 to 1967.

32.51 Möhl, Gertrud. Die Aufnahme amerikanischer Literatur in der deutschsprachigen Schweiz während der Jahre 1945–1950. Zurich, 1961.
See also 32.40.

32.52 Schirmer, Gustav. Die Schweiz im Spiegel der englischen und amerikanischen Literatur. Zurich and Leipzig, 1929.

32.53 Marjasch, Sonja. Der amerikanische Bestseller: sein Wesen und seine Verbreitung unter besonderer Berücksichtigung der Schweiz. Bern, [1946].
Incidentally revelatory; an appended bibliography lists certain editions of works of Hervey Allen, Louis Bromfield, Margaret Mitchell, Kenneth Roberts, *et al.* published in England, France, Italy, and Germany.

32.54 Mandé, Philippe. Écrivain U.S.A.; écrivain U.R.S.S. Paris, [1952].
Contains a list of works in French on various aspects of the U.S. including (pp. 100–102) literature.

32.55 Jaffe, Adrian H. Bibliography of French literature in American magazines in the 18th century. [East Lansing, Mich.], 1951.

32.56 Rabinovitz, Albert. New York University index to early American periodical literature, 1728–1870: no. 5: French fiction. N.Y., 1943.
A bibliography of articles and reviews concerned with French fiction and published in American periodicals.

32.57 Ansermoz-Dubois, Félix. L'interprétation française de la littérature américaine d'entre deux guerres (1919–1939): essai de bibliographie. Lausanne, 1944.

32.58 Jones, Howard M. America and French culture 1750–1848. Chapel Hill, N.C., 1927; Westport Conn., [1973].

32.59 Blumenthal, Henry. American and French culture, 1800–1900. Baton Rouge, La., 1975.
Deals with interchanges in literature only in part.

32.60 Mantz, Harold E. French criticism of American literature before 1850. N.Y., 1917; 1966.

32. Relations with other countries

32.61 McGee, Sidney L. La littérature américaine dans la "Revue des Deux Mondes" (1831–1900). Montpellier, 1927.

32.62 Jeune, Simon. De F. T. Graindorge à A. O. Barnabooth: les types américains dans le roman et le theâtre français (1861–1917). Paris, 1963.

    Traces the history of American types from the Revolution to World War I as reflected in French novels and plays; a very substantial study.

32.63 Falb, Lewis. American drama in Paris 1945 to 1970: a study of its critical reception. Chapel Hill, N.C., 1975.

32.64 Waldo, Lewis P. The French drama in America in the eighteenth century and its influence on the American drama of that period, 1701–1800. Baltimore, 1942.

32.65 Schoenberger, Harold W. American adaptations of French plays on the New York and Philadelphia stages from 1790 to 1833. Philadelphia, 1924.

32.66 Ware, Ralph H. American adaptations of French plays on the New York and Philadelphia stages from 1834 to the Civil War. Philadelphia, 1930.

32.67 Mason, Hamilton. French theatre in New York: a list of plays, 1899–1939. N.Y., 1940; 1966.

32.68 Åhnebrink, Lars. The beginnings of naturalism in American fiction: a study of the works of Hamlin Garland, Stephen Crane, and Frank Norris with special reference to some European influences, 1891–1903. Uppsala and Cambridge, Mass., [1950]; N.Y., 1961.

32.69 Spurlin, Paul M. Rousseau in America, 1750–1809. University, Ala., [1969].

    A carefully researched study abounding in details.

32.70 Salvan, Albert J. Zola aux États-Unis. Providence, R.I., 1943; N.Y., 1967.

32.71 Arnavon, Cyrille, Les lettres américaines devant la critique française (1887–1915). Paris, 1951.

32.72 Alexander, Jean, ed. Affidavits of genius. Port Washington, N.Y., [1971].

    Essays on Poe by 15 French poets or critics appear in translation along with a long introduction which touches on his influence on the Symbolists.

32.73 Taupin, René. L'influence du symbolisme français sur la poésie américaine de 1910 à 1930. Paris, 1929.

32.74 Smith, Thelma M., and Miner, Ward. Transatlantic migration: the contemporary American novel in France. [Durham, N.C.], 1955; Westport Conn., [1968].

    More statistical than critical.

32.75 Wickes, George. Americans in Paris. N.Y., 1969.
Popular sketches of the Parisian days (1903–1939) of Stein, Cummings, Virgil Thompson, Man Ray, Hemingway, and H. Miller.

32.76 Dommergues, Pierre, ed. Les U.S.A. à la recherche de leur identité: recontres avec 40 écrivains americains. Paris, [1967].
The authors interviewed run from Albee and Algren to Updike and T. Williams, and the topics covered are often very interesting. By way of conclusion there is a section on the intellectual in the 1960's and a glossary of Black language. In the terminal Fiches d'Identité, translations of the authors' works into French are mentioned.

32.77 Library of Congress. Spanish and Portuguese translations of U.S. books, 1955–1962. Washington, 1963.

32.78 Williams, Stanley T. The Spanish background of American literature. 2 v. New Haven, Conn., 1955; N.Y., 1968.
Influence of Spain and Spanish literature on the nineteenth century particularly.

32.79 Ferguson, J. Delancey. American literature in Spain. N.Y., 1916; 1966.

32.80 Manchester, Paul T. A bibliography and critique of the Spanish translations from the poetry of the U.S. George Peabody College for Teachers contributions to education. No. 41. Nashville, 1927.
Record incomplete; appraisal often dubious. Includes Latin American translations.

32.81 Problems of the history of the literature of the U.S.A. Moscow, 1964.
Five scholarly essays plus an extensive bibliography of Russian works on American literature and individual authors compiled by V. A. Libman. In Russian. For Libman bibliography, see following item.

32.82 Russian studies of American literature: a bibliography. Compiled by Valentina A. Libman, trans. Robert V. Allen, ed. Clarence Gohdes. Chapel Hill, N.C., 1969.
The most extensive bibliography in its field. Works on separate periods and topics are followed by works on 148 American authors. Criticism and scholarship are covered from 18th-century productions on Franklin and Jefferson to 1963 comment on Updike, Tennessee Williams, *et al.* A continuation, 1964–1968, appears in *Contemporary Literary Studies in the U.S.A.*, ed. M. O. Mendelson *et al.*, Moscow, 1969, pp. 306–343 (in Russian). Mrs. Libman has provided also a list of translations of 20th century American authors in *Problemy Literaturi SSHA XX Veka*, Moscow, 1970.

32.83 Contemporary English and American writers: bibliographical index. By the committee on affairs of cultural and enlightening institutions under the council of people's commissars to the RSFSR. Moscow, 1945.

A list—in Russian—of works translated into Russian, with lists of Soviet reviews of same. It follows *Best Representatives of English and American Literature* (1942), covering the period from the 14th century to the first part of the 20th.

32.84 Brown, Glenora W., and Brown, Deming B. A guide to Soviet Russian translations of American literature. N.Y., 1954.
Based on incomplete sources.

32.85 Brown, Deming B. Soviet attitudes toward American writing. Princeton, N.J., 1962.
A comprehensive and thorough survey, in which Dos Passos, Sinclair, London, O. Henry, Lewis, Dreiser, Fast, and Hemingway are afforded more extended discussion.

32.86 Proffer, Carl R., ed. Soviet criticism of American literature in the sixties. Ann Arbor, Mich., [1972].
An anthology which will illustrate the nature of socialist realism as applied to American productions.

32.87 Gettmann, Royal A. Turgenev in England and America. Urbana, Ill., 1941; Westport, Conn., [1975].

32.88 Sinko, Grzegorz. "American studies in Poland." Studi Americani, v. 6, pp. 365–370 (1960).

32.89 Coleman, Marion M. Polish literature in English translation: a bibliography. Cheshire, Conn., 1963.
A very considerable number of the translations listed are of American origin.

32.90 Italica. 1924——.
Contains quarterly bibliography of Italian studies in America, including those dealing with literature.

32.91 Shields, N. C. Italian translations in America. N.Y., [1931].
See also Vincent Luciani, "Modern Italian Fiction in America, 1929–1954: An Annotated Bibliography of Translations," *Bulletin of the New York Public Library*, v. 60, pp. 12–34 (1956).

32.92 Centro di Studi Americani. Repertorio bibliografico della letteratura Americana in Italia. Rome, 1966.
In two sections, covering 1945–1949 and 1950–1954, the former compiled by Robert Perrault; the latter by Alessandra Pinto Surdi.

32.93 Lombardo, Agostino, ed. "Italian criticism of American literature: an anthology." Sewanee Review, v. 68, no. 3 (1960).
Various Italians or Italian-Americans contribute essays on a variety of authors or topics. None of the essays appeared previously in English.

32.94 Pavese, Cesare. American literature: essays and opinions. Trans. Edwin Fussell. Berkeley, 1970.

A selection from Pavese's criticisms which supplies a good example of the impact of American authors on the Italian literary world 1930–1950.

32.95 Brooks, Van Wyck. The dream of Arcadia: American writers and artists in Italy, 1760–1915. N.Y., 1958.

32.96 Heiney, Donald. America in modern Italian literature. New Brunswick, N.J., [1965].
A chronological survey, from about 1930.

32.97 Peragallo, Olga. Italian-American authors and their contribution to American literature. N.Y., [1949].

32.98 Italia e Stati Uniti nell' eta del Risorgimento e della Guerra Civile. Florence, 1969.
Several of the essays deal with literary and cultural relations.

32.99 Friederich, Werner P. Dante's fame abroad, 1350–1850. Chapel Hill, N.C., 1950; 1966.
Contains a section on the U.S. See also V. Branca and E. Caccia, *Dante nel Mundo*, Florence, 1965; and William DeSua, *Dante into English*, Chapel Hill, N.C., 1964.

32.100 Scandinavian studies. 1911——.
The issues for May contain annual bibliography of books, articles, and reviews dealing with Scandinavian languages and literature published in the U.S. or Canada. See also the series, *Americana Norvegica*, ed. Sigmund Skard, Oslo and Philadelphia, 1966——.

32.101 Øksnevad, Reidar. U.S.A. in Norwegian literature: a bibliography. Oslo, 1950.
Printed in Norwegian.

32.102 White, George L. Scandinavian themes in American fiction. Philadelphia, 1937.

32.103 Skårdal, Dorothy B. The divided heart: Scandinavian immigrant experience through literary sources. Lincoln, Nebr., [1974].

32.104 Anderson, Carl L. The Swedish acceptance of American literature. Philadelphia, [1957].
Centers on fiction, especially Sinclair Lewis, from World War I to 1930. An appendix lists Swedish translations of American fiction 1916–1945. See also Stephen E. Whicher, "Swedish Knowledge of American Literature: A Supplementary Bibliography," *Journal of English and Germanic Philology*, v. 58, pp. 666–671 (October, 1959); and *Studies on American Language and Literature*, Uppsala, 1945——.

32.105 Durham, Philip, and Mustanoja, Tauno F. American fiction in Finland: an essay and bibliography. Helsinki, 1960.

32. Relations with other countries

32.106 Hungarian studies in English, no. I. Budapest, 1963.
Includes a list of American belles lettres in Hungarian translation, 1945–1961, by Anna Katona, and another on Hungarian writings, chiefly articles, on English and American literature 1957–1960.

32.107 Gergely, Emro J. Hungarian drama in New York: American adaptations, 1908–1940. Philadelphia, 1947.

32.108 Kunzová, Hela, and Rybáková, Hava. American literature in Czechoslovakia 1945–1965. Prague, 1966.

32.109 Chapman, Arnold. The Spanish American reception of United States fiction, 1920–1940. Berkeley and Los Angeles, 1966.
Reviews and interprets the reception of thirteen fiction writers, including Harte, Clemens, Louisa Alcott, London, Lewis, Faulkner, Dreiser, and Pearl Buck.

32.110 Gunn, Drewey W. Mexico in American and British letters: a bibliography of fiction and travel books. Metuchen, N.J., 1974.
A companion to the same author's *American and British Writers in Mexico, 1556–1773*, Austin, Texas, [1974].

32.111 Robinson, Cecil. With the ears of strangers: the Mexican in American literature. Tucson, Arizona, 1963.

32.112 Englekirk, John E. A litteratura Norteamericana no Brasil. [Tulane University, La.], 1950.
Bibliography of both literary and nonliterary works translated and published in Brazil.

32.113 Christy, Arthur. The Orient in American Transcendentalism. N.Y., 1932; 1963.
Principally Alcott, Emerson, and Thoreau.

32.114 Riepe, Dale M. The philosophy of India and its impact on American thought. Springfield, Ill., [1970].
Chiefly concerned with philosophers of the present century, but contains material on Emerson, Thoreau, Santayana, and other literary figures.

32.115 Fukuda, Naomi. A bibliography of translations: American literary works into Japanese, 1868–1967. Tokyo, 1968.
Printed in Japanese.

32.116 Miner, Earl R. The Japanese tradition in British and American literature. Princeton, N.J., 1958; [1966].
See also Judith Bloomingdale, "Haiku: An Annotated Checklist," *Papers of the Bibliographical Society of America*, v. 56, pp. 488–494 (1962), a list on, and history of, the reception of Japanese verse in the U.S. since 1911.

32.117 Sugiki, Takashi. "A checklist of Japanese journals in English and American literature." Bulletin of the New York Public Library, v. 65, pp. 185–199 (March, 1961).

32.118 The rising generation. 1898——.
A Japanese monthly dealing with English and American literature. In recent years contains an annual bibliography of Japanese books and articles on the two literatures (including translations). The journal is printed in Japanese. Several Japanese scholarly periodicals publish bibliography, including *American Literature*, 1964—— (in Japanese).

32.119 Sugiki, Takashi. A backward glance at the study of American literature in Japan. Tokyo, 1952.

32.120 North, William R. Chinese themes in American verse. Philadelphia, 1937; Rochester, N.Y., [1975].

32.121 Narasimhaiah, C. D. Asian response to American literature. Delhi, etc., 1972.
An anthology of studies of American authors in which are scattered a few essays on the "Asian influence" and on the response to American poetry, drama, fiction, and criticism in Malaysia, Ceylon, the Philippines, and elsewhere. To be used with caution.

32.122 Pritchard, John P. Return to the fountains: some classical sources of American criticism. Durham, N.C., 1942; N.Y., [1966].
Influence of Aristotle and Horace on fifteen writers, chiefly of the 19th century. For classical influence, see also 27.14.

32.123 Bush, Douglas. Mythology and the romantic tradition in English poetry. Rev. ed. Cambridge, Mass., 1969.
Chapter 15 surveys American poets such as Longfellow, Lowell, H. D., Pound, and Eliot; and a list of American poems connected with classical mythology appears on pp. 577–592.

32.124 Hills, Margaret T. The English Bible in America: a bibliography of editions of the Bible and the New Testament published in America, 1777–1957. Rev. ed. N.Y., 1962.

See also 8.11–15.

33. English language in the U.S.

33.1 Brenni, Vito J. American English: a bibliography. Philadelphia, [1964].

A selection of books and articles arranged under such headings as "General and Historical," "Spelling," "Dialects," "Loan Words," "Dictionaries," etc. The entries are occasionally annotated. To be used with caution.

33.2 American speech: a quarterly of linguistic usage. 1925——.
Publishes articles, reviews, and the chief current bibliography of works in its field.

33.3 Krapp, George P. The English language in America. 2 v. N.Y., 1925; [1960].
Still regarded as a standard study.

33.4 Pyles, Thomas. Words and ways of American English. [N.Y., 1952]; [1963].

33.5 Mencken, Henry L. The American language. 4th ed. N.Y., 1936.
Must be used with two supplements, which appeared in 1945 and 1948. A popular account, useful because of its extensive coverage. All three parts were reprinted, N.Y., 1961, as elements of "The American Language Reference Library.' An abridgment, made by Raven I. McDavid, Jr., and David W. Maurer, with annotations and new material appeared in N.Y., 1963.

33.6 Craigie, William A., and Hulbert, James R., eds. A dictionary of American English on historical principles. 4 v. Chicago, [1938–1944]; [1960].

33.7 Mathews, Mitford M., ed. A dictionary of Americanisms on historical principles. 2 v. Chicago, [1951]; 1 v., [1956].
An abridgment appeared in Chicago, [1966].

33.8 Kenyon, John S., and Knott, Thomas A., eds. A pronouncing dictionary of American English. 2d ed. Springfield, Mass., [1953].

33.9 Adams, Ramon F. Western words: a dictionary of the American West. Rev. ed. Norman, Okla., [1968].
Provincialisms of the cattleman's West.

33.10 Publications of the American Dialect Society. Nos. 1——, April, 1944——.
A series of word lists, monographs, etc., such as "The Argot of the Racetrack" (no. 16), "Bilingualism in the Americas: a Bibliography and Research Guide" (no. 26), or "The Phonology of the Uncle Remus Stories" (no. 22).

33.11 Dialect notes. V. 1–6. 1890–1939.
Predecessor of item above. The six volumes have been reprinted by the University of Alabama Press, 1965.

33.12 Thomas, Charles K. An introduction to the phonetics of American English. 2d ed. N.Y., [1958].

33.13 Kenyon, John S. American pronunciation. 10th ed. Ann Arbor, Mich., 1951; 1958.

33.14 Bronstein, Arthur J. The pronunciation of American English: an introduction to phonetics. N.Y., [1960].
Includes bibliographies.

33.15 Galinsky, Hans. Die Sprache des Amerikaners: eine Einführung in die Hauptunterschiede zwischen amerikanischem und britischem Englisch der Gegenwart. 2 v. Heidelberg, 1951–1952.

33.16 Horwill, Herbert W. A dictionary of modern American usage. 2d ed. Oxford, 1944.

33.17 Nicholson, Margaret. A dictionary of American-English usage, based on Fowler's Modern English Usage. N.Y., 1957.

33.18 Bryant, Margaret M., ed. Current American usage. N.Y., [1962].
About 240 entries discuss one or more points of usage; arrangement alphabetical.

33.19 Evans, Bergen, and Evans, Cornelia. A dictionary of contemporary American usage. N.Y., [1957].
Popular compilation.

33.20 Fries, Charles C. American English grammar. N.Y., [1940].

33.21 Wentworth, Harold, and Flexner, Stuart B., eds. Dictionary of American slang. 2d ed. N.Y., [1975].

33.22 Partridge, Eric. A dictionary of slang and unconventional English. 7th ed. N.Y., [1970].

33.23 Reed, Carroll E. Dialects of American English. Amherst, Mass., 1967; 1973.

33.24 Williamson, Juanita, and Burke, Virginia M., eds. A various language: perspectives on American dialects. N.Y., 1972.
An anthology of scholarly articles concerned with the history and scope of dialect studies. An appendix lists recent dissertations on the subject.

33.25 Wentworth, Harold. American dialect dictionary. N.Y., 1944.

33.26 Francis, W. Nelson. The structure of American English. N.Y., [1958].
Contains a chapter on American dialects, by Raven I. McDavid, Jr., which is a handy survey-interpretation of the dialect field. See also McDavid's article "Sense and Nonsense about American Dialects," *PMLA*, v. 81, pp. 7–17 (May, 1966), which has bibliography.

33.27 Linguistic atlas of New England. Ed. Hans Kurath. 3 v. in 6. Providence, R.I., 1939–1943; N.Y., [1975].
Provides evidence of the actual usage of selected Americans in selected

communities on selected items of grammar, pronunciation, and vocabulary. Atlases for other regions are in preparation.

33.28 Kurath, Hans. Handbook of the linguistic geography of New England. 2d ed. N.Y., [1973].

33.29 Kurath, Hans. A word geography of the eastern U.S. [Ann Arbor, Mich.], 1949; 1966.

33.30 Atwood, E. Bagby. A survey of verb forms in the eastern U.S. [Ann Arbor, Mich.], 1953.

33.31 Kurath, Hans, and McDavid, Raven I., Jr. The pronunciation of English in the Atlantic States. Ann Arbor, Mich., [1961].
Analyzes regional and social features of pronunciation of 157 "cultural speakers," Maine to Florida.

33.32 Allen, Harold B. The linguistic atlas of the upper Midwest. 2 v. Minneapolis, 1973–1975.

33.33 McMillan, James B. Annotated bibliography of Southern American English. Miami, Florida, 1971.
Contents range from about 1870 to date and cover a heterogeneous assortment of sources.

33.34 Wood, Gordon R. Vocabulary change: a study of variation in regional words in eight of the Southern States. Carbondale, Ill., [1971].
Based on a list of words collected in Alabama, Arkansas, Florida, Georgia, Louisiana, Mississippi, Oklahoma, and Tennessee.

33.35 Pederson, Lee, et al., eds. A manual for dialect research in the Southern States. 2d ed. University, Ala., [1974].
A manual for field workers. An introduction gives a brief history of "dialectology."

33.36 Reinecke, John E. Language and dialect in Hawaii: a sociolinguistic history to 1935. Honolulu, 1969.
Edited by Stanley M. Tsuzaki, this work breaks ground for the study of both the creole and the colonial English dialect now rapidly fading from the Islands.

33.37 Brasch, Ila W., and Brasch, Walter M. A comprehensive annotated bibliography of American Black English. Baton Rouge, La., [1974].
No approach is provided to subjects.

33.38 Herman, Lewis H., and Herman, Marguerite S. Manual of American dialects for radio, stage, screen and television. Chicago and N.Y., [1947]; 1959.
Instruction book for actors.

33.39 Sealock, Richard B., and Seely, Pauline A. Bibliography of place name literature: U.S. and Canada. 2d ed. Chicago, 1967.
Supplements have appeared in Names: Journal of the American Name

Society. (This journal deals with personal names and names of characters in literary works; not confined to U.S.)

33.40 Stewart, George R. American place-names: a concise and selective dictionary for the continental U.S.A. N.Y., 1970.
Has a bibliography in addition to other merits, including sound scholarship.

33.41 Stewart, George R. Names on the land: a historical account of place-naming in the U.S. 3d ed. Boston, [1967].
Emphasis is put on the process whereby places were named.

33.42 Smith, Elsdon C. New dictionary of American family names. N.Y., 1973.
A semipopular compilation.

33.43 Shankle, George E. American nicknames, their origin and significance. 2d ed. N.Y., 1955.

33.44 Carroll, John B. The study of language: a survey of linguistics and related disciplines in America. Cambridge, Mass., 1953.
Relationship of linguistic studies with science, psychology, etc.

33.45 Marckwardt, Albert H. American English. N.Y., 1958.
A brief, elementary, but clearheaded synthesis of previous investigations calculated to illustrate the "close interaction of linguistic and cultural factors in the growth of American English."

33.46 Hamp, Eric P. A glossary of American technical linguistic usage, 1925–1950. 3d ed. N.Y., 1966.

33.47 Kurath, Hans. Studies in area linguistics. Bloomington, Ind., [1972].
"The whole gamut of problems encountered in area linguistics and the techniques used in handling them are presented in the first 5 chapters of the book with reference to American English." Bibliography, pp. 186–202.

34. Folklore in the U.S.

34.1 Haywood, Charles. A bibliography of North American folklore and folksong. 2d rev. ed. 2 v. N.Y., [1961].
Indexed by state, region, race, occupation, etc. The bibliographies of local sources are immensely useful to students of the literature of the various states and regions.

34. Folklore

34.2   Brunvand, Jan H.   The study of American folklore: an introduction. N.Y., 1968.
An elementary but useful textbook which surveys the genres, using American examples.

34.3   Dorson, Richard M.   American folklore.   Chicago, [1959]; [1968].
The chief general survey, from colonial times to the present.

34.4   Dorson, Richard M.   America in legend.   N.Y., 1973.
A popular survey from colonial times to the present. The bibliography may help to update the preceding item, 34.3.

34.5   Funk and Wagnalls standard dictionary of folklore, mythology and legend.   Ed. Maria Leach.   2 v.   N.Y., [1949–1950]; [1972].
See also *Folklore Research around the World: A North American Point of View*, ed. Richard M. Dorson, Bloomington, Ind., [1961], also published as v. 74, no. 294 (October–December, 1961) of *Journal of American Folk-Lore*.

34.6   Southern folklore quarterly.   1937——.
March issues contain annual bibliographies, covering principally North and South America. (Other folklore journals of the U.S. include *Midwest Folklore, New Mexico Folklore Record, New York Folklore Quarterly, Tennessee Folklore Society Bulletin,* and *Western Folklore. Texas Folklore Society Publications* is a series of volumes. See Lawless, 19.90, for more. Beginning in 1963, the American Folklore Society has sponsored *Abstracts of Folklore Studies*, which is very wide in scope. The Folklore Institute of Indiana University publishes a *Journal*, as well as a monograph series.)

34.7   Journal of American folk-lore.   1888——.
Supplements, appearing in April, contain a bibliography of general folklore, international in scope. An analytical index covering the contents of this journal to 1958 appeared in 1958, by Tristram P. Coffin; reprinted, N.Y., 1964.

34.8   Botkin, Benjamin A., ed.   A treasury of American folklore.   N.Y., [1944]; [1956].
An anthology. Botkin has edited several different collections—on both city and regional folklore. See also the field-collected texts in Richard M. Dorson, *Buying the Wind: Regional Folklore in the U.S.*, Chicago, 1964; 1972.

34.9   Folk music: a selection of folk songs, ballads, dances, instrumental pieces, and folk tales of the United States and Latin America: catalog of phonograph records.   Washington, 1959.
Compiled under the auspices of the Archive of American Folk Song, Library of Congress, which is the chief repository of American songs and ballads. See also Lawless, 19.90, and Wilgus, 19.89.

34.10 Laws, G. Malcolm, Jr. Native American balladry: a descriptive study and a bibliographical syllabus. Rev. ed. Philadelphia, 1964; Austin, Texas, 1975.

34.11 Coffin, Tristram P. The British traditional ballad in North America. Rev. ed. Philadelphia, 1963.
A critical inventory of Child ballads transported to the New World. Bibliography, pp. 173–182.

34.12 Baughman, Ernest W. Type and motif-index of the folktales of England and North America. The Hague, 1966.
Includes 13,083 variants of types and motifs, preponderantly American.

34.13 Taylor, Archer, and Whiting, Bartlett J. A dictionary of American proverbs and proverbial phrases 1820–1880. Cambridge, Mass., 1958.

34.14 Bluestein, Gene. The voice of the folk: folklore and American literary theory. Amherst, Mass., [1972].
The influence of folk ideology on the work of high-brow authors, Emerson and Whitman particularly. Some of the sparks are better than the fire.

35. Comparative and general literature

35.1 Baldensperger, Fernand, and Friederich, Werner P. Bibliography of comparative literature. Chapel Hill, N.C., 1950; N.Y., 1960; 1964.
The most comprehensive bibliography of its subject. American literature as a source of influence is treated on pp. 668–681. Supplements enlarging or bringing this work nearer to date appear annually in *Yearbook of Comparative and General Literature*, Chapel Hill, N.C., 1952–1960, and Bloomington, Ind., 1961——.

35.2 Conover, Helen F. Current national bibliographies. Washington, 1955; Westport, Conn., [1968].
Lists works which record the current output of books and periodicals in various individual countries, from Algeria to Yugoslavia.

35.3 Index translationum . . .: international bibliography of translations. Paris, 1932——.
Co-operating nations report translations of books to UNESCO, which periodically issues this list. Record incomplete.

35. Comparative and general literature

35.4 Parks, George B., and Temple, Ruth Z., eds. The literature of the world in English translation: a bibliography. The Greek and Latin literatures, N.Y., [1968]; The Romance literatures. 2 v. N.Y., [1970].

A co-operative work with the usual uneven treatment. "Literature" is broadly conceived—not confined to belles lettres.

35.5 Revue de littérature comparée. 1921–1940, 1947——.

Each issue through January–March, 1960, contains a bibliography of its subject, including latterly a special section on North American influences.

35.6 Comparative literature. 1949——.

First American journal in its field.

35.7 Comparative literature studies. 1963——.

Has a special interest in European literary relations with South, as well as North, America.

35.8 Van Tieghem, Paul. La littérature comparée. 2d ed. Paris, 1939.

A standard work for the French school of comparatists.

35.9 Friederich, Werner P., and Malone, David H. Outline of comparative literature from Dante Alighieri to Eugene O'Neill. Chapel Hill, N.C., 1954; 1962.

An elementary but neat outline, with emphasis on literary influences.

35.10 Cassell's encyclopaedia of world literature. Rev. ed. 3 v. N.Y., [1973].

35.11 Dizionario letterario Bompiani. 12 v. Milan, 1947–1966.

Very extensive and elaborately illustrated dictionary of world literature. General terms, like *expressionism* and *symbolism*, are defined; important works are outlined; a limited group of literary characters are sketched; and a very considerable number of authors are provided with biographical accounts. Works synopsized are alphabetized according to the Italian translations of their titles. A French adaptation is available in the following: *Dictionnaire des oeuvres de tous les temps et tous les pays*, [3d ed.], 5 v., Paris, 1958–1959; *Dictionnaire des personnages littéraires et dramatiques de tous les temps et de tous les pays*, Paris, 1960; and *Dictionnaire des auteurs*, 2 v., Paris, 1957–1958.

35.12 Frauwallner, Erich, *et al.* Die Weltliteratur. 3 v. Vienna, [1951–1954].

Encyclopedia covering earliest times to 1951, articles on national literatures, literary forms, eminent authors; alphabetically arranged. The bibliographies sometimes help pick up stray works on American authors published in Europe, especially Austria.

35.13 Von Wilpert, Gero. Lexikon der Weltliteratur. 2 v. Stuttgart, [1963–1968].

A bio-bibliographical handbook with about 9,000 articles. American writers are included.

35.14 Eppelsheimer, Hanns W. Handbuch der Weltliteratur. 3d ed. Frankfurt a.M., [1960].
Covers beginnings through the 18th century; then surveys various national literatures for the 19th century and 20th century separately.

35.15 McGraw-Hill encyclopedia of world drama: an international reference work. 4 v. N.Y., 1972.
Chiefly biographical sketches of about 900 authors of plays. A "complete" chronology of scripts is provided for 300 deemed "major."

35.16 Meyers Handbuch über die Literatur. 2d ed. Mannheim, [1970].
Bio-bibliographical sketches of authors from various countries, including the U.S.

35.17 Smith, Horatio, ed. Columbia dictionary of modern European literature. N.Y., 1947.
Continental authors and literature from about 1870 to 1940.

35.18 Gassner, John, and Quinn, Edward, eds. The reader's encyclopedia of world drama. N.Y., [1969].
Almost a hundred scholars, chiefly Americans, contributed. Longer articles are supplied with bibliographies.

35.19 Fleischmann, Wolfgang B. Encyclopedia of world literature in the 20th century. 3 v. N.Y., [1967–1971].
A translation and expansion of a standard German work. Includes bibliographies.

35.20 Wakeman, John, ed. World authors 1950–1970. N.Y., 1975.
A companion volume to Kunitz and Haycraft (11.23). Almost a thousand authors are added, "most of whom came into prominence between 1950 and 1970." About half of the sketches are supplied by the authors themselves. Americans continue to preponderate.

35.21 Pownall, David E. Articles on twentieth century literature: an annotated bibliography 1954 to 1970. 7 v. Milwood, N.Y., 1973——.
Cumulates "Current Bibliography" from the journal *Twentieth Century Literature* and adds materially others. American literature is only a part of the coverage.

35.22 Saintsbury, George E. B. A history of criticism and literary taste in Europe from the earliest texts to the present day. 4th–5th ed. 3 v. Edinburgh, 1922–1929; N.Y., 1961.
"Present day" means beginning of the present century.

35.23 Wellek, René. A history of modern criticism: 1750–1950. 5 or 6 v. planned. New Haven, Conn., 1955——.

35.24 Highet, Gilbert. The classical tradition: Greek and Roman influences on Western literature. Oxford, 1949; 1957.

35. Comparative and general literature

35.25 Olbrich, Wilhelm. Der Romanführer. Stuttgart, 1950———.
Digests of novels and stories; first volumes cover Germany, in particular, and various other European countries. North America, up to 1900, enters in v. 7.

35.26 Frenzel, Elisabeth. Stoff- und Motivgeschichte. [Berlin, 1966.]
Contains a good bibliography.

35.27 Thompson, Stith. Motif-Index of folk-literature. Rev. ed. 6 v. Bloomington, Ind., [1955–1958].
Classifies "narrative elements" in folk tales, ballads, myths, etc.

35.28 Pichois, Claude, and Rousseau, André-M. La littérature comparée. Paris, 1967.

35.29 Corstius, Jan Brandt. Introduction to the comparative study of literature. N.Y., 1968.
For other works on methodology, see 2.25–2.28.

Index of subjects

Abstracts, American history, 9.6; American literature, 7.15, 20.12, 20.17; dissertations, 1.29; historical, 2.4; methodology of, 3.24; services available, 3.24
Advertising, 15.32
Aesthetics, 19.8, 25.2–3
Affluence, 15.32
Agrarianism, 28.10, 28.32
Almanacks, 26.34
American Authors and Critics Series, 21.43
American civilization, *see* American studies
American Dialect Society, 33.10
American English, *see* English language in U.S.
American Guide Series, 30.3
American Historical Association, 9.2, 9.4, 9.7
American Historical Review, 9.7
American history, articles on, 9.3–8; articles abstracted, 9.6; colonial, 10.1–3; dissertations on, 9.6, 9.10–11; encyclopedias, 9.16–20; general tools for study, 9.1–44; historiography of, 9.28–40; manuscript collections, 9.12; special studies of, 10.1–43; statistics, 9.21; societies, 9.24–27
American imprints, 6.1–21
American Imprints Inventory, 30.4
Americanisms, 33.5–7
American Literary Realism, 20.18
American Literature, 20.9; index to, 20.10
American Literature Abstracts, 20.17
American mythology, 15.25–33
American Quarterly, 8.2
American Society of Composers, Authors and Publishers, 19.103
American Speech, 33.2
American studies, 8.1–20; abroad, 8.11–

20; method and problems, 8.6–10, 21.17; periodicals, 8.2, 8.14–19; sources for study, 8.1, 8.3, 8.5, 8.20
American Studies News, 8.14
American Thought, 15.1ff.
American Transcendental Quarterly, 17.7
American Writers Series, 20.19
Amerikastudien, 8.18
Annuals, 7.14; literary, 26.33
Anonyms, 3.26–27
Anti-slavery, in literature, 29.18
Architecture, 8.1, 19.53–71
Archive of American Folk Song, 34.9
Archive of New Orleans Jazz, 19.98
Archive of Recorded Poetry and Literature, 22.12
Archives, guide to, 1.16
Archives of American Art, 19.5
Area linguistics, 33.47
Armenian American authors, 31.55
Armory Show, 19.35
Art and architecture, 8.1; *see also* Architecture, Fine arts, Painting, Sculpture
Asia, response to American literature, 32.115–121
Asian-American authors, 31.51
Atlases, historical geography, 9.23; international, 1.37; linguistic, 33.27–34, 33.47; religious sects, 18.10
Autobiographies, 11.12–14; of actors and show people, 11.3; journalists, 11.3; Plains Indians, 30.28; psychologists, 16.22

Ballads, 34.9–11, 35.27; *see also* Folk music
Beatniks, 10.20; verse by, 22.37
Best sellers, 14.21–25; sales in Europe, 35.53
Bible, editions of in U.S., 32.124; use in fiction, 18.5

Index of subjects

Bibliography, descriptive, 3.2–5; general aids to, 1.1–38; in field of American literature, 20.1–36

Biographies, dictionaries of American, 11.5–7; actors and theater people, 23.47, 23.60, 23.68–69; architects, 19.66; artists, 19.13–16; authors, 11.17–25, 21.20–22, 21.42–44; editors and journalists, 13.1–3; European authors, 35.10–20; jazz performers, 19.100; musicians, 19.102–104; Negroes, 11.14; scientists, 10.16; scholars, 11.27; sculptors, 19.16, 19.46–68; universal, 11.1–4; women of U.S., 11.9; *see also* Autobiographies

Biography, as craft, 3.22–23

Bohemianism, 10.20, 28.16, 30.46

Book clubs, 14.16

Book design, 5.3, 5.15

Book prices, 14.19–20

Book reviews, indexes, 7.6–7, 7.11, 7.16; effect on readers, 14.27

Book trade, 6.5; 14.1–28

Boston, in fiction, 24.30

Brazil, American books in, 32.112

Brookgreen Gardens, 19.47

Bulletin of Bibliography, 1.22

California, literature of, 30.1, 30.40–47

Cartoons, 19.41, 19.43

Catholics, 18.24

Censorship, 15.41

Center for Editions of American Authors, 3.16, 21.34

Centro di Studi Americani, 32.92

Chandler Facsimile Series in American Literature, 21.45

Charles E. Merrill Checklists, 20.36

Chautauquas, 10.18

Chicago, authors, 28.30–31; magazines, 12.13

Children's literature, 26.35–37

Chinese, characters in literature, 31.53; themes in verse, 32.120

City directories, 10.33

City planning, 19.59

Civil War, effect on ideas, 15.42, 21.39; in literature, 21.38–39

Classical literature, 35.24; influence, 27.14, 32.122–123; translations, 35.4

Clergy, New England, 18.13

Cliometrics, 10.36; *see also* computers

Colonial literature, 27.1–31; classical tradition in, 27.14; forms of, 27.12; in newspapers, 27.13; in Maryland, 27.26; in New York, 27.28; in Pennsylvania, 29.29; in South, 30.9; in Virginia, 27.30–31; theology in, 27.17

Comics, 14.23, 19.42

Communism, in U.S., 15.19; in literature, 28.34; *see also* Marxism

Comparative literature, 35.1–29; methodology, 2.25–28, 35.29

Comparative Literature, 35.6

Composers, 19.103–104

Computers, 3.30–33

Comstockery, 15.41

Concerts, 19.110

Concordances, 3.33

Confederate States, 30.13; *see also* Civil War

Connecticut Wits, 27.25

Dance, 8.1, 23.81

Darwinism, 15.13–14, 24.42; *see also* Evolution

Dates, dictionaries of, 1.31; in U.S. history, 9.18

Deism, 18.15–16

Democratic idealism, 29.3–4

Depression, 15.39, 23.27

Detective stories, 26.22–26

Determinism, 29.7; *see also* Naturalism

Dialects, 33.1–3, 33.9–11, 33.23–25; for actors, 33.38

Diaries, 11.15–16; early New England, 27.27

Dictionaries, American English, 33.6–9, 33.16–19, 33.25; slang, 33.21–22; various languages, 1.32; world drama, 35.15, 35.18; world literature, 35.10–20

Digests, of novels, 1.38, 35.25; of plays, 23.23, 23.57, 23.85

Dime novels, 26.19–20

Doctoral dissertations, in all fields, 1.27–28; in American literature, 1.27, 20.14; in history departments, 9.10–11, 9.5; in speech, etc., 26.38–42; in theater and drama of all kinds, 23.7

Drama and theater, 23.1–93; acting, 23.40; "Best Plays Series," 23.19–22; bibliography on, 7.5, 23.1–11, 23.25, 23.86–88; collections in libraries, 23.1–

154

3; copyright entries, 23.17; digests of plays, 23.23, 23.57, 23.85; federal, 23.72; finances of, 23.80–83; in colleges, 23.25; in colonies, 23.43–44; in New York, 23.32; in Philadelphia, 23.48–50; in San Francisco, 23.51; in South, 23.46; left-wing, 23.73, 23.76–77; "little" theaters, 23.70–71; local and state, 23.9–10, 23.74; "lost" plays, 23.18–22; melodramas, 23.42; minstrel shows, 23.53–54; musical comedies, 23.57–58 (*see also* Music); off-Broadway, 23.67; periodicals devoted to, 23.26–29; Pulitzer Prize plays, 23.84–85; showboats, 23.56; tent shows, 23.55; twentieth-century, 23.60–93; vaudeville, 23.59; workers', 23.73

Dramatic critics, 25.16

Dramatic Index, 7.5

Dutch in New York, 27.28

Early American Literature, 27.5

Economic history, 8.1, 10.7, 15.12

Economics, in fiction, 24.37–39, 24.65; of authorship, 14.10, 28.28; of learned societies, 9.27; of performing arts and theater, 23.80–83; of slavery, 10.36

Economic ideas, 15.12

Editing manuscripts, 3.14–16; copy editing, 5.10

Education, 8.1, 10.22–29; college and university, 10.23, 10.28–29; schoolbooks, 10.27

Emerson Society Quarterly, 17.7

Encyclopedias, 1:30; of world literature, 35.10–20

England, literary relations with, 32.5–25

English language in U.S., 8.11, 8.20, 33.1–47

Engravers, 19.16, 19.40

Entertainment, 8.1

Essay, 26.1–3

Europe, relations of American literature with, 32.1–108; *see also* England, France, etc.

European Association for American Studies, 8.11

Evolution, 15.4, 15.14, 22.13, 24.42

Existentialism, 15.4; in fiction, 24.47, 24.79

Expatriates, 10.15, 15.30, 28.19, 29.21; in France, 32.75; in Italy, 32.95

Explication, 22.10; of short stories, 24.18

Explication de textes, 2.23

Far West, *see* West, California

Federal Theater Project, 23.72–73

Federal Writers' Project, 10.38

Festschrifts, 1.31

Fiction, 20.31, 24.1–83; American life in, 24.7–8; by Jews, 31.31–40; by Negroes, 31.26–28; city in, 24.8, 24.30; college life in, 24.41; criticism of, 24.12–13, 24.60; economic problems in, 24.37–39, 24.54; historical, 24.29, 24.70; indexes of, 24.1–8, 24.34, 24.70; military, 24.33–34; of absurd, 24.72, 24.80–81; Pulitzer Prizes, 24.77; "radical" or political, 24.36, 24.64–65; regional, 24.66, 24.68; sentimental, 24.31–32; *see also* Novels, Short stories

Films, 14.23, 23.89–93

Fine arts, 19.1–71; *see also* Art, Architecture, Museums, Music

Finland, American fiction in, 32.105

First editions of literary works, 20.20–22, 32.5

Folk art, 8.1, 19.18–19

Folklore, 8.1, 34.1–14; journals, 34.6–7; motifs, 35.26–27; and literary study, 34.14; study of, 34.2

Folk music, 34.9–11

Folktales, 34.12

Footnotes, style of, 5.2–4

Foreign influences, 10.15; *see also* England, France etc.

Foreign languages, editorial style of, 5.5

France, literary relations with, 17.10, 21.9, 25.15, 32.54–76

Free religion, 17.13

Free-thought, 18.18–19

Free verse, 22.8

Freudianism, 15.4, 23.75, 28.12, 28.17, 28.29

Frick Art Reference Library, 19.22

Frontier, hypothesis, 10.19, 15.27–28, 15.32; in literature, 29.11–12; in novels, 24.68

Fugitives, 25.24, 28.32

Fundamentalism, 18.22

Genealogy, 11.28–30

Genteel tradition, 15.4, 15.37; decline of, 15.44, 25.26; sex and sentiment in, 29.9

union lists, 12.2, 12.18; *see also* Journalism, Little magazines

Major authors, ranking of, 21.40

Manuscripts, collections in American history, 8.4–5, 9.12; collections in various fields, 1.15–16, 1.18–19; copyright restrictions, 3.14; of American authors, 20.24; pertaining to theater, 23.3; preparation for publication, 5.1–15; scientific aids for study, 3.12; search for, 3.7, 3.10; use of, 3.12–16; union catalogs, 1.15, 1.16; variants, 3.13

Maps, international, 1.37; of U.S., 9.42; *see also* Atlases

Marxism, in historiography, 2.12; in literature and criticism, 25.10, 25.28, 25.33, 28.10, 28.23–24, 28.34, 29.8

Maryland, colonial writers in, 27.26

Master's essays, preparation of, 2.14–17, 2.20–21, 9.1; list of, in field of American literature, 20.15

Methodology of research, in comparative literature, 2.25–28; in history, 2.2, 2.16–19; in literature, 2.1, 2.13–15; in social history, 2.6, 2.18–19; techniques, 3.1–33

Mexico, literary relations with, 32.110–111

Microform Review, 3.20

Microforms, 1.23–26; recordings, 3.17–21, 6.4

Middle West, linguistic atlas of, 33.32; literature of, 30.22–27

Minority groups, literature on or by, 31.1–55; *see also* Jews, Negroes

Minstrel shows, 23.53–54

Mississippi Valley Historical Review, 9.8

Motion pictures, 6.4, 23.89–93

Mountaineers in literature, 29.13

Muckracking movement, 10.21

Museums, 19.7; *see also* Painting

Music, 8.1, 19.72–113; country, 19.91; economics of, 19.110–111; folk, 19.89–91, 19.109, 34.9; influence on poetry, 22.14; musical comedy, 19.85–88; Negro, 19.106; opera, 19.82–85; popular songs, 19.108, 19.113; rock, 19.101; *see also* Jazz

Myth, Adamic, 15.25; American, 15.28, 15.30; classical influence on poetry, 32.123; in fiction, 24.40; in vaudeville,

23.59; pastoral idea, 15.26; relations with literary study, 2.34; West as myth and symbol, 15.27–28; *see also* Success motif

Names, of persons, 33.42; of places, 33.39–41; nicknames, 33.43

Names: Journal of the American Name Society, 33.39

National Academy of Design, 19.28

Nationalism, in literature, 2.1, 10.3, 29.1; problem of identifying, 15.32

National bibliographies, 35.2; of U.S., 6.1–17

Naturalism, 15.4, 15.38, 28.10; in literature, 24.42–44, 24.76, 29.6–7

Nature in literature, 29.2

Negroes, as artists, 19.17, 31.14; as characters in literature, 31.12–13; as authors, 13.1–30; as playwrights, 31.29–30; as producers of humor, 26.16; newspapers of, 13.24; Black English, 33.37

New Criticism, 25.3, 25.19–23, 28.6, 28.10; ancestor of, 2.24

New England Quarterly, 30.6

New Humanism, 25.24, 25.26–27, 25.29–30, 28.6, 28.10; applied to fiction, 24.52

New Left, 15.20

New Literary History, 2.37

New Netherland, literary culture in, 27.28

Newspapers, 13.1–26; colonial, 27.13; columnists, 13.23; directories, 13.9–10; German-American, 13.25–26; history of, 13.1–3, 13.11–17; indexes of, 13.18–22; in microfilm, 13.8; Negro, 13.24; union list, 13.6; *see also* Journalism

New York, in fiction, 24.39; *see also* Drama and Theater

Northwest, literature of, 30.1, 30.38–39

Norway, literary relations with, 32.100–103

Novels, digests of, 1.38, 35.25; on farms, 24.8, 30.27; war novels, 24.33–34, 28.28; *see also* Fiction

Obituaries, 11.8

Oenology, 10.43

Opera, *see* Music

Index of subjects

Oral history, 3.11, 9.43–44
Orient, literary relations with, 32.113–121

Pacific Northwest, 30.39
Painting and drawing, 8.1, 19.21–44; abstract, 19.38–39; genre, 19.30; landscape, 21.32; prints, 19.26; still life, 19.29
Paperbacks, 6.21, 14.11–12, 28.28
Parodies, 26.18
Pastoral ideal, 15.26
Pennsylvania, early Quaker culture, 27.29; see also Philadelphia
Pennsylvania Germans, as authors, 31.52
Periodicals, directory, 7.14; indexes, 7.1–16; on drama and theater, 23.26–29; publishing literary research, 5.11–13; see also Magazines, Newspapers
Perspectives in American History, 9.9
Pessimism, see Naturalism
Phenomenology, 2.30
Philadelphia, in fiction, 24.30; magazines of, 12.12; theater in, 23.43, 23.48–50
Philanthropy, 10.34
Philosophy, 8.1, 16.1–21; of American literature, 2.13; of authors, 16.20; of historical studies, 2.2–4, 2.6ff; of literary studies, 2.1, 2.5, 2.34, 2.37
Phonograph, 19.98
Photography, 19.4
Phrenology, 16.27
Plays, see Drama and Theater
Poetry, 22.1–43; colonial, 22.16, 27.24–25; explication, 22.10; free verse, 22.8; in anthologies, 22.1, 22.26; index to criticisms of, 22.2; of 20th century, 22.20–43; recordings, 22.11–12
Poland, literary relations with, 32.88–89
Political ideas, 15.5–11, 15.16–23, 25.13
Political parties, 10.9–11
Popular books, 14.21–25, 32.53
Portraits, dictionary of, 9.41
Portugal, translations of U.S. books, 32.77
Pottery, 19.11
Pragmatism, 15.4, 16.8–12
Preaching, in early New England, 27.23
Pre-Raphaelites, 32.12, 32.23
Printing, 6.5–16, 14.1–7; mechanics of, 5.15
Prizes and awards, 5.14; see also Pulitzer Prizes

Proof: The Yearbook of American Bibliographical and Textual Studies, 20.34
Proofreading, 5.10
Prosody, 22.7, 22.27
Prospects, 10.42
Proverbs, 34.13
Pseudonyms, 3.26, 3.28
Psychoanalysis, 16.24–25; in criticism, 25.32; see also Freudianism
Psychology, 8.1, 16.22–23, 16.26; relations with literature and literary study, 2.1, 2.25, 2.34
Publication of research, 5.1–15
Publications of the American Dialect Society, 33.10
Publications of the Modern Language Association, 20.11–12
Publishers, directory of, 5.12; pioneer, 6.5, 14.3, 14.9; see also Publishing
Publishers' Weekly, 6.18
Publishing, 3.1, 8.1, 14.1–28; economic survey, 14.14, 14.18; textbooks, 14.18
Pulitzer prizes, 10.37, 24.77
Puritanism, 15.4; decline of, 21.19; effect on American "identity," 27.22
Puritans, as philosophers, 16.6, 16.14; as writers, 21.23, 27.16–22, 27.24

Quarterly Journal of Speech, 26.42
Quakers, in early culture, 27.29; influence in literature, 29.17

Radio, 13.1, 13.12, 14.23, 26.38; book programs on, 5.14
Recordings, of folk music, etc., 19.55–56, 34.9; of poetry, 22.11–12
Regionalism, in literature, 2.19, 15.4, 20.23, 24.66, 24.68, 30.1–47; in speech, 33.23–33; see also New England, South, West, etc.
Religion, 8.1, 15.10, 18.1–35; historiography of, 18.3; in literature, 18.28–34; religious bodies, 18.26–27; Supreme Court on, 18.25; see also Catholics, Free-thought, Free Religion, Puritanism, Transcendentalism
Resources for American Literary Study, 20.13
Revolt against formalism, 15.29, 15.36, 15.40
Revolt from village, 29.20

Revolutionary War, literature of, 27.7, newspapers in, 13.17; political satire in, 27.15
Revue de Littérature Comparée, 35.5
Rhetoric, 26.41–43
Rocky Mountains, 30.35–39
Romanticism, 2.25, 21.19; in theater, 23.41
Russia, literary relations with, 32.81–87

San Francisco, stage, 23.51
Scandinavia, literary relations with, 32.101–104
Science and technology, 8.1; fiction, 26.27–31; in colonial era, 27.8–10; in philosophical thought, 16.13; in 20th-century poetry, 22.39; influence on criticism, 25.15; relations with linguistic study, 33.44; technical word usage, 33.46
Sculpture, 19.45–51
Sectional feeling, 15.4, 30.5
Sentimentalism, 24.31–32, 29.9
Serif Series, 20.32
Serials, 1.20, 7.14, 12.2
Sermons, 27.23
Short stories, criticism of, 24.16–19, 24.26–28, 24.49, 24.51, 24.58; detective, 26.22; index of, 24.3; since 1947, 24.74
Showboats, 23.56
Slang, 33.21–22
Slavery, 10.36, 29.18
Small town in literature and theater, 29.10, 29.20
Social Darwinism, 15.13
Social gospel, 18.20
Socialism, 15.15
Social sciences, guide to, 1.36; in historical study, 2.5; *see also* Economics, History, Sociology
Societies, learned, 2.27
Sociology, 10.5–6
South, criticism in, 25.14, 25.24; effect on national character, 15.42; folklore of, 34.6; history of, 10.4, 10.36; humor of, 26.14–15; literature of, 30.8–21, 30.32–34; speech of, 33.33–35; theater, 23.46
Southern Literary Journal, 30.8
Southwest, literature of, 30.1, 30.32–34; *see also* California

Spain, literary relations with, 32.77–80
Spanish America, literary relations with, 32.109–112
Speech Monographs, 26.40
Speeches and oratory, 26.38–43
Spiritism, 29.22
Sports and recreation, 8.1
Statistical study of vocabulary, 2.36
Statistics of U.S., 9.21
Structuralism, 2.30
Studies in Bibliography, 3.1
Studies in American Fiction, 24.10
Style manuals, 5.2–3
Success motif, 29.19
Supreme Court, on religion, 13.35; *see also* Constitution of U.S.
Sweden, literary relations with, 32.100, 32.102–104
Switzerland, literary relations with, 32.51–53
Symbolism, 2.35, 29.5

Television, 13.1, 13.12, 14.23–24, 26.38
Terms, definitions of, architecture, 4.1; ballet, 4.1; librarians', 4.6; linguistic, 4.13; literary, 4.2–5, 4.7–8, 4.14–17; 35.10–16, 35.19; music, 4.1, 19.89; New Criticism, 25.30; painting, 4.1; poetry, 4.15–16; printing and publishing, 4.9–12, 5.3; theater, 4.17
Textbooks, 10.27
Textual criticism, 2.29, 2.31, 3.2–5
Theater, *see* Drama and theater
Themes in American literature, 29.1–22
Theology, *see* Puritanism, Religion
Theory of American literature, 25.18
Transcendentalism, 17.1–13, 12.15, 15.4, 21.19, 29.1, 32.42, 32.46, 32.113
Translation, 2.32–33; international, 35.3–4; methods, 3.25
Travel books, 26.44
Twayne's U.S. Authors Series, 21.44
Twentieth-century literature, 28.1–34, 35.21; critical writing, 25.19–34; drama and theater, 23.60–93; fiction, 24.48–83; poetry, 22.20–43
Typology, 18.21

Union catalogs, of books, 3.6, 6.4; of microfilms, 1.23; of microforms, 1.24; of serials, 1.20

Index of subjects

Unitarianism, 17.1–2
UNESCO, index of translations, 35.3
U.S. government publications, 1.34–35
U.S. National Archives, guide to, 9.22
University of Minnesota Pamphlets, 21.42
University presses, 14.16, 14.26, 14.28

Vaudeville, 23.59
Versification, 4.14–16
Virginia, literature and culture in, 27.30–31
Vocabulary, statistical study of, 2.28; *see also* Computers

Washington, George, 29.16
West, artists of, 19.15; as symbol, 15.27; literature of, 30.29–31, 30.35–36, 30.37–47; vocabulary of, 33.9; *see also* Southwest
"Western," 30.1, 30.31
Western American Literature, 30.7
Wills, 3.10
Wines, 10.43
Winterthur Museum, 19.31
Women's rights, 10.31–32
Works Progress Administration, 2.15, 7.10, 7.12, 30.4

Yearbook of Comparative and General Literature, 35.1
"Young America," 25.13

Names of authors, editors, and compilers

Aaron, Daniel, 21.38, 28.34
Abrams, M. H., 4.3
Abramson, D. E., 31.30
Adams, G. P., 16.18
Adams, J. T., 9.16, 9.20
Adams, L. D., 10.43
Adams, O. F., 11.18
Adams, R. F., 33.9
Adelman, Irving, 24.60
Adler, Sidney, 31.38
Agnew, J. M., 30.17
Ahlstrom, S. E., 18.4, 18.9
Åhnebrink, Lars, 24.44, 32.68
Aldridge, A. O., 2.26
Aldridge, J. W., 24.62
Alexander, Jean, 32.72
Allen, F. L., 28.17, 28.23
Allen, G. W., 22.7
Allen, H. B., 33.32
Alman, Miriam, 8.4
Alter, Robert, 31.35
Altick, R. D., 2.14
Andersen, W. V., 19.52

Anderson, C. L., 32.104
Anderson, P. R., 16.3
Andrews, C. M., 10.2
Andrews, Wayne, 9.16, 19.55
Ansermoz-Dubois, Félix, 32.57
Arms, George, 22.17
Arnavon, Cyrille, 21.9, 32.71
Arndt, K. J., 13.25, 13.26
Arrowsmith, William, 2.33
Ash, Lee, 1.18, 6.14
Auer, J. J., 26.39
Austin, G. C., 14.24
Ayer, A. J., 16.9
Ayer, N. W., 13.9

Bacon, J. C., 7.1
Bahm, A. J., 16.16
Baigell, Matthew, 19.24
Bailyn, Bernard, 9.9
Baird, N. D., 30.42
Baker, B. M., 23.1
Baker, H. A., Jr., 31.9
Baker, J. A., 22.2

160

161

Names of authors, editors, and compilers

Brown, G. W., 32.84
Brown, H. R., 24.31
Brown, M. W., 19.35
Browne, R. B., 21.33
Brownell, W. C., 21.30
Bruccoli, M. J., 14.10, 20.36, 21.34
Brumm, Ursula, 18.21
Brummel, L., 1.21
Brunvand, J. H., 34.2
Brussel, I. R., 32.5
Bryan, W. A., 29.16
Bryant, J. H., 24.79
Bryant, M. M., 33.18
Bryer, J. R., 20.30, 20.31, 31.34
Buchanan, W. W., 1.34
Buchloch, P. E., 26.26
Buell, Lawrence, 17.12
Bungert, Hans, 24.17
Burchard, John, 19.55
Burke, J. G., 30.5
Burke, Russell, 19.29
Burke, V. M., 33.24
Burke, W. J., 11.19
Burnette, O. L., Jr., 3.9
Burns, E. M., 15.31
Burr, N. R., 18.1, 18.2
Bush, Douglas, 32.123
Bush-Brown, Albert, 19.55
Butcher, M. J., 31.14
Butts, R. F., 10.25
Byrd, M. B., 5.11

Cady, E. H., 24.24, 29.14
Cairns, W. B., 32.7, 32.8
Cameron, K. W., 17.7
Cantrell, C. H., 30.10
Cappon, L. J., 11.28
Carman, H. J., 8.3
Carpenter, E. H., 14.9
Carroll, J. B., 33.44
Carruth, Gorton, 9.18
Carter, John, 4.11
Cartwright, W. A., 19.13
Cartwright, W. H., 15.1
Cawelti, J. G., 29.19
Cederholm, T. D., 19.17
Chalmers, D. M., 10.21
Chamberlin, M. W., 19.2
Chandler, Sue, 31.18
Chapman, Arnold, 32.109
Chapman, John, 23.19
Charvat, William, 14.10, 25.11

Chase, Gilbert, 19.75
Chatterton, Wayne, 30.37
Cheney, O. H., 14.14
Chielens, E. E., 20.31
Chin, Frank, 31.51
Chipp, H. B., 19.20
Chisholm, R. M., 16.2
Christadler, Martin, 26.1, 28.26
Christensen, E. O., 19.13, 19.18
Christy, Arthur, 32.113
Cirker, Blanche, 9.41
Cirker, Hayward, 9.41
Clark, A. J., 5.7
Clark, H. H., 20.8, 20.19, 21.19, 25.15,
    27.9
Clark, T. D., 2.19, 9.8
Cleary, J. W., 26.42
Clebsch, W. A., 18.8
Clendenning, John, 20.31
Clifford, J. L., 2.23
Cline, G. S., 22.2
Coan, O. W., 24.7
Coffin, T. P., 34.7, 34.11
Coffman, S. K., 22.33
Cohen, Hennig, 8.2
Cohen, Saul, 5.8
Cohn, Ruby, 23.79
Colburn, W. E., 20.33
Cole, M. D., 6.8
Coleman, Arthur, 23.86
Coleman, E. D., 31.43
Coleman, M. M., 32.89
Coleman, R. A., 30.38
Collingwood, R. G., 2.10
Collison, R. L., 1.30
Collison, Robert, 3.6, 3.24
Commager, H. S., 9.13, 9.14, 15.7
Conlin, J. R., 12.11
Conner, F. W., 22.13
Conover, H. F., 35.2
Cook, Bruce, 22.37
Cook, D. E., 24.3
Cook, E. C., 27.13
Cooke, G. W., 17.2
Cooperman, Stanley, 24.33
Cordasco, Francesco, 10.23
Corrigan, R. H., 20.31
Corstius, J. B., 35.29
Cotton, G. B., 24.2
Coulter, E. M., 10.4
Cowan, Louise, 28.32
Cowdrey, Bartlett, 19.27

Cowie, Alexander, 24.20
Cowley, Malcolm, 28.12, 28.15, 28.19, 28.28, 28.33
Cox, E. G., 26.44
Craigie, W. A., 33.6
Crain, W. H., Jr., 25.16
Craven, Wayne, 19.45
Cremin, L. A., 10.24, 10.25, 10.26
Crick, B. R., 8.4
Cumming, John, 3.8
Cummings, Paul, 19.44
Cunliffe, Marcus, 9.36
Currier, T. F., 3.5
Curti, Merle, 10.34, 15.1, 16.17
Cushing, H. G., 7.2
Cushing, William, 3.27

Dargan, Marion, 11.11
Davidson, L. J., 30.36
Davidson, Martha, 19.11
Davies, J. D., 16.27
Davis, A. P., 31.16
Davis, R. B., 27.3, 27.31
Davis, R. L., 19.83
Dawdy, D. O., 19.15
Day, A. G., 31.48
Day, D. B., 26.29
Deakin, Motley, 21.35
de Camp, L. S., 10.16
Degler, C. N., 15.43
Dembo, L. S., 22.41
DeMille, G. E., 25.9
DeMott, Robert, 21.36
den Hollander, A. N. J., 8.11
Denisoff, R. S., 19.109
Denny, Margaret, 32.2
Deodene, Frank, 31.20
Dessauer, J. P., 14.17
DeSua, William, 32.99
Detweiler, F. G., 13.24
Deutsch, Babette, 4.15
Dickason, D. H., 32.12
Dickinson, A. T., Jr., 24.70
Ditzion, Sidney, 12.1
Doane, G. H., 11.28
Dobie, J. F., 30.32
Dommergues, Pierre, 32.76
Dondore, Dorothy, 30.24
Dorfman, Joseph, 15.12
Dormon, J. H., 23.46
Dorson, R. M., 2.19, 34.3, 34.4, 34.5, 34.8
Downer, A. S., 23.63

Downs, R. B., 1.5, 13.7
Duckles, V. H., 19.73
Duffey, Bernard, 28.30
Dukore, B. F., 23.11
Dumbauld, Edward, 10.8
Dunlap, G. A., 24.30
Dunlap, L. W., 9.26
Dunlap, William, 19.33
Durham, Philip, 32.105
Duyckinck, E. A., 11.21
Duyckinck, G. L., 11.21
Dworkin, Rita, 24.60
Dyment, A. G., 23.90
Dyson, A. J., 23.88

Eagle, Dorothy, 4.8
Edwards, H. W., 15.4
Egbert, D. D., 15.15
Egger, E., 1.21
Ehresmann, D. L., 19.3
Eichelberger, C. L., 24.13
Eisinger, C. E., 24.76
Ekirch, A. A., Jr., 15.3
Ellis, C. M., 17.6
Ellis, J. T., 18.24
Elson, R. M., 10.27
Elton, William, 25.30
Emerson, Everett, 27.1
Emery, Edwin, 13.12
Engerman, S. L., 10.36
Englekirk, J. E., 32.112
Enkvist, N. E., 32.11
Eppelsheimer, H. W., 35.14
Esdaile, Arundell, 3.5
Etulain, R. W., 30.29
Evans, Bergen, 33.19
Evans, Charles, 6.5
Evans, Cornelia, 33.19
Evans, Paul, 19.114
Everton, G. B., 11.28
Ewen, David, 19.107, 19.113, 23.57

Fadiman, Clifton, 16.20
Fairchild, H. N., 18.32
Falb, Lewis, 32.63
Falk, Robert, 21.37, 24.35
Falk, R. P., 26.18
Faris, R. E. L., 10.6
Fay, J. W., 16.26
Feather, Leonard, 19.100
Feidelson, Charles, Jr., 29.5
Felheim, Marvin, 23.47

163

Fenn, W. P., 31.53
Ferguson, J. D., 32.79
Fielding, Mantle, 19.16
Fidell, E. A., 23.13, 24.1
Filler, Louis, 10.21
Findlay, R. R., 23.39
Firkins, I. T. E., 23.13
Fisch, Harold, 31.39
Fisch, M. H., 16.3, 16.7
Fisher, M. L., 31.6
Fishman, J. A., 10.12
Fishman, Solomon, 28.10
Fishwick, M. W., 8.7
Fiske, H. S., 24.43
Fitch, J. M., 19.65
Flanagan, J. T., 2.19, 30.26
Fleischmann, W. B., 35.19
Fleming, Donald, 9.9
Fleming, H. E., 12.13
Flexner, Eleanor, 10.32
Flexner, S. B., 33.21
Flory, C. R., 24.37
Foerster, Norman, 21.18, 25.7, 29.2
Fogel, W. R., 10.36
Foley, Martha, 24.49
Foley, P. K., 20.22
Folsom, J. K., 30.31
Foote, H. W., 26.32
Forbes, Harriette, 27.27
Fox, D. R., 9.15
Fraiberg, Louis, 25.32
Francis, W. N., 33.26
Frauwallner, Erich, 35.12
Frederick, J. T., 18.33
Freese, Peter, 24.74
Freidel, Frank, 9.1
Freitag, R. S., 1.20
French, Warren, 28.24
Frenz, Horst, 2.25, 32.29
Frenzel, Elizabeth, 35.26
Friederich, W. P., 32.3, 32.99, 35.1, 35.9
Friedman, L. M., 10.30
Fries, C. C., 33.20
Frohock, W. M., 24.71
Frothingham, O. B., 17.4
Fukuda, Naomi, 32.115

Gabriel, R. H., 9.19, 15.2
Gagey, E. M., 23.51, 23.61
Gaines, F. P., 30.14
Galinsky, Hans, 32.44, 33.15
Galloway, D. D., 24.81

Gardner, A. T. E., 19.48, 19.50
Garland, Hamlin, 21.25
Garraty, J. A., 3.22
Garrett, W. D., 19.9
Gaskell, Philip, 3.3
Gassner, John, 23.64, 35.18
Gaustad, E. S., 18.3, 18.7, 18.10, 18.11
Geduld, H. M., 23.89
Geismar, Maxwell, 24.55, 24.56, 24.61, 24.63
Gelfant, B. M., 24.67
Georgiu, Constantine, 26.36
Gérard, Albert, 24.47
Gerdts, W. H., 19.29, 19.49
Gergely, E. J., 32.107
Gerlach, J. C., 23.92
Gerlach, Lana, 23.92
Gerstenberger, Donna, 5.12, 24.12
Gettmann, R. A., 32.87
Gibson, Jeremy, 3.10
Giedion, Sigfried, 19.59
Gilbert, D. B., 19.13
Gilbert, Douglas, 23.59
Gilbert, J. B., 12.21
Gilman, Witt, 32.2
Gilmer, G. C., 12.14
Glaister, G. A., 4.9
Glazer, Nathan, 18.25
Gleason, Harold, 19.105
Gloster, H. M., 31.28
Goddard, H. C., 17.5
Gohdes, Clarence, 12.15, 20.23, 21.17, 23.10, 30.1, 32.9, 32.82
Goldsmith, A. L., 5.11
Goldstein, Malcolm, 23.77
Goode, S. H., 7.8
Goodrich, Lloyd, 19.34
Gordon, G. S., 32.6
Gossett, L. Y., 24.71
Gottesman, Ronald, 23.89
Graff, H. F., 11.28
Graham, Philip, 23.56
Granger, B. I., 27.15
Grannis, C. B., 14.16
Green, Stanley, 19.86
Greene, E. B., 8.3
Greenlaw, Edwin, 2.5
Greenwood, Robert, 30.42
Greenwood, V. D., 11.29
Greer, Louise, 32.24
Greg, W. W., 3.13
Gregor, Carl, 19.93, 19.97

Howard, Leon, 21.5, 27.25
Howard, P. C., 20.15
Howe, D. W., 17.2
Howe, G. F., 2.2, 9.2
Howells, W. D., 11.9, 21.24
Hoyt, C. A., 24.25
Hubbell, J. B., 21.40, 30.11
Hudson, W. S., 18.6
Huggins, N. I., 31.24
Hughes, C. M., 31.27
Hughes, Glenn, 22.34, 23.34
Hulbert, J. R., 33.6
Hunter, Sam, 19.37
Hurley, Paul, 20.31
Hurt, Peyton, 5.4
Hutchinson, W. T., 9.32
Hutchison, W. R., 17.1
Hyamson, A. W., 11.1
Hyman, S. E., 25.31

Icolari, Daniel, 31.45
Iggers, G. G., 2.12
Inge, M. T., 26.17
Irish, W. R., 22.20
Isaacs, E. J. R., 31.29

Jackson, Richard, 19.72
Jaffe, H. H., 32.55
James, A. E., 26.33
James, E. T., 11.9
James, R. D., 23.49
Jameson, A. L., 18.5, 18.9
Janis, Sidney, 19.39
Janssen, G. A., 12.20
Jantz, H. S., 27.24, 32.36
Jenkins, F. B., 1.5
Jeune, Simon, 32.62
Johannsen, Albert, 26.20
Johnson, A. E., 25.16
Johnson, M. D., 20.21
Johnson, T. H., 20.1, 27.17
Jones, A. E., 24.42
Jones, H. M., 2.13, 15.34, 27.30, 28.1, 32.58
Jones, Joseph, 20.24
Jones, M. A., 10.12
Jordan, P. D., 3.7
Jordy, W. H., 19.70
Josephson, B. E., 3.7

Kallen, H. M., 16.19
Kanely, E. M., 1.34

Kaplan, Harold, 29.3
Kaplan, Louis, 11.12
Kaser, David, 2.19
Katona, Anna, 32.106
Katz, Joseph, 20.21, 20.36
Kazin, Alfred, 28.9
Keaveney, S. C., 19.21
Keiser, 31.46
Keller, D. H., 23.4
Keller, H. R., 1.31
Kelly, A. H., 10.8
Kelly, James, 6.13
Kempkes, Wolfgang, 19.42
Kennedy, A. G., 20.33
Kenner, Hugh, 22.36, 28.14
Kennington, Donald, 19.94
Kenyon, J. S., 33.8, 33.13
Kerr, Howard, 29.22
Key, Vladimer, 10.9
Kherdian, David, 30.41
Kiefer, Monica, 26.37
Kiger, J. C., 9.27
Kindilien, C. T., 22.18
Kinnamon, Keneth, 31.1, 31.23
Kinne, W. P., 23.69
Kirby, D. K., 20.31, 24.9
Kitzhaber, A. R., 26.41
Klein, B. T., 31.45
Klein, Marcus, 24.73
Klinkowitz, Jerome, 24.83
Knight, G. C., 21.26, 28.11
Knott, T. A., 33.8
Knox, G. A., 23.73
Koch, D. A., 14.24
Koch, G. A., 18.16
Koehmstedt, C. L., 1.38
Koht, Halvdan, 32.4
Konnye, Leslie, 31.54
Kopp, W. L., 32.35
Kramer, Dale, 28.32
Krapp, G. P., 33.3
Kraus, Michael, 9.31
Krause, S. J., 29.7
Kreymborg, Alfred, 22.5
Krichmar, Albert, 10.31
Kroeger, Karl, 19.74
Krohn, E. C., 19.111
Krutch, J. W., 28.20
Kruzas, A. T., 1.19
Kuehl, W. F., 9.10
Kunitz, S. J., 11.17, 11.23
Kuntz, H. W., 22.10

Names of authors, editors, and compilers

Ulrich, Carolyn, 12.17
Unger, Irwin, 15.20
Untermeyer, Louis, 22.30
Upjohn, E. M., 19.62

VanDerhoof, Jack, 24.68
Van Doren, Carl, 24.22
Van Doren, Charles, 11.7
Van Hoff, Henry, 2.32
Van Patten, Nathan, 20.27
Van Tassel, D. D., 9.33
Van Tieghem, Paul, 35.8
Vaughan, A. T., 10.1
Veinstein, André, 23.2
Veysey, L. R., 10.29
Vigneron, Robert, 2.23
Vogel, S. M., 32.46
Vogt, Jochen, 26.25
Von Eckard, Wolf, 19.69
Von Ostermann, G. F., 5.5
Von Wilpert, Gero, 35.13
Voss, Arthur, 24.27

Wagenknecht, Edward, 24.23
Waggoner, H. H., 22.39
Wagner, Jean, 31.23
Wakeman, John, 35.20
Waldmeir, J. J., 24.33
Waldo, L. P., 32.64
Walford, A. J., 1.9
Walker, F. D., 30.43, 30.44, 30.46
Walker, R. H., 8.12, 22.19
Walker, W. S., 24.18
Wall, C. E., 7.1
Wallace, D. H., 19.14
Wallace, W. S., 11.22
Walsh, D. D., 4.13
Ware, R. H., 32.66
Warfel, H. R., 24.69
Warren, Austin, 2.1
Warren, R. P., 21.39
Warren, Sidney, 18.19
Waserman, M. J., 9.43
Washburn, W. E., 10.40
Wasserstrom, William, 29.9
Waters, W. O., 6.7
Watson, E. S., 13.14
Watson, R. L., 15.1
Weales, Gerald, 23.65
Weber, Alfred, 28.8
Wegelin, Oscar, 22.15, 23.15

Weimann, Robert, 25.29
Weingarten, J. A., 23.62
Weiser, I. H., 22.24
Weisstein, Ulrich, 2.27
Weitenkampf, Frank, 19.40, 19.43
Welch, d.A., 26.35
Welch, W. L., 19.98
Wellek, René, 2.1, 25.8, 25.23, 25.25, 32.46
Wells, H. W., 22.9, 22.35
Wells, R. V., 17.11
Welter, Rush, 14.28, 15.6
Wentworth, Harold, 33.21, 33.25
Werkmeister, W. H., 16.5
West, D. H., 23.13
West, R. B., Jr., 24.51, 30.35
Wetherill, P. M., 2.21
Whicher, S. E., 32.104
Whipple, T. K., 28.22
White, C. M., 1.36
White, G. L., 32.102
White, M. G., 15.36, 16.13
White, W., 20.31
Whitehill, W. M., 9.26
Whiteman, Maxwell, 31.26
Whiting, B. J., 34.13
Whitlow, Roger, 31.7
Wickes, George, 32.75
Wiener, P. P., 25.4
Wilbur, E. M., 17.3
Wilder, A. N., 18.28
Wilgus, D. K., 19.89
Williams, S. T., 32.78
Williamson, Juanita, 33.24
Wilson, A. H., 23.50
Wilson, Edmund, 21.23, 21.39, 30.47
Wilson, G. B., 23.38, 23.40
Wilson, H. S., 12.22
Winchell, C. W., 1.3
Winks, R. W., 9.36
Wisbey, R. A., 3.32
Wish, Harvey, 9.30, 15.8
Withey, E. R., 19.66
Withey, H. F., 19.66
Witt, S. H., 31.50
Wittenberg, Philip, 5.7
Wittke, C. F., 10.13, 23.53
Wodehouse, Lawrence, 19.56
Wölcken, Fritz, 26.24
Wolf, M. L., 4.1
Wood, G. R., 33.34

For Reference

Not to be taken from this room